Mastering Research

A Guide to the Methods of Social and Behavioral Sciences

SHEYING CHEN
The College of Staten Island
The City University of New York

Nelson-Hall Publishers
Chicago

are: (1) Opening and introduction. The conversation usually begins informally. In an individual interview, it can be started before both the interviewee and you get seated. In a group session, there is often a while of chatting before you have all the participants in. The formal beginning of the data collection may not appear "formal," but it is marked by the introduction of the topic of discussion, and the introduction of each participant if necessary. (2) Questioning and discussion. Key questions are asked at this stage. These are the substantive data you need for analysis. Great care should be taken in the selection of the questions and their wording. For a focus group discussion, the number of the key questions is rarely more than ten, and typically it is no more than five. (3) Ending and summary. Before you close up the discussion, one or more questions are needed to ask the respondent(s) to reflect back on the answers given to the key questions. The ending question(s) may help to identify the most important points, confirm the major ideas, and make up potentially missing information.

To ensure the effectiveness of these data collection methods and the validity of the measurement tools chosen for a particular research project, a pilot study can be carried out before a large-scale data collection is conducted. For the purpose of scale development, such a pilot study is often needed to ensure the reliability and validity of the scales to be employed.

Computerizing and managing your data

After you have completed your data collection, you still have a lot to do before you can start data analysis and derive the results. These tasks can be divided into two general steps or topics. First, we will talk about quantification and computerization; then, we will discuss data cleaning and manipulation.

Quantification and computerization

Quantification is the process of using numbers to represent the information or data collected. In chapter seven we have discussed different measurement levels. Data obtained at any measurement level may be presented in a numeric form, though the numbers at different levels have different meanings and mathematical properties.

Quantification is realized through a special process of coding. Coding is the use of a set of symbols, which include but are not limited to numbers, to rupted. When obstruction occurs, the symptoms include an increased ventilatory rate and cough, which is greatly aggravated by recumbancy. Clinically, this condition is called *superior vena cava syndrome.*

GENERAL MANAGEMENT OF CANCER OF THE LUNG

The treatment of lung cancer falls into three major categories: curative, palliative, and adjunctive. These treatments may be used individually or in combination. The most commonly used treatment modalities for lung cancer are surgery, radiation, and chemotherapy. Recently, immunotherapy and interferon have also been incorporated in the treatment of cancer on an experimental basis.

Surgery

Surgery is used in diagnosis of the disease, in removal of the tumor, and for the relief of symptoms (palliative) when a cure is not possible. Small tumors can often be completely removed. When the tumor is large or involves vital organs, surgical removal may not be possible.

Radiation Therapy

Radiation therapy is used in about 50% of the cancer cases, either alone or in combination with other forms of treatment. Radiation therapy involves the use of sophisticated equipment that generates high-voltage x-ray and electronic beams that deliver radiation to the tumor without causing lethal damage to the surrounding tissues. Radioactive particles kill tumor cells by causing chemical bonds to break, by disrupting DNA, and by interfering with cellular mitosis.

Chemotherapy

Chemotherapy has evolved as a major treatment for cancer. Drugs may be used as the only treatment modality or in combination with other treatments. Drugs used for chemotherapy act at the cellular level in several ways, including disrupting enzyme production; inhibiting DNA, RNA, and protein synthesis; and interfering with cell mitosis.

Immunotherapy and Interferon

Immunotherapy and interferon are used only experimentally in combination with other forms of treatment.

Respiratory Care

Mobilization of Bronchial Secretions.—Because of the excessive mucus production and accumulation associated with lung cancer, a number of respiratory therapy modalities may be used to enhance the mobilization of bronchial secretions (see Appendix XI).

Hyperinflation Techniques.—Hyperinflation techniques may be ordered to offset the alveolar compression and consolidation associated with lung cancer (see Appendix XII).

Supplemental Oxygen.—Because of the hypoxemia associated with lung cancer, supplemental oxygen may be required. It should be noted, however, that because of the alveolar compression and consolidation produced by lung cancer, capillary shunting may be present. Hypoxemia caused by capillary shunting is often refractory to oxygen therapy.

SELF-ASSESSMENT QUESTIONS

Multiple Choice

1. Which of the following is the most common form of bronchogenic carcinoma?
   a. Squamous cell carcinoma.
   b. Oat cell carcinoma.
   c. Large-cell carcinoma.
   d. Adenocarcinoma.
   e. Small-cell carcinoma.
2. Which of the following arises from the mucus glands of the tracheobronchial tree?
   a. Small-cell carcinoma.
   b. Adenocarcinoma.
   c. Squamous cell carcinoma.
   d. Oat cell carcinoma.
   e. Large-cell carcinoma.
3. Which of the following is/are strongly associated with cigarette smoking?
   I. Adenocarcinoma.
   II. Small-cell carcinoma.
   III. Large-cell carcinoma.
   IV. Squamous cell carcinoma.
   a. I only.
   b. III only.
   c. II and IV only.
   d. I and III only.
   e. II, III, and IV only.
4. Which of the following has the fastest growth rate?
   a. Large-cell carcinoma.
   b. Small-cell carcinoma.
   c. Adenocarcinoma.
   d. Squamous cell carcinoma.
   e. Epidermoid carcinoma.
5. Which of the following is associated with bronchogenic carcinoma?
   I. Alveolar consolidation.
   II. Pleural effusion.
   III. Alveolar hyperinflation.

IV. Atelectasis.
   a. III only.
   b. II and III only.
   c. I and IV only.
   d. II and III only.
   e. I, II, and IV only.

True or False

1. Necrosis, ulceration, and cavitation are commonly associated with malignant tumors.   True _____   False _____
2. It is estimated that about 85% of lung cancer cases are due to cigarette smoking.   True _____   False _____
3. Small-cell carcinoma arises from the Kulchitsky cells in the bronchial epithelium.   True _____   False _____
4. Benign tumors are metastatic.   True _____   False _____
5. Adenocarcinoma is most commonly found in the peripheral portion of the lung parenchyma.   True _____   False _____

Answers appear in Appendix XVII.

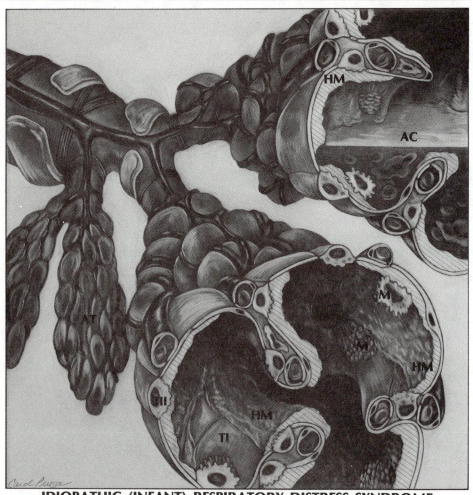

IDIOPATHIC (INFANT) RESPIRATORY DISTRESS SYNDROME

FIG 18–1.
Idiopathic (infant) respiratory distress syndrome. *HM* = hyaline membrane; *AC* = alveolar consolidation; *AT* = atelectasis; *TI* = type I cell; *TII* = type II cell; *M* = macrophages.

IDIOPATHIC (INFANT) RESPIRATORY DISTRESS SYNDROME

ANATOMIC ALTERATIONS OF THE LUNGS

On gross examination the lungs are dark red and liverlike. Under the microscope the lungs appear solid because of countless areas of alveolar collapse. The pulmonary capillaries are congested, and the lymphatic vessels are distended. There is extensive interstitial and intra-alveolar edema and hemorrhage.

In what appears to be an effort to offset alveolar collapse, the respiratory bronchioles, alveolar ducts, and some alveoli are dilated. As the disease intensifies, the intra-alveolar walls become lined with a dense, ripply hyaline membrane identical to the hyaline membrane that develops in the adult respiratory distress syndrome (ARDS). The membrane contains fibrin and cellular debris.

During the later stages of the disease, leukocytes are present, and the hyaline membrane is often fragmented and partially ingested by macrophages. Type II cells begin to proliferate, and secretions begin to accumulate in the tracheobronchial tree. The anatomic alterations in infant respiratory distress syndrome (IRDS) produce a restrictive type of lung disorder (Fig 18–1).

To summarize, the major pathologic or structural changes associated with IRDS are as follows:

- Interstitial and intra-alveolar edema and hemorrhage
- Alveolar consolidation
- Intra-alveolar hyaline membrane
- Pulmonary surfactant deficiency or abnormality
- Atelectasis

In alphabetical order, the following are some of the terms that have been used as synonyms for IRDS:

- Asphyxial membrane
- Congenital alveolar dysplasia
- Hyaline atelectasis
- Hyaline-like membrane

- Hyaline membrane disease (perhaps the most popular although an incorrect term)
- Myelin formation in the lungs
- Neonatal atelectasis
- Neonatal pulmonary ischemia
- Pulmonary hypoperfusion syndrome
- Surfactant deficiency syndrome
- Vernix membrane

ETIOLOGY

Although the exact cause of IRDS is controversial, the most popular theory suggests that the disorder develops as a result of (1) a pulmonary surfactant abnormality or deficiency and (2) pulmonary hypoperfusion evoked by hypoxia.

Some of the known factors that predispose an infant to a pulmonary surfactant abnormality or deficiency are as follows:

- Cesarean birth
- Diabetic mother
- Maternal bleeding
- Premature birth (birth weight less than 2.5 kg)
- Prenatal asphyxia
- Prolonged labor
- Second-born twin

The pulmonary hypoperfusion evoked by hypoxia is probably a secondary response to the surfactant abnormality. The probable steps in the development of IRDS are as follows:

1. Because of the pulmonary surfactant abnormality alveolar compliance decreases,* and this results in alveolar collapse.

*See the section on compliance, page 24.

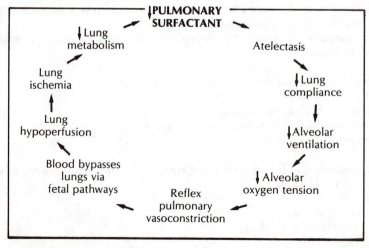

FIG 18–2.
Probable etiologic steps in the development of IRDS.

2. The pulmonary atelectasis causes the infant's work of breathing to increase.
3. Alveolar ventilation decreases in response to the decreased lung compliance, as well as infant fatigue, and causes the alveolar oxygen tension (Pa_{O_2}) to decrease.
4. The decreased Pa_{O_2} (alveolar hypoxia) stimulates a reflex pulmonary vasoconstriction.
5. Because of the pulmonary vasoconstriction, blood bypasses the infant's lungs through fetal pathways—the patent ductus and the foramen ovale.
6. The lung hypoperfusion in turn causes lung ischemia and decreased lung metabolism.
7. Because of the decreased lung metabolism, the production of pulmonary surfactant is reduced even further, and a vicious cycle develops (Fig 18–2).

OVERVIEW OF THE CARDIOPULMONARY CLINICAL MANIFESTATIONS ASSOCIATED WITH INFANT RESPIRATORY DISTRESS SYNDROME

INCREASED RESPIRATORY RATE

Normally a newborn infant's respiratory rate is about 40 to 60 breaths per minute. In IRDS, the respiratory rate is generally well over 60 breaths per minute. On the basis of anatomic alterations of the lung associated with IRDS, there may be several pathophysiologic mechanisms operating simultaneously that lead to an increased ventilatory rate. The possible mechanisms are as follows (see page 23):

- Stimulation of peripheral chemoreceptors
- Decreased lung compliance/increased work of breathing relationship
- Stimulation of central chemoreceptors

INCREASED HEART RATE, CARDIAC OUTPUT, AND BLOOD PRESSURE (see page 57)

PULMONARY FUNCTION STUDIES (see page 37)

LUNG VOLUME AND CAPACITY FINDINGS
- Decreased VC
- Decreased RV
- Decreased FRC
- Decreased TLC
- Decreased Vт

CLINICAL MANIFESTATIONS ASSOCIATED WITH INCREASED NEGATIVE INTRAPLEURAL PRESSURES DURING INSPIRATION

- Intercostal retractions
- Substernal retraction/abdominal distension ("seesaw" movement)
- Cyanosis of the dependent portion of the thoracic/abdominal area

The thorax of the newborn infant is very flexible, i.e., the compliance of the infant's thorax is high.* This is due to the large amount of cartilage found in the

*See the section on compliance, page 24.

skeletal structure of newborns. Because of the structural alterations associated with IRDS, however, the compliance of the infant's lungs is low.

In an effort to offset the decreased lung compliance, the infant must generate increased negative intrapleural pressure during inspiration. This causes the following:

- The soft tissues between the ribs retract during inspiration.
- The substernal area retracts, and the abdominal area protrudes in a seesaw fashion during inspiration. The substernal retraction is due to increased negative intrapleural pressure, and the abdominal distension is due to the increased contraction—or depression—of the diaphragm during inspiration
- The blood vessels in the more dependent portions of the thoracic/abdominal area dilate and pool blood. This causes these areas to appear cyanotic (Fig 18–3).

FLARING NOSTRILS

Flaring nostrils are frequently observed in infants in respiratory distress. This is probably a facial reflex to facilitate the movement of gas into the tracheobronchial tree. The *dilator naris*, which originates from the maxilla and inserts into the ala of the nose, is the muscle responsible for this clinical manifestation. When activated, the dilator naris pulls the alae laterally and widens the nasal aperture. This provides a larger orifice for gas to enter during inspiration.

EXPIRATORY GRUNTING

An audible expiratory grunt is frequently heard in infants with IRDS. Depending on the auditory perception of the listener, the expiratory grunt may sound like an expiratory sigh or cry. It is often first detected on auscultation.

The expiratory grunt is a natural physiologic mechanism that generates greater positive pressures in the alveoli. This effect counteracts the hypoventilation associated with the disorder, that is, as the gas pressure in the alveoli increases, the infant's $P_{A_{O_2}}$ increases. During exhalation the infant's epiglottis covers the glottis,

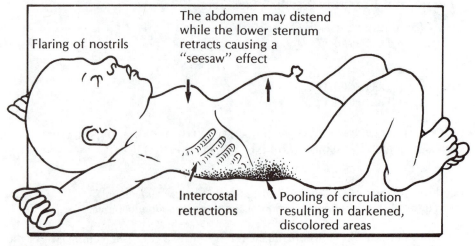

FIG 18–3.
Clinical manifestations associated with an increased negative intrapleural pressure during inspiration in infants with IRDS.

which causes the intrapulmonary air pressure to increase. When the epiglottis abruptly opens, gas rushes past the infant's vocal cords and produces an expiratory grunt or cry.

CHEST X-RAY FINDINGS

INCREASED OPACITY (GROUND-GLASS APPEARANCE)

On chest x-ray films of infants with IRDS, the air-filled tracheobronchial tree typically stands out against a dense opaque (or white) lung. This white density is often described as having a fine ground-glass appearance throughout the lung fields.

Because of the pathologic processes the density of the lungs is increased. Increased lung density resists x-ray penetration and is revealed on x-ray films as increased opacity. Thus, the more severe the IRDS, the whiter the x-ray film will be (Fig 18–4).

ARTERIAL BLOOD GASES:

ADVANCED STAGES OF IRDS
ACUTE VENTILATORY FAILURE WITH HYPOXEMIA (SEE PAGE 52)
- Pa_{O_2}: decreased
- Pa_{CO_2}: increased
- HCO_3^-: increased
- pH: decreased

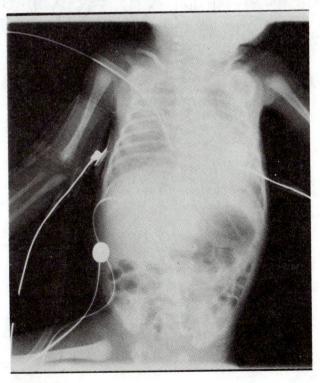

FIG 18–4.
Chest x-ray film of an infant with IRDS.

represent the information to be processed and conveyed. Although you can use nonnumeric symbols, and modern computers have the capability to process such symbols as alphabetic letters and strings, it is to your advantage to quantify your data whenever feasible by using numbers. Computers are much better at numbers than at alphabetic letters and strings.

There are two kinds of coding practice, that is, precoding and postcoding. To understand what precoding is, one must be able to distinguish between two different forms of question or questionnaire design. The first kind is called "open-ended," meaning that the respondent is free to provide her own answer to the question. The second form is called "closed-ended," which is essentially a multiple-choice type question. For the latter, all possible answers should be identified and listed (exhaustiveness), and the logical requirement for mutual exclusiveness must be met. If you are not sure whether or not your list of choices is exhaustive, you should add a category called "Other" for the respondent to consider and, if needed, you can further ask the respondent to specify it. There may still be some problems with closed-ended questions, depending on how you structure the predetermined categories of responses. But this format offers great convenience in data management and analysis. You know beforehand all the possible answers to a question, and the limited categories of answers are standardized across your research sample. Therefore, you can assign a code (a numeric value if you want to quantify it) to each potential answer (a uniform category). If you assign codes to all your closed-ended questions before data collection is started, then these questions and answers are said precoded. The precodings (numeric or alphabetical values) may be printed on the questionnaire next to the answers they represent, or recorded on a separate codebook. The easiest way to learn how to lay out your precodings is to find a questionnaire designed by other researchers and see how they have done it. You do not have to precode the questionnaire, however. The codes can be made up after data are collected. In other words, you can always postcode your data.

If your questions are closed-ended, the postcoding is not very much different from the precoding, which is a simple assignment of codes or numbers to the predetermined categories of answers. If you have open-ended questions, usually you cannot precode all the answers because you never know what responses you will receive from the respondents. And the postcoding for an open-ended question will be much more difficult and time-consuming since every answer could be different. Unlike the use of precoding by which you have uniform answers or standardized categories, the postcoding of the answers to an open-

Decreased Pa$_{O_2}$

There are three major mechanisms responsible for the decreased Pa$_{O_2}$ observed in IRDS: (1) pulmonary shunting and venous admixture, (2) persistent fetal circulation, and (3) infant fatigue.

The infant's Pa$_{O_2}$ decreases in IRDS because of the reduced $\dot{V}/\dot{Q}$ ratio,* intrapulmonary shunting,† and venous admixture‡ associated with the disorder.

As the infant's Pa$_{O_2}$ declines, a reflex pulmonary vasoconstriction may be stim-

*See the section on the ventilation-perfusion ratio, page 16.
†See the section on pulmonary shunting, page 18.
‡See the section on venous admixture, page 19.

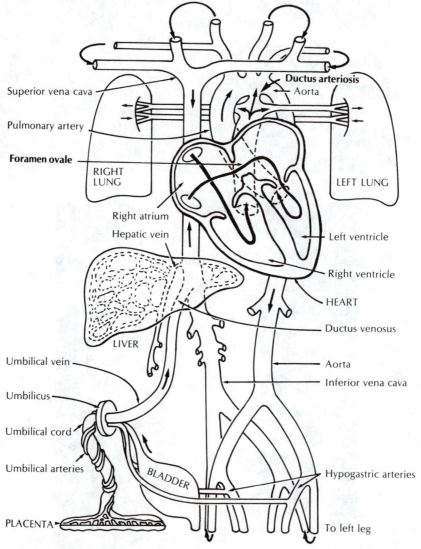

FIG 18–5.
Fetal circulation.

ulated. Because of the pulmonary vasoconstriction, nonreoxygenated blood begins to bypass the infant's lungs through fetal pathways—the patent ductus and foramen ovale. This is known as *persistent fetal circulation* (Fig 18–5).

If the pathologic processes persist for a long period of time, the infant becomes *fatigued* (because of the increased work of breathing) and begins to hypoventilate. This causes a further reduction of the Pa_{O_2}

INCREASED Pa_{CO_2}

There are two major mechanisms responsible for the increased Pa_{CO_2} noted in IRDS: (1) decreased lung compliance* and (2) infant fatigue.

Due to the pulmonary surfactant abnormality, alveolar compliance decreases, and alveolar hypoventilation ensues. This in turn causes the Pa_{CO_2} to increase.

Because of the increased work of breathing required, the infant may become fatigued and begin to hypoventilate even more. When this occurs, alveolar ventilation slowly decreases and causes the Pa_{O_2} to decrease and the Pa_{CO_2} to increase (Fig 18–6).

INCREASED HCO_3^-
DECREASED pH

When acute ventilatory failure and a progressive increase in Pa_{CO_2} develop during the advanced stages of IRDS, a secondary increase in the HCO_3^- level and a decreased pH will be present. The decreased pH may also be due to the decreased Pa_{O_2} and the metabolic acidosis that result from anaerobic metabolism and lactic acid accumulation.* If this is the case, the calculated HCO_3^- reading and pH will be lower than expected for a particular Pa_{CO_2} level.

*See the section on compliance, page 24.
*See the section on the $P_{CO_2}/HCO_3^-/pH$ relationship, page 50.

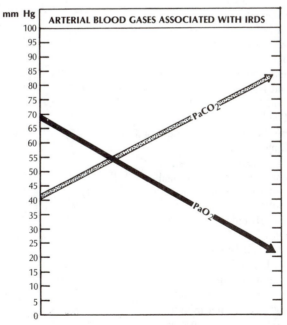

FIG 18–6.
Pa_{O_2} and Pa_{CO_2} trends associated with IRDS.

CYANOSIS (see page 16)

CHEST ASSESSMENT FINDINGS (see page 3)

- Bronchial (or harsh) breath sounds
- Fine crackles/rhonchi

GENERAL MANAGEMENT OF IRDS

During the early stages of IRDS, continuous positive-airway pressure (CPAP) is the treatment of choice. Mechanical ventilation is usually avoided as long as possible. CPAP generally works well with these patients since it increases the functional residual capacity, decreases the work of breathing, and works to increase the Pa_{O_2} while the infant is receiving a lower inspired concentration of oxygen. A Pa_{O_2} between 40 and 70 mm Hg is normal for newborn infants. No efforts should be made to get the infant's Pa_{O_2} within the normal adult range.

Special attention should be given to the thermal environment of the infant with IRDS since the infant's oxygenation could be further compromised if the body temperature is above or below normal.

SELF-ASSESSMENT QUESTIONS

Multiple Choice
1. When persistent fetal circulation exists in IRDS, blood bypasses the infant's lungs through the
     I. Ductus venosus.
    II. Umbilical vein.
   III. Ductus arteriosus.
    IV. Foramen ovale.
        a. I only.
        b. I and II only.
        c. I and III only.
        d. II and III only.
        e. III and IV only.
2. It is suggested that IRDS is a result of a
     I. Vernix membrane.
    II. Decreased perfusion of the lungs.
   III. Pulmonary surfactant abnormality.
    IV. Congenital alveolar dysplasia.
        a. I and III only.
        b. II and III only.
        c. I and IV only.
        d. II, III, and IV only.
        e. I, II, III, and IV.
3. What is the normal respiratory rate of a newborn infant?
        a. 12–15 breaths per minute.
        b. 15–20 breaths per minute.
        c. 20–30 breaths per minute.
        d. 30–40 breaths per minute.
        e. 40–60 breaths per minute.

4. What is the normal tidal volume (V_T) of a newborn infant?
    a. 15 mL.
    b. 20 mL.
    c. 25 mL.
    d. 50 mL.
    e. 100 mL.

5. The blood-brain barrier is very permeable to
    I. CO_2.
    II. H^+.
    III. HCO_3^-.
    IV. $H_2CO_3^-$.
    a. I only.
    b. II and III only.
    c. II, III, and IV only.
    d. I, II, and III only.
    e. I, II, III, and IV.

6. Infants with severe IRDS have a/an
    I. Increased RV.
    II. Decreased FRC.
    III. Increased V_T.
    IV. Decreased VC.
    a. I and II only.
    b. III and IV only.
    c. I and IV only.
    d. II and IV only.
    e. II, III, and IV only.

7. What is the normal heart rate of a newborn infant?
    a. 70 beats per minute.
    b. 90 beats per minute.
    c. 120 beats per minute.
    d. 140 beats per minute.
    e. 160 beats per minute.

8. When an infant with IRDS creates a greater-than-normal negative intrapleural pressure during inspiration, the
    I. Soft tissue between the ribs bulges outward.
    II. Substernal area protrudes outward.
    III. Abdominal area retracts inward.
    IV. Dependent blood vessels dilate and pool blood.
    a. II only.
    b. IV only.
    c. II and III only.
    d. I, III, and IV only.
    e. II, III, and IV only.

9. Infants with severe IRDS often have
    I. Diminished breath sounds.
    II. Bronchial breath sounds.
    III. Hyperresonate percussion notes.
    IV. Fine rales.
    a. I only.
    b. I and IV only.
    c. III and IV only.
    d. II and III only.
    e. II and IV only.

10. Continuous positive-airway pressure (CPAP) is often administered to infants with IRDS in an effort to
    I. Increase the infant's FRC.
    II. Decrease the infant's work of breathing.
    III. Increase the infant's Pa_{O_2}.
    IV. Decrease the $F_{I_{O_2}}$ necessary to oxygenate the infant.
        a. I and III only.
        b. II and III only.
        c. III and IV only.
        d. II, III, and IV only.
        e. I, II, III, and IV.

True or False

1. The intra-alveolar hyaline membrane seen in IRDS is identical to the hyaline membrane seen in adult respiratory distress syndrome (ARDS).   True _____   False _____
2. Alveolar consolidation develops in IRDS.   True _____   False _____
3. When activated, the dilator naris muscle widens the glottis.   True _____   False _____
4. Chest x-ray films of infants with severe IRDS appear more translucent.   True _____   False _____
5. The Pa_{O_2} of infants with IRDS should be maintained between 80 and 100 mm Hg.   True _____   False _____

Fill in the Blank

1. A premature birth is when the infant's weight is less than _____

Answers appear in Appendix XVII.

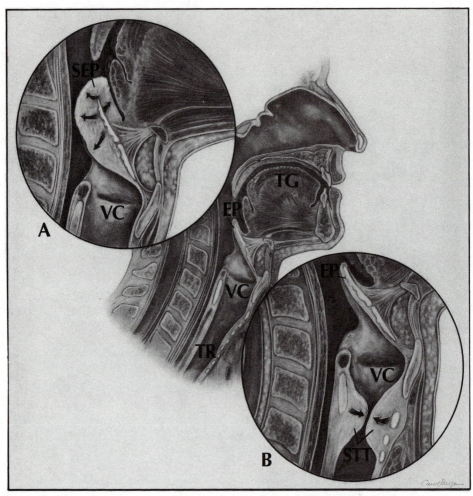

EPIGLOTTITIS AND LARYNGOTRACHEOBRONCHITIS

FIG 19–1.
A, epiglottitis: obstruction due to tissue swelling above the vocal cords. **B,** croup: airway obstruction due to tissue swelling below the vocal cords. *TG* = tongue; *EP* = epiglottis; *VC* = vocal cords; *TR* = trachea; *SEP* = swollen epiglottis; *STT* = swollen trachea tissue.

CROUP SYNDROME: LARYNGOTRACHEO-BRONCHITIS AND ACUTE EPIGLOTTITIS

Croup is a general term used to describe the inspiratory, barking sound associated with the partial upper airway obstruction that develops in the following two disease entities: (1) *laryngotracheobronchitis (subglottic croup)* and (2) *acute epiglottitis (supraglottic croup)* (Fig 19–1). Clinically, the inspiratory, sound heard in croup is also called an *inspiratory stridor*.

ANATOMIC ALTERATIONS OF THE UPPER AIRWAY

Laryngotracheobronchitis

Because this disease entity can affect the lower laryngeal area, trachea, and occasionally the bronchi, the term *laryngotracheobronchitis* (LTB) is used as a synonym for "classic" *subglottic croup*. Pathologically, LTB is an inflammatory process that causes edema and swelling of the mucous membranes. Although the laryngeal mucosa and submucosa are vascular, the distribution of the lymphatic capillaries is either uneven or absent in this region. Consequently, when edema develops in the upper airway, fluid spreads and accumulates quickly throughout the connective tissues, which causes the mucosa to swell and the airway lumen to narrow. The inflammation also causes the mucous glands to increase their production of mucus and the cilia to lose their effectiveness as a mucociliary transport mechanism.

Because the subglottic area is the narrowest region of the larynx in a infant or small child, even a slight degree of edema can cause a significant reduction in the cross-sectional area. The edema in this area is further aggravated by the rigid, cricoid cartilage, which surrounds the mucous membrane and prevents external swelling as fluid engorges the laryngeal tissues. The edema and swelling in the subglottic region also decreases the ability of the vocal cords to abduct (move apart) during inspiration. This further reduces the cross-sectional area of airway in this region.

Acute Epiglottitis

Acute epiglottitis is a life-threatening emergency. In contrast to LTB, epiglottitis is an inflammation of the supraglottic region. The supraglottic region includes the epiglottis, aryepiglottic folds, and false vocal cords. Epiglottitis does not involve the pharynx, trachea, or other subglottic structures. As the edema in the epiglottis increases, the lateral borders curl, and the tip of the epiglottis protrudes in a posterior and inferior direction. During inspiration, the swollen epiglottis is pulled (or sucked) over the laryngeal inlet. In severe cases, this may completely block the laryngeal opening. Clinically, the "classic" finding is a swollen, cherry-red epiglottis.

To summarize, the major pathologic or structural changes associated with croup are as follows:

- LTB: airway obstruction due to tissue swelling just below the vocal cords
- Epiglottitis: airway obstruction due to tissue swelling just above the vocal cords

ETIOLOGY

Laryngotracheobronchitis

The most common cause of LTB is a viral infection. The *parainfluenza viruses* 1, 2, and 3, transmitted via aerosol droplets, are the most frequently identified etiologic agents, with type 1 being the most prevalent. LTB may also be caused by *influenza A and B, respiratory syncytial viruses, rhinovirus,* and *adenoviruses.*

LTB is predominantly seen in children between 3 months and 3 years of age. Males are affected slightly more often than females are. The onset of LTB is relatively slow (i.e., symptoms progressively increase over a period of 24 to 48 hours), and it is most often seen during the winter months. A cough is commonly present. The child's voice is usually hoarse, and the inspiratory stridor is typically loud and high in pitch. Unlike epiglottitis, the patient usually does not have a fever, drooling, swallowing difficulties, or a toxic appearance.

Acute Epiglottitis

Acute epiglottitis is a bacterial infection almost always caused by *Haemophilus influenzae* B. It is transmitted via aerosol droplets. Although rare, other causative agents such as *Streptococcus pneumoniae, Staphylococcus aureus,* and *Haemophilus parainfluenzae* have been reported. It is estimated that epiglottitis accounts for fewer than 1 per 1,000 pediatric cases. There is no clear-cut geographic or seasonal incidence. Males are affected more than females. Although acute epiglottitis may develop in all age groups (neonatal to adulthood), it most often occurs in children between 2 and 4 years of age. The onset of epiglottitis is usually abrupt.

Although the initial clinical manifestations are usually mild, they progress rapidly over a 2- to 4-hour period. A common scenario includes a sore throat or mild upper respiratory problem that quickly progresses to a high fever, lethargy, and difficulty in swallowing and handling secretions. The child usually appears pale. As the supraglottic area becomes swollen, breathing becomes noisy, the tongue is often thrust forward during inspiration, and the child may drool. Compared with LTB, the inspiratory stridor is usually softer and lower in pitch. The voice and cry

TABLE 19–1.
General History/Physical Findings of Laryngotracheobronchitis and Epiglottitis

Clinical Finding	LTB	Epiglottitis
Age	3 mo–3 yr	2–4 yr
Onset	Slow (24–48 hr)	Abrupt (2–4 hr)
Fever	Absent	Present
Drooling	Absent	Present
Lateral neck x-ray	Haziness in subglottic area	Haziness in supraglottic area
Inspiratory stridor	High pitched and loud	Low pitched and muffled
Hoarseness	Present	Absent
Swallowing difficulty	Absent	Present
White blood count	Normal (viral)	Elevated (bacterial)

is usually muffled rather than hoarse. Older children commonly complain of a sore throat and pain during swallowing. A cough is usually absent in patients with epiglottitis.

The general history and physical findings of LTB and epiglottis are listed in Table 19–1.

OVERVIEW OF THE CLINICAL MANIFESTATIONS ASSOCIATED WITH LARYNGOTRACHEOBRONCHITIS AND EPIGLOTTITIS

INCREASED RESPIRATORY RATE

Several pathophysiologic mechanisms operating simultaneously may lead to an increased ventilatory rate. These are (see page 23):

- Stimulation of peripheral chemoreceptors
- Anxiety

INCREASED HEART RATE, CARDIAC OUTPUT, AND BLOOD PRESSURE (see page 57)

ARTERIAL BLOOD GASES

EARLY STAGES OF LTB OR EPIGLOTTITIS
ACUTE ALVEOLAR HYPERVENTILATION WITH HYPOXEMIA (see page 48)
- Pa_{O_2}: decreased
- Pa_{CO_2}: decreased
- HCO_3^-: decreased
- pH: increased

ADVANCED STAGES OF LTB OR EPIGLOTTITIS
ACUTE VENTILATORY FAILURE WITH HYPOXEMIA (see page 52)
- Pa_{O_2}: decreased
- Pa_{CO_2}: increased
- HCO_3^-: increased
- pH: decreased

ended question requires you to analyze and understand the meaning of every answer, summarize the answers of all the respondents by setting up some general categories (values), and then classify each answer by assigning an appropriate value to it. In research practice, open-ended questions sometimes fail to be coded because the postcoding turns out to be too complicated for a relatively simple project. Occasionally the answers to an open-ended question are found to be useless for quantitative analysis since they might be too dispersive to be summarized for a categorical variable as compared with the limited size of the sample. It is reasonable, therefore, for you to try to ask closed-ended questions whenever feasible, though this format has certain problems as well.

The computerization of data means the setting up of a database and the transferring of data from the original records (e.g., questionnaires) into the computer database. Setting up a database is like inputting the questionnaire, or generally a structure of inquiry, into the computer. By computerization you will have a special computer file to contain your questionnaire and the data structure. You may have used the computer to create your questionnaire. That computer file, however, is different from a database file. They are created by different computer software packages. The questionnaire is compiled with the use of a word processing program such as WordPerfect, while the database file is usually created with the use of a data management program (e.g., dBASE or EXCEL) or a statistical package that has data entry and management functions (e.g., SPSS for Windows). To create a database structure, each item of inquiry (i.e., a question or a sub-question) must be represented by a variable with a name of no more than eight characters including numbers and alphabetic letters (the names should not begin with numbers). In addition to the substantive variables derived from the specific questions, an identification variable needs to be created to give a unique ID to each respondent, questionnaire, or case record. The definition of a variable not only includes the name that represents a question, but also contains the specifications for the answers, i.e., their type (numeric or character), maximum length, and specific codes. When the types and maximum lengths are specified for all the variables and codes for all the answers, the computer database structure represents the questionnaire with a standard text, and in some aspect becomes more specific. The variable names, however, are reduced from the original questions and the codes are reduced from the original answers. Frequent cross-references will be needed during data analysis, although usually you do not need to bother about the lengths once they are determined. A separate codebook is not mandated, however. Not only can the codes be printed on the

Cyanosis (see page 16)

Use of Accessory Muscles During Inspiration (see page 61)

Sternal and Intercostal Retractions (see page 72)

Chest Assessment Findings (see page 3)

- Diminished breath sounds
- Crackles/rhonchi/wheezing

Inspiratory Stridor

Under normal circumstances, the slight narrowing that naturally occurs during inspiration is nonsignificant. Because the upper airway is relatively small in infants and children, even a slight degree of edema may become significant during inspiration. Thus, when the cross section of the upper airway is reduced because of the edema, the child will generate stridor during inspiration, when the upper airway naturally becomes smaller. It should also be noted that if the edema becomes very severe, the patient may generate both an inspiratory and expiratory stridor.

Lateral Neck X-ray Film

- Haziness in the subglottic area (LTB)
- Haziness in the supraglottic area (epiglottitis)
- Classic thumb sign

Although the diagnosis of epiglottitis or LTB can generally be made on the basis of the patient's clinical history, a lateral neck x-ray film is sometimes used to confirm the diagnosis. When the patient has LTB, a white haziness is demonstrated in the subglottic area. When the patient has acute epiglottitis, there is a white haziness in the supraglottic area. In addition, epiglottitis often appears on a lateral neck x-ray film as the classic "thumb sign." The epiglottis is swollen and rounded, which gives it an appearance of the distal portion of a thumb (Fig 19–2).

GENERAL MANAGEMENT OF LARYNGOTRACHEOBRONCHITIS AND EPIGLOTTITIS

It is important to stress that early recognition of epiglottitis may be lifesaving. A history of upper airway obstruction and a general examination should be secured as soon as possible. A lateral neck x-ray may be necessary to differentiate LTB, epiglottitis, or some other upper airway obstruction. Once established, the general management of LTB and acute epiglottitis is as follows:

Supplemental Oxygen

Because hypoxemia is associated with both LTB and epiglottitis, supplemental oxygen is usually required.

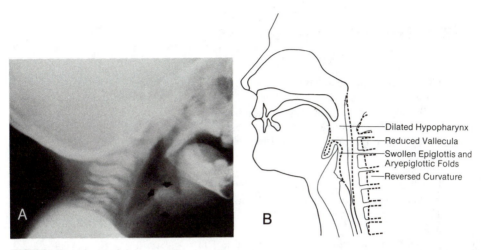

FIG 19–2.
The classic "thumb sign" of an edematous epiglottis is evident in this lateral neck film (see *arrows* in **A**). The schematic illustrates the findings to look for in a lateral film in a patient with suspected epiglottitis **(B)**. Such films are superfluous in a child with the classic history, signs, and symptoms of epiglottitis; they can be of tremendous help, however, in the diagnosis of mild or questionable cases—particularly when explaining to parents the need for aggressive treatment. (From Ashcraft CK, Steele RW: *J Respir Dis* 1988; 9:48–60. Used by permission.)

Cool Aerosol Mist

Cool aerosol mist therapy is a primary mode of treatment for LTB. It is administered to liquify thick secretions and to cool and reduce the subglottic edema.

Racemic Epinephrine (Micronefrin, Vaponefrin)

Aerosolized racemic epinephrine is usually administered to children with LTB. This α-adrenergic agent is used for its mucosal vasoconstriction and is an effective and safe aerosol decongestant.

Endotracheal Intubation

Because acute epiglottitis is a life-threatening situation, endotracheal intubation, in the operating room with a fully trained team, is the treatment of choice.*

Antibiotic Therapy

Because acute epiglottitis is almost always caused by *Haemophilus influenzae,* appropriate antibiotic therapy should be part of the treatment plan.

*Note: In cases of suspected epiglottitis, examination or inspection of the pharynx and larynx are absolutely contraindicated, except in the operating room or as indicated above.

SELF-ASSESSMENT QUESTIONS

True or False

 1. LTB is a supraglottic croup.   True _____   False _____
 2. Acute epiglottitis is a life-threatening emergency.   True _____   False _____
 3. LTB is most predominately seen in children be-
    tween 2 and 4 years of age.   True _____   False _____
 4. Acute epiglottitis is usually caused by *Haemophilus*
    influenzae B.   True _____   False _____
 5. The onset of LTB is relatively slow (24 to 48 hours). True _____   False _____
 6. Drooling is usually present in LTB.   True _____   False _____
 7. A fever is associated with acute epiglottitis.   True _____   False _____
 8. The inspiratory stridor is usually low pitched and
    muffled in LTB.   True _____   False _____
 9. The white blood count is usually elevated in LTB.   True _____   False _____
10. Swallowing is usually difficult in patients with LTB. True _____   False _____

Answers appear in Appendix XVII.

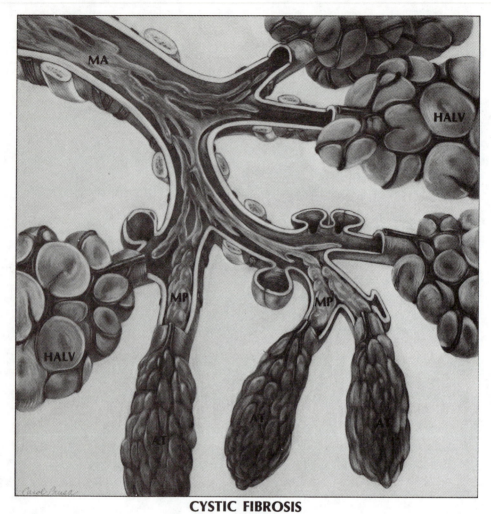

CYSTIC FIBROSIS

FIG 20–1.
Cystic fibrosis. *MP* = mucus plugging; *HALV* = hyperinflated alveoli; *AT* = atelectasis;
MA = mucus accumulation.

• 20

CYSTIC FIBROSIS

ANATOMIC ALTERATIONS OF THE LUNGS*

Although the lungs of patients with cystic fibrosis appear normal at birth, abnormal structural changes develop quickly. Initially there are bronchial gland hypertrophy and metaplasia of goblet cells, which secrete large amounts of thick, tenacious mucus. Because the mucus is particularly tenacious in cystic fibrosis, impairment of the normal mucociliary clearing mechanism ensues, and many small bronchi and bronchioles become partially or totally obstructed. Partial obstruction leads to overdistension of the alveoli, and complete obstruction leads to patchy areas of atelectasis. Hyperinflation of the lungs is the predominant feature of cystic fibrosis in the advanced stages.

The abundance of stagnant mucus in the tracheobronchial tree also serves as an excellent culture medium for bacteria, particularly *Staphylococcus aureus* and *Pseudomonas aeruginosa*. The infection stimulates additional mucus production and further compromises the mucociliary transport system. Finally, as the disease progresses, the patient may develop signs and symptoms of chronic bronchitis, bronchiectasis, and lung abscesses (Fig 20–1).

To summarize, the major pathologic or structural changes associated with cystic fibrosis are as follows:

- Excessive production and accumulation of thick, tenacious mucus in the tracheobronchial tree
- Partial or total bronchial obstruction
- Atelectasis
- Hyperinflation of the alveoli

ETIOLOGY

Cystic fibrosis is genetically transmitted as an autosomal recessive trait. It is estimated that as many as 10 million Americans carry the cystic fibrosis gene and approximately 175,000 carriers are born each year. Presently there is no reliable test to identify carriers, and clinically the carrier does not demonstrate any signs of cystic fibrosis.

The distribution of homozygotes vs. heterozygotes in the offspring of two cystic

---

*Cystic fibrosis does not exclusively affect the lungs. It also affects the function of exocrine glands in other parts of the body. In addition to the abnormally viscid secretions of the pulmonary system, the disease is clinically manifested by pancreatic deficiency and high electrolyte concentrations in sweat.

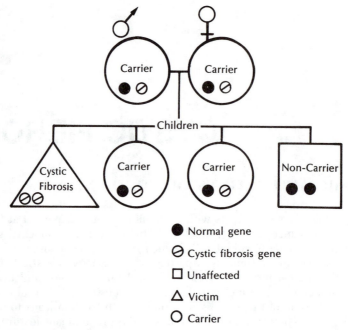

FIG 20–2.
Standard mendelian pattern.

fibrosis carriers follows the standard mendelian pattern: there is a 25% chance that an individual offspring will have cystic fibrosis, a 25% chance that it will be completely normal, and a 50% chance that it will be a carrier (Fig 20–2).

OVERVIEW OF THE CARDIOPULMONARY CLINICAL MANIFESTATIONS ASSOCIATED WITH CYSTIC FIBROSIS

INCREASED RESPIRATORY RATE

Several pathophysiologic mechanisms operating simultaneously may lead to an increased ventilatory rate. These are (see page 23):

- Stimulation of peripheral chemoreceptors
- Anxiety

PULMONARY FUNCTION STUDIES

EXPIRATORY MANEUVER FINDINGS (see page 38)
- Decreased FVC
- Decreased $FEF_{200-1200}$
- Decreased $FEF_{25\%-75\%}$
- Decreased FEV_T
- Decreased FEV_1/FVC ratio
- Decreased MVV

- Decreased PEFR
- Decreased $\dot{V}_{max\ 50}$

LUNG VOLUME AND CAPACITY FINDINGS (see page 47)
- Increased VT
- Increased RV
- Increased RV/TLC ratio
- Increased FRC
- Increased CV
- Decreased VC
- Decreased IRV
- Decreased ERV

INCREASED HEART RATE, CARDIAC OUTPUT, AND BLOOD PRESSURE (see page 57)

INCREASED ANTEROPOSTERIOR CHEST DIAMETER (BARREL CHEST) (see page 67)

PURSED-LIP BREATHING (see page 67)

USE OF ACCESSORY MUSCLES DURING INSPIRATION (see page 61)

USE OF ACCESSORY MUSCLES DURING EXPIRATION (see page 64)

COUGH AND SPUTUM PRODUCTION (see page 58)

ARTERIAL BLOOD GASES

EARLY STAGES OF CYSTIC FIBROSIS
ACUTE ALVEOLAR HYPERVENTILATION WITH HYPOXEMIA (see page 48)
- Pa_{O_2}: decreased
- Pa_{CO_2}: decreased
- HCO_3^-: decreased
- pH: increased

ADVANCED STAGES OF CYSTIC FIBROSIS
CHRONIC VENTILATORY FAILURE WITH HYPOXEMIA (see page 53)
- Pa_{O_2}: decreased
- Pa_{CO_2}: increased
- HCO_3^-: increased
- pH: normal

CYANOSIS (see page 16)

POLYCYTHEMIA/COR PULMONALE (see page 67)

- Distension of neck veins
- Enlarged and tender liver
- Peripheral edema

Digital Clubbing (see page 70)

Chest Assessment Findings (see page 3)

- Decreased tactile and vocal fremitus
- Hyperresonant percussion note
- Diminished breath sounds
- Crackles/rhonchi/wheezing

Chest X-ray Findings

- Translucencies
- Depressed or flattened diaphragm
- Enlarged heart

During the later stages of cystic fibrosis, the alveoli become hyperinflated, which causes the residual volume and functional residual capacity to increase. This condition decreases the density of the lungs. Consequently, the resistance to x-ray penetration is not as great, and the x-ray films become darker in appearance.

Because of the increased residual volume and functional residual capacity, the diaphragm is depressed or flattened and appears so on x-ray films (Fig 20–3). Since ventricular heart enlargement and failure often develop as secondary problems during the advanced stages of cystic fibrosis, an enlarged heart may be identified on x-ray films.

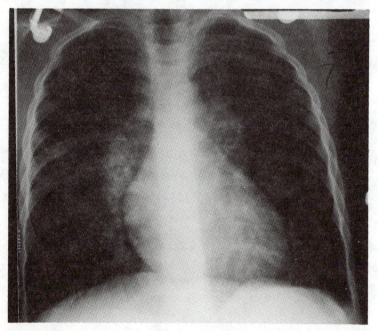

FIG 20–3.
Chest x-ray film of a patient with cystic fibrosis.

COMMON NONRESPIRATORY CLINICAL MANIFESTATIONS

MECONIUM ILEUS

Meconium ileus is an obstruction of the small intestine of the newborn that is caused by the impaction of thick, dry, tenacious meconium, usually at or near the ileocecal valve. This results from a deficiency in pancreatic enzymes and is the earliest manifestation of cystic fibrosis. The disease is suspected in newborn infants who demonstrate abdominal distension and fail to pass meconium within 12 hours after birth. Meconium ileus may occur in up to 25% of infants with cystic fibrosis.

MECONIUM ILEUS EQUIVALENT

Meconium ileus equivalent is an intestinal obstruction (similar to meconium ileus in neonates) that occurs in older children and young adults with cystic fibrosis.

MALNUTRITION AND POOR BODY DEVELOPMENT

In cystic fibrosis, the pancreatic ducts become plugged with mucus, which leads to fibrosis of the pancreas. The pancreatic insufficiency that ensues inhibits the digestion of protein and fat, and this results in vitamin A, E, D, and K deficiency. Vitamin K deficiency may be the basis of easy bruising and bleeding. Approximately 80% of all patients with cystic fibrosis have the aforementioned vitamin deficiency and therefore show signs of malnutrition and of poor body development throughout life.

ELEVATED CONCENTRATION OF SODIUM AND CHLORIDE IN SWEAT

Although the sweat glands of cystic fibrosis patients are described as normal, the glands secrete up to four times the normal amount of sodium and chloride. The actual amount of sweat, however, is no greater than that produced by a normal individual. A concentration of sodium greater than 60 mEq/L is considered to be diagnostic of the disease.

GENERAL MANAGEMENT OF CYSTIC FIBROSIS

Mobilization of Bronchial Secretions

Because of the excessive mucus production and accumulation, a number of respiratory therapy modalities may be used to enhance the mobilization of bronchial secretions (see Appendix XI). Vigorous bronchial hygiene should be performed on cystic fibrosis patients both in the hospital and at home.

Although controversial, nightly mist tent therapy is sometimes used for these patients.

Medications

Mucolytic Agents.—Mucolytics may be used to break down the large amounts of thick tenacious mucus associated with cystic fibrosis (see Appendix VI).

Sympathomimetics.—Sympathomimetic drugs are administered to patients with cystic fibrosis when bronchial spasm is present (see Appendix II).

Parasympatholytic Agents.—Parasympatholytic agents are also used to offset bronchial smooth muscle constriction (see Appendix III).

original questionnaire, but also the types of the codes as well as the variable names representing the questions or inquiry items. It is often convenient to use a blank hard copy of the questionnaire as the codebook. Later we will discuss recoding in data manipulation. All the recodings should also be recorded in such a "codebook" to avoid confusion in data analysis. Sometimes additional codes might have been added during data collection due to the inadequacy of the precoding scheme. The "codebook" should keep a complete record of such additions as well.

An important issue with coding is the treatment of missing information. For the various reasons that we will discuss later, you may often find some questions on a questionnaire left unanswered after the data collection is completed. If you are using another source of information such as administrative records, missing information could also be a frequently seen problem. In your coding scheme, you need to use one or more codes, in addition to those representing the valid answers, to indicate such an "information missing" situation. These codes are called missing values. Missing values can be ordinary codes as long as they remain distinguished from the valid ones. For the variable "gender," for instance, you can use the number 9 as a missing value if you code male as 0 and female as 1. Or you may use 0 as a missing value if you code male as 1 and female as 2. Of course, you can always use other numbers as valid codes, such as 2 for female and 3 for male, and choose to use another number for missing value, such as 8, as long as these codes remain distinct from one another. As a natural habit, researchers tend to begin with the number 1 for valid values. They also tend to use 9 (or 0) for missing values if the number of valid answer categories (including the "Other" category if necessary) is less than 10, 99 as a missing value if the number of valid answer categories is less than 100, and so on. But you do not have to use the 9's or 99's; you can use -1 or something else as missing values. If the number of valid answer categories is less than 9 or 8, the researchers may also use 8 as a missing value, especially when they feel they need to use more than one code to distinguish between different missing information situations such as "Don't know" and "Refused." In presenting data it is a good practice to report both percentages and valid percentages in frequency tables, especially when it is difficult to deal with such cases as "don't knows" and "refused".

A variable with only two valid values is called a dichotomy or dichotomous variable. It is often expedient to code dichotomies as "dummy variables" whose valid values are 0's and 1's, which have special use and convenience in statistical

Xanthine Bronchodilators.—Xanthine bronchodilators are used to enhance bronchial smooth muscle relaxation (see Appendix IV).

Expectorants.—Expectorants are prescribed to loosen bronchial secretions and facilitate expectoration (see Appendix VII).

Antibiotic Agents.—Antibiotics are commonly employed to prevent secondary respiratory tract infections (see Appendix VIII).

Other

Time-release pancreatic enzymes such as Pancrease are prescribed to patients with cystic fibrosis to aid food digestion. They are also encouraged to replace body salts either by heavily salting their food or in pill form. Supplemental multivitamins and minerals are also very important. Patients should have regular medical check-ups for comparative purposes to determine their general health, weight, height, pulmonary function abilities, sputum culture status, and interior lung status.

The patient and the patient's family should be instructed as to the type of disease the patient has and how it affects body functions. They should be taught home care therapies, the goals of these therapies, and how to administer medications. Patients with severe cystic fibrosis are commonly managed by a pulmonary rehabilitation team. Such teams include a respiratory therapist, physical therapist, respiratory nurse specialist, occupational therapist, dietitian, social worker, and psychologist. An internist trained in respiratory rehabilitation outlines and orchestrates the patient's therapeutic program.

Supplemental Oxygen

Because of the hypoxemia associated with cystic fibrosis, supplemental oxygen may be required. The hypoxemia that develops in cystic fibrosis is most commonly caused by the hypoventilation and shuntlike effect associated with the disorder. Hypoxemia caused by a shuntlike effect can generally be corrected by oxygen therapy.

It should be noted, however, that when a patient demonstrates chronic ventilatory failure during the advanced stages of cystic fibrosis, caution must be taken not to eliminate the patient's hypoxic drive to breathe.

SELF-ASSESSMENT QUESTIONS

Multiple Choice
1. Which of the following is commonly found in the tracheobronchial tree secretions of patients with cystic fibrosis?
   I. *Staphylococcus.*
   II. *Haemophilus influenzae.*
   III. *Streptococcus.*
   IV. *Pseudomonas aeruginosa.*
       a. I only.
       b. II only.
       c. IV only.

    d. I and IV only.

    e. I, II, III, and IV.

2. When two carriers of cystic fibrosis produce children, there is a

    I. 75% chance that the baby will be a carrier.

    II. 25% chance that the baby will be completely normal.

    III. 50% chance that the baby will have cystic fibrosis.

    IV. 25% chance that the baby will have cystic fibrosis.

        a. I only.

        b. III only.

        c. II and IV only.

        d. I and II only.

        e. I, III, and IV only.

3. When arranged for pressure (P), Poiseuille's law states that P is

    I. Directly related to l.

    II. Indirectly related to $\dot{V}$

    III. Directly related to r^4.

    IV. Indirectly related to n.

        a. I only.

        b. III only.

        c. II and III only.

        d. III and IV only.

        e. II, III, and IV only.

4. In cystic fibrosis, the patient commonly demonstrates a(an)

    I. Increased FEV_T.

    II. Decreased MVV.

    III. Increased RV.

    IV. Decreased FEV_1/FVC ratio.

        a. I only.

        b. II only.

        c. III only.

        d. III and IV only.

        e. II, III, and IV only.

5. During the advanced stages of cystic fibrosis, the patient generally demonstrates

    I. Bronchial breath sounds.

    II. Dull percussion notes.

    III. Diminished breath sounds.

    IV. Hyperresonant percussion notes.

        a. I and III only.

        b. II and IV only.

        c. I and IV only.

        d. III and IV only.

        e. II and III only.

6. Approximately 80% of all patients with cystic fibrosis demonstrate a deficiency in which vitamin

    I. A.

    II. B.

    III. D.

    IV. E.

    V. K.

        a. III and IV only.

        b. I, IV, and V only.

        c. II, III, and IV only.

    d. I, III, IV, and V only.

    e. I, II, III, IV, and V.

7. The patient is considered to have cystic fibrosis when the concentration of sodium in sweat is greater than

    a. 50 mEq/L.

    b. 60 mEq/L.

    c. 70 mEq/L.

    d. 80 mEq/L.

    e. 90 mEq/L.

8. In regard to the secretion of sodium and chloride, the sweat glands of patients with cystic fibrosis secrete:

    a. 2 times the normal amount.

    b. 4 times the normal amount.

    c. 6 times the normal amount.

    d. 8 times the normal amount.

    e. 10 times the normal amount.

9. Which of the following is/are a mucolytic agent?

    I. N-acetylcysteine.

   II. Aristocort.

  III. Crystodigin.

  IV. Aldactone.

    a. I only.

    b. II only.

    c. IV only.

    d. II and IV only.

    e. III and IV only.

10. Assuming pressure remains constant, decreasing the radius of a tube by 16% decreases gas flow through the tube to

    a. ¼ of its original flow rate.

    b. ⅓ of its original flow rate.

    c. ½ of its original flow rate.

    d. ¾ of its original flow rate.

    e. ¹⁄₁₆ of its original flow rate.

True or False

1. Carriers of the cystic fibrosis gene can be identified clinically.   True _____   False _____

2. Meconium ileus results from a deficiency in pancreatic enzymes.   True _____   False _____

3. During the advanced stages of cystic fibrosis, the patient's $\dot{V}/\dot{Q}$ ratio increases.   True _____   False _____

4. The peripheral chemoreceptors are found in the upper pons.   True _____   False _____

5. During the advanced stages of cystic fibrosis, the patient's HCO_3^- level is increased.   True _____   False _____

Answers appear in Appendix XVII.

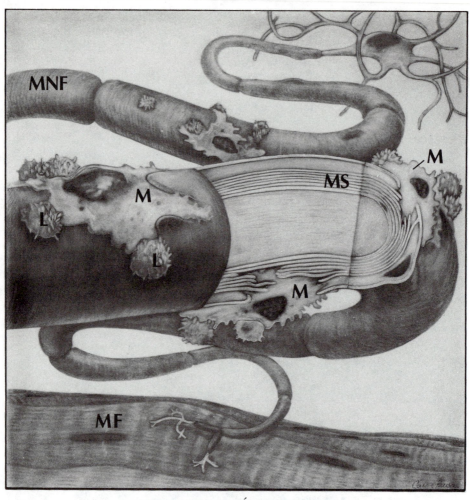

GUILLAIN-BARRÉ SYNDROME

FIG 21–1.
Guillain-Barré syndrome. *MNF* = myelinated nerve fibers; *L* = lymphocyte; *M* = macrophage; *MS* = myelin sheath; *MF* = muscle fiber.

GUILLAIN-BARRÉ SYNDROME

ANATOMIC ALTERATIONS ASSOCIATED WITH THE GUILLAIN-BARRÉ SYNDROME

The Guillain-Barré syndrome is a relatively rare disorder of the peripheral nervous system in which flaccid paralysis of the skeletal muscles and loss of reflexes develop in a previously healthy patient. In severe cases, paralysis of the diaphragm and ventilatory failure can develop. Clinically, this is a medical emergency. If the ventilatory failure is not properly managed, mucus accumulation, airway obstruction, alveolar consolidation, and atelectasis can develop (see Fig 1–1).

Paralysis of the skeletal muscles develops in response to various pathologic changes in the peripheral nerves. Microscopically, the nerves show demyelination, inflammation, and edema. As the anatomic alterations of the peripheral nerves intensify, the ability of the neurons to properly transmit nerve impulses to the muscles decreases, and eventually paralysis ensues (Fig 21–1).

Other names found in the literature for the Guillain-Barré syndrome are as follows:

- Infectious polyneuritis
- Acute idiopathic polyneuritis
- Landry-Guillain-Barré-Strohl syndrome
- Landry's paralysis
- Acute polyneuropathy
- Acute polyradiculitis
- Polyradiculoneuropathy

To summarize, the major pathologic or structural changes of the lungs associated with the ventilatory failure may accompany the Guillain-Barré syndrome are as follows:

- Mucus accumulation
- Airway obstruction
- Alveolar consolidation
- Atelectasis

ETIOLOGY

The precise cause of the Guillain-Barré syndrome is not known. It is probably an immune disorder (humoral factor) that causes inflammation and deterioration of the patient's peripheral nervous system. Studies of serial serum samples have shown high antibody titers during the early stages of the disorder. Elevated levels of specific antibodies include IgM and the presence of what are called the *complement-activating antibodies* against isolated human peripheral nerve myelin, or anti-PNM antibodies. Studies have shown that the serum antibody titers fall very rapidly during the recovery period.

Lymphocytes and macrophages appear to attack and strip off the myelin sheath of the peripheral nerves and leave swelling and fragmentations of the neural axon (see Fig 21–1). It is believed that it is the myelin sheath covering the peripheral nerves (or the myelin-producing Schwann cell) that is the actual target of the immune attack.

The onset of the Guillain-Barré syndrome frequently follows a febrile episode such as an upper respiratory or gastrointestinal illness within 1 to 4 weeks. Multiple viruses and some bacterial agents have been implicated as precursors to the Guillain-Barré syndrome. Infectious mononucleosis, for example, has been associated with as many as 25% of the cases. Other possible infectious agents include parainfluenza 2, vaccinia, variola, measles, mumps, hepatitis A and B viruses, *Mycoplasma pneumoniae*, *Salmonella typhi*, and *Chlamydia psittaci*. Although the significance of the association is controversial, during the nationwide immunization campaign in the United States in 1976, more than 40 million adults were vaccinated with swine influenza vaccine, and more than 500 cases of the Guillain-Barré syndrome were reported among the vaccinated individuals, with 25 deaths.

The annual incidence of the Guillain-Barré syndrome in the United States is about 1.7 cases per 100,000. Although uncommon in early childhood, the condition may occur in all age groups and in either sex. A greater incidence has been noted among people 45 years of age and older, among males, and among whites (50% to 60% greater in whites). There is no obvious seasonal clustering of cases.

If diagnosed early, patients with the Guillain-Barré syndrome have an excellent prognosis. The diagnosis is typically based on the history of the neurologic symptoms, the nature of the cerebrospinal fluid, and electrodiagnostic studies. If the Guillain-Barré syndrome is present, the cerebrospinal fluid shows an increased protein concentration with a normal cell count. Serial electrodiagnostic studies in multiple nerves in both the upper and lower extremities provide important data in making the diagnosis as well as in determining the locations and severity of the lesions. Functional, spontaneous recovery is expected in about 85% to 95% of the cases, although about 40% may have some minor residual symptoms.

COMMON NONCARDIOPULMONARY MANIFESTATIONS

- Progressive ascending skeletal muscle paralysis
  - Tingling sensation and numbness (distal paresthesia)
  - Loss of deep tendon reflexes
  - Sensory nerve impairment
  - Peripheral facial weakness
  - Decreased gag reflex
  - Decreased ability to swallow

The early symptoms of the Guillain-Barré syndrome include fever, malaise, nausea, and prostration, with a subsequent tingling sensation and numbness in the the extremities (distal paresthesia). The feet and lower portions of the legs are usually affected first. The tingling and numbness is followed by skeletal muscle paralysis and the loss of deep tendon reflexes.

The muscle paralysis then moves upward (ascending paralysis) to the arms, neck, and pharyngeal and facial muscles (cranial nerves IX and X). The muscle weakness and paralysis commonly develop over a single day, although it may develop more slowly over a period of a few days. Paralysis generally peaks in less than 10 days. Sensory nerve impairment may also be present. The patient's gag reflex is generally decreased or absent, and swallowing is usually difficult (dysphagia). Thus, the handling of oral secretions is usually a problem.

Although the Guillain-Barré syndrome is typically an ascending paralysis (i.e., moving from the lower portions of the legs upward), muscle paralysis may affect the facial and arm muscles first and then move downward. While it is more common for the weakness to be symmetric, a single arm or leg may be involved before paralysis spreads. The paralysis may also affect all four limbs simultaneously. Progression of the paralysis may stop at any point. Once the paralysis reaches its maximum, it usually remains unchanged for a few days or weeks. Improvement generally begins spontaneously and continues for weeks or, in rare cases, months.

OVERVIEW OF THE CARDIOPULMONARY CLINICAL MANIFESTATIONS ASSOCIATED WITH THE GUILLAIN-BARRÉ SYNDROME

ARTERIAL BLOOD GASES

ACUTE VENTILATORY FAILURE WITH HYPOXEMIA (see page 52)
- Pa_{O_2}: decreased
- Pa_{CO_2}: increased
- HCO_3^-: increased
- pH: decreased

CYANOSIS (see page 16)

PULMONARY FUNCTION STUDIES (see page 37)

LUNG VOLUME AND CAPACITY FINDINGS
- Decreased VC
- Decreased RV
- Decreased FRC
- Decreased TLC

CHEST ASSESSMENT FINDINGS (see page 3)

- Diminished breath sounds
- Crackles/rhonchi

CHEST X-RAY FINDINGS

- Normal
- Increased opacity

If the ventilatory failure associated with Guillain-Barré syndrome is properly managed, the chest x-ray findings should be normal. If improperly managed, however, alveolar consolidation and altelectasis develop from excess secretion accumulation in the tracheobronchial tree. This increases the density of the lungs.

AUTONOMIC NERVOUS SYSTEM DYSFUNCTIONS

- Heart rate and rhythm abnormalities
- Blood pressure abnormalities

Autonomic nervous system dysfunction develops in about 50% of the cases. The autonomic dysfunction involves the overreaction or underreaction of the sympathetic or parasympathetic nervous system. Clinically the patient may manifest various cardiac arrhythmias such as sinus tachycardia (the most common), bradycardia, ventricular tachycardia, atrial flutter, atrial fibrillation, and asystole. Blood pressure changes such as hypertension and hypotension may also be seen. Although the loss of bowel and bladder sphincter control is uncommon, transient sphincter paralysis may occur during the evolution of symptoms. The autonomic involvement may be very transient or may persist throughout the duration of the disorder.

GENERAL MANAGEMENT OF THE GUILLAIN-BARRÉ SYNDROME

The Guillain-Barré syndrome is a medical emergency that must be monitored closely after the diagnosis has been made. The primary treatment should be directed at stabilization of vital signs and supportive care for the patient. Initially, such patients should be managed in an intensive care unit. Frequent measurements of the patient's vital capacity, blood pressure, and arterial blood gases should be performed. Mechanical ventilation should be administered when the clinical data demonstrate impending, or acute, ventilatory failure. Routine pulmonary toilet should be instituted to prevent mucus accumulation, airway obstruction, alveolar consolidation, and atelectasis.

As in any patient who is paralyzed, the risk of thromboembolic events increases. Because of this, the patient commonly receives subcutaneous heparin, elastic stockings, and passive range-of-motion exercises (every 3 to 4 hours) for all extremities.

To prevent skin breakdown and bedsores, the patient should be turned frequently from side to side. A rotary bed or Stryker frame may be required. Urinary catheterization is required in the completely paralyzed patient.

A pulmonary catheter and cardiac monitoring may be needed in some cases. Blood pressure disturbances and cardiac arrhythmias require immediate attention. For example, nitroprusside (Nipride) or phentolamine (Regitine) are commonly administered during severe hypertensive episodes. Episodes of bradycardia may be treated with atropine.

In severe cases, *plasmapheresis* has been shown to be effective in decreasing the morbidity and shortening the clinical course of Guillain-Barré syndrome. Plasmapheresis is the removal of plasma from withdrawn blood, with retransfusion of the formed elements. This procedure has been shown to reduce antibody titers during the early stages of the disorder. Type-specific fresh frozen plasma or albumin is generally used to replace the withdrawn plasma. As a general rule, a fairly conservative plasmapheresis regimen is performed: an exchange of 200 to 250 mL/kg over a period of 7 to 14 days. In the normal-sized adult, a total of five exchanges of 3 L each over a period of 8 to 10 days is usually adequate. Recent studies have shown that plasmapheresis within the first 7 days of the onset of neurologic symptoms significantly decreases the number of days the patient requires mechanical ventilation. It is recommended, however, that only the severely affected and worsening patients receive plasmapheresis. Patients with mild symptoms or symptoms that have improved or plateaued should not undergo plasmapheresis.

Because the Guillain-Barré syndrome is believed to be immunologically mediated, anti-inflammatory and immunosuppressive agents are commonly administered. Corticosteroids are frequently used, but their effectiveness is controversial.

Mobilization of Bronchial Secretions

Because of the mucus accumulation associated with Guillain-Barré syndrome, a number of respiratory therapy modalities may be used to enhance the mobilization of bronchial secretions (see Appendix XI).

Hyperinflation Techniques

Hyperinflation techniques may be ordered to offset the alveolar consolidation and atelectasis associated with Guillain-Barré syndrome (see Appendix XII).

Supplemental Oxygen

Because hypoxemia may develop in Guillain-Barré syndrome, supplemental oxygen may be required. It should be noted, however, that because of the alveolar consolidation and atelectasis associated with Guillain-Barré syndrome, capillary shunting may be present. Hypoxemia caused by capillary shunting is often refractory to oxygen therapy.

SELF-ASSESSMENT QUESTIONS

Multiple Choice
1. In Guillain-Barré syndrome, which of the following pathologic changes develop in the peripheral nerves?
  I. Inflammation.
  II. Increased ability to transmit nerve impulses.
  III. Demyelination.
  IV. Edema.
     a. I and IV only.
     b. II and III only.
     c. III and IV only.
     d. II, III, and IV only.
     e. I, III, and IV only.
2. Which of the following is associated with Guillain-Barré syndrome?
  I. Alveolar consolidation.
  II. Mucus accumulation.
  III. Alveolar hyperinflation.

analysis. For the purpose of scale development, it may also be advantageous to assign numeric values to valid categories of answers based on some metric theories and justifications (e.g., to approach interval assignment while coding an ordinal variable). These are considered better than an arbitrary coding scheme since they may save a lot of work of recoding in data manipulation.

The process of transferring data from such original records as questionnaires and code sheets of content analysis into an established computer database structure is called data entry or input. Generally speaking, after the database structure is set or the variables are defined, the task of data entry appears simple and straightforward. In formally organized research projects, this is often the job of junior staff with low pay and little training. The importance of data entry, however, is typically under-stressed even though a research project could easily be damaged by the poor quality of the work. Data entry can be a very demanding job due to the requirements for: (1) speed, (2) accuracy, and (3) judgment. Good judgment is needed in dealing with confusing answers, missing values, questionnaire design defects or limits, and information recording problems. Both life and research experiences are crucial to the ability of making good judgments. Familiarity with data management and analysis process is particularly important. If the data entry person does not possess all such desired qualities, at least somebody with experience should be readily available during data entry to provide the needed directions and assistance.

The computerization of qualitative data is different from creating a database and keying in the codes. Since the data are not quantified, you may need to use a word processing system such as WordPerfect to do the job. This kind of work is also referred to as data entry, and is frequently seen in all kinds of regular business. For the purpose of research, your computerized qualitative data may come from the following sources: (1) Original computer files. Following the popularization of the computer technology, it becomes more and more likely that you will be able to ask people for a "soft" copy of the documents or records you wish to study. Those people who created the documents and records and granted you the access would be willing to provide you with a copy of the computer files if they have one. There should be no essential difference between the soft copies and the hard copies except that the former will give you by far the greater convenience. You may directly read the file in to your computer and work on it by using the same or compatible software program(s). (2) Recreated computer files. For historical documents and those whose soft copies are not obtainable, the information needs to be reproduced in the computerized format. Yet, unless you

    IV. Atelectasis.
      a. I only.
      b. I and II only.
      c. III and IV only.
      d. I, II, and IV only.
      e. II, III, and IV only.

3. The incidence of Guillain-Barré syndrome is greater in
    I. People older than 45 years of age.
    II. Blacks than in whites.
    III. Males than in females.
    IV. Early childhood.
      a. I only.
      b. IV only.
      c. I and III only.
      d. III and IV only.
      e. II and III only.

4. Which of the following is/are possible precusors to the Guillain-Barré syndrome?
    I. Mumps.
    II. Swine influenza vaccine.
    III. Infectious mononucleosis.
    IV. Measles.
      a. I and III only.
      b. II and IV only.
      c. III and IV only.
      d. II, III, and IV only.
      e. I, II, III, and IV.

5. Spontaneous recovery from Guillain-Barré syndrome is expected in about what percentage of cases?
      a. 45–55.
      b. 55–65.
      c. 65–75.
      d. 75–85.
      e. 85–95.

True or False

1. In Guillain-Barré syndrome a tingling sensation and numbness usually begins in the feet and lower portions of the legs.   True ____   False ____
2. Guillain-Barré syndrome is called a descending paralysis.   True ____   False ____
3. Paralysis in Guillain-Barré syndrome usually takes about 12 weeks to peak.   True ____   False ____
4. Both hypertension and hypotension are associated with Guillain-Barré syndrome.   True ____   False ____
5. Plasmapheresis has been shown to reduce the antibody titers during the early stages of Guillain-Barré syndrome.   True ____   False ____

Answers appear in Appendix XVII.

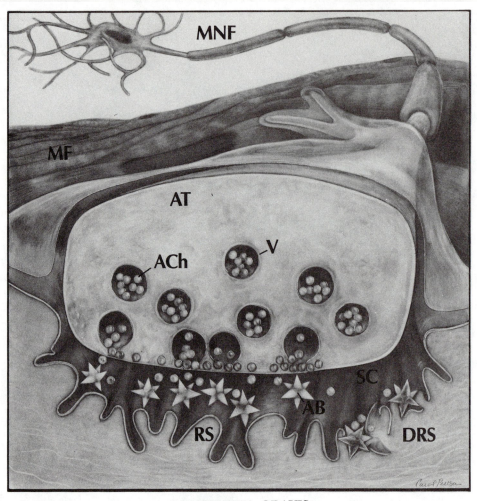

MYASTHENIA GRAVIS

FIG 22–1.
MNF = myelinated nerve fiber; *MF* = muscle fiber; *AT* = axonal terminal; *V* = vesicles
containing acetylcholine; *ACh* = acetylcholine; *AB* = antibodies; *RS* = receptor site;
SC = synaptic cleft; *DRS* = destruction of receptor sites by circulating antibodies.

278

• 22

MYASTHENIA GRAVIS

ANATOMIC ALTERATIONS ASSOCIATED WITH MYASTHENIA GRAVIS

Myasthenia gravis is a chronic disorder of the neuromuscular junction that interferes with the chemical transmission of acetylcholine (ACh) between the axonal terminal and the receptor sites of voluntary muscles (Fig 22–1). It is characterized by periods of rapid fatigue, with improvement following rest. Because the disorder affects only the myoneural junction, there is no loss of sensory function.

The abnormal fatigability may be confined to an isolated group of muscles (e.g., the drooping of the one or both eyelids), or it may be a generalized weakness that, in severe cases, may include the diaphragm. When the diaphragm is involved, ventilatory failure can develop. If the ventilatory failure is not properly managed, mucus accumulation, airway obstruction, alveolar consolidation, and atelectasis can develop (see Fig 1–1).

ETIOLOGY

The cause of myasthenia gravis appears to be related to circulating antibodies of the autoimmune system (anti-ACh receptor antibodies). It is believed that the antibodies disrupt the chemical transmission of ACh at the neuromuscular junction by (1) blocking the ACh from the receptor sites of the muscular cell, (2) accelerating the breakdown of ACh, and (3) actually destroying the receptor sites (see Fig 22–1). While it is not clear what events activate the formation of the antibodies, the thymus gland is almost always abnormal. Because of this fact, it is generally presumed that the antibodies arise within the thymus or in related tissue.

The incidence of myasthenia gravis ranges between 1 in 10,000 and 1 in 25,000 persons in the United States. It is at least twice as common in women as in men. The disease usually has a peak age of onset in females between 15 and 35 years as compared with 40 to 70 years of age in males. The clinical manifestations associated with myasthenia gravis are often provoked by emotional upset, physical stress, exposure to extreme temperature changes, febrile illness, or pregnancy. Death caused by myasthenia gravis is possible, especially during the first few years after onset. After the disease has been in progress for 10 years, however, death from myasthenia gravis is rare.

The diagnosis of myasthenia gravis is based on the clinical history, the clinical response to an intravenous injection of edrophonium chloride (Tensilon), electrical tests of neuromuscular transmission, and the amount of circulating antibodies in the blood.

In regard to the clinical history, muscular weakness without sensory involvement, changes in consciousness, or autonomic dysfunctions are early signs of myasthenia gravis. Because the disease is relatively uncommon and because the symptoms fluctuate from hour to hour, day to day, and week to week, the patient is often misdiagnosed or not diagnosed until the disorder has progressed to a more generalized and consistent weakness.

The diagnosis is usually confirmed with the Tensilon test. Tensilon, which is a short-acting drug used to treat myasthenia gravis, blocks cholinesterase from breaking down ACh after it has been released from the terminal axon. This action increases the concentration of ACh, which in turn works to offset the influx of antibodies at the neuromuscular junction. When muscular weakness is caused by myasthenia gravis, a dramatic transitory improvement in muscle function (lasting about 10 minutes) is seen after the administration of Tensilon.

To further support the diagnosis of myasthenia gravis, electromyography is usually performed to confirm the diagnosis, identify specific muscles involved, and determine the degree of fatigability. Electromyography entails the repetitive stimulation of a nerve, such as the ulnar, with the simultaneous recording of the muscle response. Clinically, the degree of fatigability is often evaluated by having the patient use certain muscles for a sustained period of time. For example, the patient may be instructed to gaze upward for an extended period of time, to blink continuously, to hold both arms outstretched as long as possible, or to count aloud as long as possible in one breath (normal is about 50). A dynamometer is sometimes used to measure the force of repetitive muscle contractions.

Finally, measurement of the circulating anti-ACh receptor antibodies in the blood may also be helpful. Antibody titers are detectable in the serum of 50% to 85% of myasthenic patients. Special chest x-ray films can show an enlarged thymus gland, which may also support the diagnosis of myasthenia gravis.

COMMON NONCARDIOPULMONARY MANIFESTATIONS

- Weakness of striated muscles
  - Eye muscles (ptosis)
    - Drooping of the upper eyelids
  - Extraocular muscles (diplopia)
    - Double vision
  - Muscles of the lower portion of the face
    - Speech impairment
  - Chewing and swallowing muscles
  - Muscles of the arms and legs

The onset of myasthenia gravis is usually gradual. The drooping of one or both upper eyelids (ptosis), followed by double vision (diplopia) due to weakness of the external ocular muscles, is usually the first symptom. Weakness of the external ocular muscles is usually asymmetric and may progress to complete external paralysis in one or both eyes. For some patients, these may be the only symptoms. Clinically, this condition is called ocular myasthenia.

In many patients, however, the disease progresses to a generalized skeletal muscle disorder. In such patients, the lower facial and neck muscles are almost always affected. The orbicularis oris is usually weak, which causes a vertical snarl when attempting to smile. Chewing and swallowing become difficult as the muscles of the jaw, soft palate, and pharynx weaken. The patient may also regurgitate food and fluid through the nose when swallowing. Muscle fatigue in the pharyngeal area represents a significant danger since food and fluids may be aspirated. During periods of muscle fatigue, the patient's ability to articulate frequently deteriorates, and the voice is usually high and nasal in quality. Weakness of the neck muscles commonly causes the patient's head to fall forward. Clinically, the patient is often seen to support the chin with one hand to either hold the head up or to assist in speaking.

As the disorder becomes more generalized, weakness develops in the arms and legs. The muscle weakness is usually more pronounced in the proximal parts of the extremities. The patient has difficulty in climbing stairs, lifting objects, maintaining balance, and walking. In severe cases, the weakness of the upper limbs may be such that the hand cannot be lifted to the mouth. Muscle atrophy or pain is rare. A notable characteristic of myasthenia gravis is that the tendon reflexes almost always remain intact.

Finally, it should be stressed that the clinical manifestations during the early stages of the disorder are often elusive. The patient may (1) demonstrate normal health for weeks or months at a time, (2) only show signs of weakness late in the day or evening, or (3) develop a sudden and transient generalized weakness that includes the diaphragm. Ventilatory failure is always a sinister possibility.

OVERVIEW OF THE CARDIOPULMONARY CLINICAL MANIFESTATIONS ASSOCIATED WITH MYASTHENIA GRAVIS

ARTERIAL BLOOD GASES

ACUTE VENTILATORY FAILURE WITH HYPOXEMIA (see page 52)
- Pa_{O_2}: decreased
- Pa_{CO_2}: increased
- HCO_3^-: increased
- pH: decreased

CYANOSIS (see page 16)

PULMONARY FUNCTION STUDIES (see page 37)

LUNG VOLUME AND CAPACITY FINDINGS
- Decreased VC
- Decreased RV
- Decreased FRC
- Decreased TLC

CHEST ASSESSMENT FINDINGS (see page 3)

- Diminished breath sounds
- Crackles/rhonchi

CHEST X-RAY FINDINGS

- Normal
- Increased opacity

If the ventilatory failure associated with myasthenia gravis is properly managed, the chest x-ray findings should be normal. If improperly managed, however, alveolar consolidation and atelectasis develop from excess secretion accumulation in the tracheobronchial tree.

GENERAL MANAGEMENT OF MYASTHENIA GRAVIS

Formerly many patients with myasthenia gravis died within the first few years of the disease. Today, there are a number of therapeutic measures that provide many patients with marked relief of symptoms and allow them to live a normal life span. Because there is the possibility of ventilatory failure in patients with myasthenia gravis, the patient should be monitored closely during critical periods. Frequent measurements of the patient's vital capacity, blood pressure, and arterial blood gases should be performed. Mechanical ventilation should be administered when the patient's clinical data demonstrate impending, or acute, ventilatory failure. Routine pulmonary toilet should be instituted to prevent mucus accumulation, airway obstruction, alveolar consolidation, and atelectasis.

During a myasthenic crisis, the following treatment modalities may also be used:

Drug Therapy

Drugs used to enhance the action of ACh are used to treat myasthenia gravis. The most popular agents are edrophonium chloride (Tensilon), neostigmine (Prostigmin), and pyridostigmine (Mestinon). These agents inhibit the function of cholinesterase. This action in effect increases the concentration of ACh to compete with the circulating anti-ACh antibodies, which interfere with the ability of ACh to stimulate the muscle receptors. Although the anticholinesterase drugs are very effective in mild cases of myasthenia gravis, they are not completely effective in severe cases.

Corticosteroid Therapy.—During periods of remission, the patient's strength often improves strikingly with steroids (e.g., prednisone). Patients receiving long-term steroid therapy, however, frequently develop various complications such as cateracts, gastrointestinal bleeding, infections, aseptic necrosis of the bone, osteoporosis, myopathies, and psychoses.

Adrenocorticotropic Hormone Therapy.—The administration of adrenocorticotropic hormone (ACTH) has proved useful in the severely ill myasthenia gravis patient. A disadvantage to this therapy, however, is that patients tend to worsen before improving. Paradoxically, patients who demonstate the greatest initial weakness often show the most improvement later.

Thymectomy

Although controversial, thymectomy has been helpful in many myasthenia gravis patients, especially in young adult females. The thymus gland in the myasthenic patient frequently appears to be the source of anti-ACh receptor antibodies.

In some patients, muscle strength improves soon after surgery, while in others it takes months or years.

Respiratory Care

Mobilization of Bronchial Secretions.—Because of the mucus accumulation associated with myasthenia gravis, a number of respiratory therapy modalities may be used to enhance the mobilization of bronchial secretions (see Appendix XI).

Hyperinflation Techniques.—Hyperinflation techniques may be ordered to offset the alveolar consolidation and atelectasis associated with myasthenia gravis (see Appendix XII).

Supplemental Oxygen.—Because hypoxemia may develop in myasthenia gravis, supplemental oxygen may be required. It should be noted, however, that because of the alveolar consolidation and atelectasis associated with myasthenia gravis, capillary shunting may be present. Hypoxemia caused by capillary shunting is often refractory to oxygen therapy.

SELF-ASSESSMENT QUESTIONS

True or False

1. Alveolar hyperinflation is associated with myasthenia gravis.   True ____   False ____
2. The cause of myasthenia gravis appears to be related to circulating antibodies that disrupt the transmission of acetylcholine.   True ____   False ____
3. Myasthenia gravis is more common in men than women.   True ____   False ____
4. Tensilon is used to confirm the diagnosis of myasthenia gravis because of its ability to block cholinesterase.   True ____   False ____
5. The onset of myasthenia gravis is usually sudden.   True ____   False ____
6. In myasthenia gravis, the extremity muscles (arms and legs) are usually the first to weaken.   True ____   False ____
7. Neostigmine is used to treat patients with myasthenia gravis.   True ____   False ____
8. A thymectomy may be beneficial in young adult females with myasthenia gravis.   True ____   False ____
9. In males, the incidence of myasthenia gravis is greatest between 15 and 35 years of age.   True ____   False ____
10. After the disease has been in progress for 10 years, death from myasthenia gravis is rare.   True ____   False ____

Answers appear in Appendix XVII.

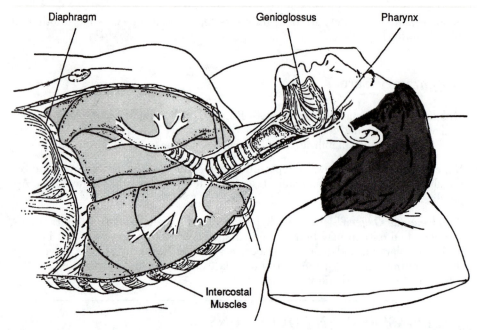

FIG 23–1.
Obstructive sleep apnea. When the genioglossus muscle fails to oppose the collapsing force on the airway passage during inspiration, the tongue moves into the oropharyngeal area and obstructs the airway.

SLEEP APNEA

Despite the fact that the clinical characteristics of sleep apnea have been described in the literature for centuries, it was not until the late 1970s or early 1980s that this disorder became generally acknowledged by the medical community. Prior to this time, it was assumed that individuals who breathed normally while awake also did so during sleep. It was also assumed that patients with lung disorders were not likely to develop more severe respiratory problems when asleep than when awake. Both of these assumptions are now recognized as being incorrect.

STAGES OF SLEEP AND CHARACTERISTIC CARDIOPULMONARY PATTERNS

During sleep, the normal individual slips in and out of two major stages: *non-rapid eye movement* (non-REM) sleep (also called quiet or slow-wave sleep) and *rapid eye movement* (REM) sleep (also called active or dreaming sleep). Each stage is associated with characteristic electroencephalographic (EEG), behavioral, and breathing patterns.

Non-REM Sleep

Non-REM sleep usually begins immediately after an individual dozes off. This stage consists of four separate phases, each progressing into a deeper sleep. During phases 1 and 2, the ventilatory rate and tidal volume continually increase and decrease, and brief periods of apnea may also be seen. The EEG tracing shows an increased slow-wave activity (slow-wave sleep) and loss of alpha rhythm. The occurrence of apnea is greater in persons over 40 years of age. Cheyne-Stokes breathing is also commonly seen in older adult males during non-REM sleep, especially at high altitudes.

During phases 3 and 4, ventilation becomes slow and regular. The minute ventilation is commonly 1 to 2 L less than during the quiet wakeful state. Typically, the Pa_{CO_2} levels are higher (4 to 8 mm Hg), the Pa_{O_2} levels are lower (3 to 10 mm Hg), and the pH is lower (0.03 to 0.05 units).

Normally, non-REM sleep lasts for about 60 to 90 minutes. Although an individual typically moves in and out of all four phases during non-REM sleep, most of the time is spent in phase 2. An individual may move into REM sleep at any time and directly from any of the four non-REM sleep phases, although the lighter phases 1 and 2 are commonly the levels of sleep just prior to REM sleep.

are studying only a very limited volume of documents, you cannot afford the time to retype all of them into your computer. You may just want to take some notes for further computerized analysis. Using a scanner will be much faster than retyping, though considerable time may be involved in taking out various strange symbols, especially when the originals are not very neat. For certain important documents, there may be some people who have spent enormous amount of time and completely computerized them. You need to keep your eyes open for the opportunity to share such resources. (3) Computerization of first-hand data. If you have tape-recorded a focus group session, you can use a transcribing machine to help transfer the data into a computer file. If you have taken notes in a case interview using paper and pencil, you need to retype them. If possible you may bring a laptop or notebook computer to the field and directly use it in place of the paper and pencil instrument. But its effect depends on how fast you type, and you also need to consider the potential impact of such equipment on the particular situation of data collection.

Once the qualitative data are computerized, you can use your word processing system to do such analytical work as searching, numbering, and counting. There are also software packages specifically designed to handle this kind of data, such as Alpha, TextBase, and Ethnograph. However, it is those fully quantified data that best demonstrate the strengths of computer-assisted data management and analysis. In the following, we will focus on the handling of quantitative data.

Data cleaning and manipulation

The completion of data entry seems to suggest that you are ready to perform intended data analysis. In doing the excises for your research classes this might have appeared straightforward: You entered your data and almost immediately analyzed them. In a real research situation, however, weeks or even months of exhausting work may be required before you can really embark on your data analysis tasks. And computer programs with hundreds or even thousands of lines may need be carefully compiled to deal with the data management tasks. One of the major reasons is very simple, and almost for sure: The data are too "dirty." Let us look back at all the links of the research chain. Every step of the data collection process may involve problems caused by, for instance, misunderstanding, confusion, omission, refusal, pretending, and even cheating. Detecting such problems and remedying them to the maximum possible extent is the task for data cleaning.

REM Sleep

During REM sleep, there is a burst of fast alpha rhythms on the EEG tracing. During this period, the ventilatory rate becomes rapid and shallow. Sleep-related hypoventilation and apnea are frequently demonstated during this period. Apnea in the normal adult lasts for about 15 to 20 seconds; in the normal infant, apnea lasts for about 10 seconds. There is a marked reduction in both the hypoxic ventilatory response and the hypercapnic ventilatory response during REM sleep. The heart rate also becomes irregular, and the eyes move rapidly. Dreaming occurs mainly during REM sleep, and there is a profound paralysis of movement. The muscle paralysis primarily affects the arms, legs, and intercostal and upper airway muscles. The activity of the diaphragm is maintained.

The muscle paralysis that occurs during REM sleep can affect an individual's ventilation in two major ways: first, since the muscle tone of the intercostal muscles is low during this period, the negative intrapleural pressure generated by the diaphragm often causes a paradoxical motion of the rib cage. That is, during inspiration the tissues between the ribs move inward, and during expiration the tissues bulge outward. This paradoxical motion of the rib cage causes the functional residual capacity to decrease. During the wakeful state, the intercostal muscle tone tends to stiffen the tissue between the ribs. Second, the loss of muscle tone in the upper airway involves muscles that normally contract during each inspiration and hold the upper airway open. These muscles include the posterior muscles of the pharynx, the genioglossus (which normally causes the tongue to protrude outward), and the posterior cricoarytenoid (the major abductor of the vocal cords). The loss of muscle tone in the upper airway may result in airway obstruction. The negative pressure produced when the diaphragm contracts during inspiration tends to (1) bring the vocal cords together, (2) collapse the pharyngeal wall, and (3) suck the tongue back into the oral pharyngeal cavity.

REM sleep lasts for about 10 to 20 minutes and recurs about every 60 to 90 minutes. The intervals of REM sleep lengthen and become more frequent toward the end of a night's sleep. REM sleep constitutes about 20% to 25% of sleep time. Most studies show that it is more difficult to awaken a subject during REM sleep than during non-REM sleep.

TYPES OF SLEEP APNEA

Apnea is defined as the cessation of breathing for a period of 10 seconds or longer. Sleep apnea is diagnosed in patients who have at least 30 episodes of apnea that occur in both non-REM and REM sleep over a 6-hour period. Generally, the episodes of apnea are more frequent and severe during REM sleep. They last about 20 to 30 seconds and, occasionally, may exceed 100 seconds. Some patients have as many as 500 periods of apnea per night. It may occur in all age groups; in infants, it may play an important role in sudden infant death syndrome (SIDS).

Sleep apnea is classified as either obstructive, central, or mixed apnea. Patients often have more than one type and are classified according to the predominant type.

Obstructive Sleep Apnea

Obstructive sleep apnea is the syndrome most commonly encountered in the clinical setting. It is caused by an anatomic obstruction of the upper airway in the presence of continued ventilatory effort (Fig 23–1). During periods of obstruction, patients commonly appear quiet and still, as if holding their breath, followed by increasingly desperate efforts to inhale. Often, the apneic episode ends only after an intense struggle. In severe cases, the patient may suddenly awaken, sit upright in bed, and gasp for air. Interestingly, however, patients with obstructive sleep apnea usually demonstrate perfectly normal and regular breathing patterns during the wakeful state.

Obstructive sleep apnea is seen more often in males than in females (8:1 ratio), and it is especially common in middle-aged men. It is estimated that 1% to 4% of the male population may be affected. It is commonly associated with obesity and with individuals who have a short neck, a combination that may significantly narrow the pharyngeal airway. In fact, a large number of patients with obstructive sleep apnea demonstrate the pickwickian syndrome (named after the fat boy in Charles Dickens' *The Posthumous Papers of the Pickwick Club*, published in 1837). Charles Dickens' description of Joe, the fat boy who snored and had excessive daytime sleepiness, included many of the classic features of what are now recognized as the sleep apnea syndrome. It should be emphasized, however, that many patients with sleep apnea are not obese and, therefore, clinical suspicion should not be limited to this group.

Some clinical disorders associated with the cause of obstructive sleep apnea are as follows:

- Obesity (hypoventilation syndrome)
- Anatomic narrowing of upper airway
  - Excessive pharyngeal tissue
  - Enlarged tonsils or adenoids
  - Deviated nasal septum
  - Laryngeal stenosis
  - Laryngeal web
  - Pharyngeal neoplasms
  - Micrognathia
  - Macroglossia
  - Goiter
- Hypothyroidism
- Testosterone administration
- Myotonic dystrophy
- Shy-Drager syndrome

The general noncardiopulmonary clinical manifestations of obstructive sleep apnea can be summarized as follows:

- Loud snoring
- Morning headaches
- Nausea
- Excessive daytime sleepiness (hypersomnolence)
- Intellectual and personality changes
- Depression
- Sexual impotence
- Nocturnal enuresis

Central Sleep Apnea

Central sleep apnea occurs when the respiratory centers of the medulla fail to send signals to the respiratory muscles. It is characterized by cessation of airflow at the nose and mouth along with cessation of inspiratory efforts (absence of diaphragmatic excursions), as opposed to obstructive sleep apnea, which is characterized by the presence of inspiratory efforts during apneic periods. Central sleep apnea is associated with central nervous system disorders. As already mentioned, a small number of brief central apneas normally occur with the onset of sleep or the onset of REM sleep. Central sleep apnea, however, is diagnosed when the frequency of the apnea episodes is excessive (over 30 in a 6-hour period).

Clinical disorders associated with central sleep apnea include the following:

- Idiopathic (hypoventilation syndrome)
- Encephalitis
- Brain stem neoplasm
- Brain stem infarction
- Bulbar poliomyelitis
- Cervical cordotomy
- Spinal surgery
- Hypothyroidism

The general noncardiopulmonary clinical manifestations of central sleep apnea can be summarized as follows:

- Tendency for the patient to be of normal weight
- Mild snoring
- Insomnia
- Although not as great as in obstructive apnea, there may be some of the following:
  - Daytime fatigue
  - Depression
  - Sexual dysfunction

Mixed Sleep Apnea

Mixed sleep apnea is a combination of both obstructive and central sleep apnea. It usually begins as central apnea followed by the onset of ventilatory effort without airflow (obstructive apnea). Clinically, patients with predominantly mixed apneas are classified as having obstructive sleep apnea.

Figure 23–2 summarizes the patterns of (1) airflow, (2) respiratory effort (reflected through the esophageal pressure), and (3) arterial oxygen staturation demonstrated in central, obstructive, and mixed apneas.

DIAGNOSIS

The diagnosis of sleep apnea begins with a general history of the patient, especially the presence of snoring, sleep disturbance, and persistent daytime sleepiness. This is followed by a careful examination of the upper airway and pulmonary function studies to determine whether there is an upper airway obstruction.

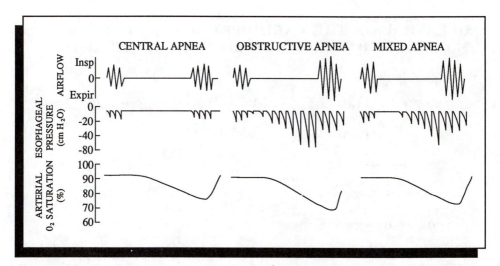

FIG 23–2.
Patterns of *(1)* airflow, *(2)* respiratory efforts (reflected through the esophageal pressure), and *(3)* arterial oxygen saturation produced by central, obstructive, and mixed apneas.

The patient's blood is evaluated for the presence of polycythemia and thyroid function. Arterial blood gas values are obtained to determine the oxygenation and acid-base status. A chest x-ray film and electrocardiogram (ECG) are helpful in evaluating the presence of pulmonary hypertension, the state of right and left ventricular compensation, as well as the presence of any other cardiopulmonary disease.

The diagnosis and type of sleep apnea is confirmed with polysomnographic sleep studies, which include (1) an EEG and an electro-oculogram to identify the sleep stages; (2) a monitoring device for airflow in and out of the patient's lungs; (3) an ECG to identify cardiac arrhythmias; (4) either impedance pneumography, intercostal electromyography, or esophageal manometry to monitor the patient's ventilatory rate and effort; and (5) ear oximetry or transcutaneous oxygen monitoring to detect changes in the patient's oxygen saturation.

Patients diagnosed as having predominantly central sleep apnea are evaluated carefully for lesions involving the brain stem. Patients diagnosed as having obstructive sleep apnea generally undergo a computed tomographic evaluation of the upper airway to determine the site(s) and severity of the pharyngeal narrowing.

The steps typically involved in diagnosing sleep apnea can be summarized as follows:

- History
- Examination of the neck and upper airway
- Spirometry (flow-volume loops)
- Arterial blood gases
- Hemoglobin
- Thyroid function
- Chest radiograph
- Electrocardiogram
- Polysomnographic sleep study
- Computed axial tomographic scan of the upper airway (obstructive apnea)

OVERVIEW OF THE CARDIOPULMONARY CLINICAL MANIFESTATIONS ASSOCIATED WITH SLEEP APNEA

ARTERIAL BLOOD GASES

ACUTE VENTILATORY FAILURE WITH HYPOXEMIA (see page 52)
- Pa_{O_2}: decreased
- Pa_{CO_2}: increased
- HCO_3^-: increased
- pH: decreased

CYANOSIS (see page 16)

PULMONARY FUNCTION STUDIES

- Sawtooth pattern on maximal inspiratory and expiratory flow-volume loops
- $FEF_{50\%}/FIF_{50\%}$ ratio greater than 1.0
- Decreased vital capacity (VC)
- Decreased reserve volume (RV)
- Decreased functional residual capacity (FRC)
- Decreased total lung capacity (TLC)

Patients with obstructive sleep apnea commonly demonstrate a sawtooth pattern on maximal inspiratory and expiratory flow-volume loops. Also characteristic of obstructive sleep apnea is a ratio of expiratory-to-inspiratory flow rates at 50% of the vital capacity ($FEF_{50\%}/FIF_{50\%}$) that exceeds 1.0 in the absence of obstructive airway disease.

In addition, because the muscle tone of the intercostal muscles is low during periods of REM apneas, the negative intrapleural pressure generated by the diaphragm often causes a paradoxical motion of the rib cage, that is, during inspiration the tissue between the ribs moves inward, and during expiration the tissue bulges outward. This paradoxical motion of the rib cage may cause the VC, RV, FRC, and TLC to decrease. This pathologic condition further contributes to the nocturnal hypoxemia seen in patients with sleep apnea syndrome.

ACUTE HEMODYNAMIC CHANGES

- Decreased heart rate
- Decreased cardiac output
- Systemic hypertension
- Pulmonary hypertension
- Cor pulmonale
- Polycythemia

During periods of apnea, the heart rate decreases, followed by an increase after the termination of apnea. It is believed that the carotid body peripheral chemoreceptors are responsible for this response, that is, when ventilation is kept constant or absent (e.g., apneic episode), it is known that hypoxic stimulation of the carotid body peripheral chemoreceptors slows the cardiac rate. Thus, it follows that when the lungs are unable to expand (e.g., periods of obstructive apnea), the depressive effect of the carotid bodies on the heart rate predominates. The increased heart rate noted when ventilation resumes is activated by the excitation of the pulmonary stretch receptors.

Although changes in cardiac output during periods of apnea have been difficult to study, several studies have reported a reduction in cardiac output (about 30%) during periods of apnea, followed by an increase (10% to 15% above controls) after the termination of apnea.

Both pulmonary and systemic arterial blood pressure increase in response to the nocturnal oxygen desaturation that develops during periods of sleep apnea. The magnitude of the pulmonary hypertension is related to the severity of the alveolar hypoxia and hypercapnic acidosis. It is believed that repetition of these transient episodes of pulmonary hypertension, many times a night every night for years, may contribute to the development of the ventricular hypertrophy, cor pulmonale, and eventual decompensation seen in such patients. Systemic vasoconstriction secondary to sympathetic adrenergic neural activity is believed to be responsible for the elevation in systemic blood pressure that is seen during apneas.

The recurrent nocturnal hypoxemia associated with sleep apnea may contribute to the development of secondary polycythemia. The polycythemia that results from chronic hypoxemia is an adaptive mechanism that increases the oxygen-carrying capacity of the blood.

Chest X-Ray Findings

• Right- or left-heart failure

Because of the pulmonary hypertension and polycythemia associated with persistent periods of apnea, right- and left-heart failure may develop. This condition is readily identified on a chest x-ray film and may help in diagnosis.

Cardiac Arrhythmias

• Sinus arrhythmia
• Sinus bradycardia
• Sinus pauses
• Atrioventricular block (second degree)
• Premature ventricular contraction
• Ventricular tachycardia

In severe cases of sleep apnea, there is always a possibility of a sudden arrhythmia-related death. Periods of apnea are commonly associated with sinus arrhythmias, sinus bradycardia, and sinus pauses (greater than 2 seconds). The extent of sinus bradycardia is directly related to the severity of the oxygen desaturation. Obstructive apneas are usually associated with the greatest degrees of cardiac slowing. To a lesser extent, atrioventricular heart blocks (second degree), premature ventricular contractions, and ventricular tachycardia are seen. Identification of apnea-related ventricular tachycardia is viewed as a life-threatening event.

GENERAL MANAGEMENT OF SLEEP APNEA

Over the past few years, it has become apparent that sleep apnea is frequently associated with many disorders: hyoxemia, fragmented sleep, cardiac arrhythmias, and neurologic disorders. In general, the prognosis is more favorable for obstructive and mixed apneas than for central sleep apnea.

Weight Reduction

Because of the fact that many patients with obstructive sleep apnea are overweight and although weight by itself is not the cause of the apnea, weight reduction clearly parallels the reduction in apnea severity. The precise reason is not known. Because weight reduction may take several weeks and because it is often difficult to maintain a certain weight loss, weight reduction as a form of therapy often fails.

Sleep Posture

It is generally believed that periods of obstructive apnea are more severe in the supine position and, in fact, may only be present in this position. Although the long-term effectiveness has not been evaluated, it has been reported that apnea and daytime hypersomnolence have significantly improved in patients who have been instructed to sleep on their sides and avoid the supine posture.

Oxygen Therapy

Because of the hypoxemia-related cardiopulmonary complication of apnea (arrhythmias and pulmonary hypertension), oxygen therapy is commonly used to offset or minimize the oxygen desaturation.

Drug Therapy

There are two major types of drugs used to treat sleep apnea: REM inhibitors and respiratory stimulants.

REM Inhibitors

Protriptyline.—The most frequent and severe episodes of apnea occur during REM sleep in patients with obstructive sleep apnea. Protriptyline, which is a tricyclic antidepressant agent, causes a marked decrease in REM sleep. By decreasing the amount of REM sleep, the incidence of REM apneic episodes is also decreased. Some patients demonstrate improved upper airway muscle tone during REM and non-REM sleep when administered protriptyline. A reduction in daytime hypersomnolence may also be seen. Protriptyline is not therapeutic for central sleep apnea.

Central Nervous System Stimulants

Methylphenidate.—Methylphenidate, which is structurally related to amphetamine, is helpful in managing the symptoms of excessive daytime sleepiness in patients with either central or obstructive sleep apnea. It does not, however, have any therapeutic effects on sleep apnea. It is commonly used in patients who refuse surgical therapy and in patients who do not respond favorably to other drug therapy.

Surgery

Many patients with obstructive sleep apnea benefit from surgical correction or bypass of the anatomic defect or obstruction that is responsible for the apneic episodes. The following procedures are presently available:

Tracheostomy.—A tracheostomy is often the treatment of choice in emergency situations and in patients who do not respond satisfactorily to drug therapy or to other treatment interventions.

Palatopharyngoplasty.—A palatopharyngoplasty is a relatively new procedure in treating obstructive sleep apnea. In general, the soft palate is shortened by removing the posterior third, including the uvula. The pillars of the palatoglossal arch and the palatopharyngeal arch are sewn together, and the tonsils are removed if they are still present. As much excess lateral posterior wall tissue is removed as possible. Palatopharyngoplasty is effective in only about 40% of the cases.

Mandibular Advancement.—Approximately 6% of patients with obstructive sleep apnea have a mandibular malformation. For example, patients who have obstructive sleep apnea because of retrognathia or mandibular micrognathia will likely benefit from surgical mandibular advancement.

Mechanical Ventilation

Continuous Positive Airway Pressure.—As mentioned earlier, the cause of many obstructive sleep apneas is related to (1) an anatomic problem of the pharynx and (2) the decreased muscle tone that normally develops in the pharynx during REM sleep. When these patients inhale, the pharyngeal muscles and surrounding tissues are sucked inward in response to the negative pressure generated by the contracting diaphragm. Nocturnal continuous positive airway pressure (CPAP) may be useful in preventing the inward collapse of the hypotonic airway. CPAP is not indicated in central sleep apnea.

Continuous Mechanical Ventilation.—Intubation and continuous mechanical ventilation may be used for short-term therapy when acute ventilatory failure develops in either central or obstructive sleep apnea.

Negative-Pressure Ventilation.—In patients with central sleep apnea, the noninvasive approach of negative pressure ventilation without an endotracheal tube may be useful. For example, a negative-pressure cuirass, which is applied to the patient's chest and upper portion of the abdomen, may effectively control a patient's ventilation throughout the night. A negative-pressure cuirass is convenient for home use. Negative-pressure ventilation is contraindicated in obstructive sleep apnea.

Phrenic Nerve Pacemaker

The implantation of an external phrenic nerve pacemaker may be useful in patients with central sleep apnea since these patients experience apnea because of the absence of a signal sent from the central nervous system to the diaphragm by way of the phrenic nerve. This procedure, however, has not received wide application.

TABLE 23–1.
Therapy Modalities for Sleep Apnea

Therapy	Obstructive	Central
Oxygen therapy	Therapeutic	Therapeutic
Drugs		
REM Inhibitor		
Protriptyline	Therapeutic	Not indicated
Central nervous system stimulant		
Methylphenidate	Symptomatic	Symptomatic
Surgical		
Tracheostomy	Therapeutic (100%)	Not indicated
Palatopharyngoplasty	Therapeutic (40%)	Not indicated
Mandibular advancement	Therapeutic	Not indicated
Mechanical ventilation		
Continuous positive airway pressure	Therapeutic	Not indicated
Mechanical ventilation	Short-term	Short-term
Negative-pressure ventilation	Contraindicated	Therapeutic
Endotracheal tube at night	Short-term	Not indicated
Phrenic pacemaker	Not indicated	Experimental
Medical devices	Experimental	Not indicated

Medical Devices

Tongue-retaining Device.—In some patients whose obstructive sleep apnea is caused by a large tongue, a tongue-retaining device may be helpful. A major problem with this therapy, however, is that it is quite uncomfortable and, because of this fact, patient compliance is often low.

Neck Collar.—It has been reported that a small number of patients have used a collar (similar to those used to stabilize cervical fractures) to increase the diameter of the airway and reduce the apnea. The therapeutic success of this procedure is questionable.

Other Therapeutic Approaches

Regardless of the type of sleep apnea, the patient should be advised to avoid drugs that depress the central nervous system. For example, alcohol and sedatives have been shown to increase the severity and frequency of sleep apnea. Weight loss should be encouraged in all obese apnea patients.

Table 23–1 summarizes the major therapy modalities for obstructive and central apnea and their effectiveness.

SELF-ASSESSMENT QUESTIONS

Multiple Choice
1. Nonrapid eye movement (non-REM) sleep is also called
    I. Slow-wave sleep.
    II. Active sleep.
    III. Dreaming sleep.

IV. Quiet sleep.
    a. I only.
    b. III only.
    c. IV only.
    d. I and IV only.
    e. II and III only.

2. During non-REM sleep, ventilation becomes slow and regular during which phase(s)?
    I. Phase 1.
    II. Phase 2.
    III. Phase 3.
    IV. Phase 4.
    a. II only.
    b. III only.
    c. I and II only.
    d. II and III only.
    e. III and IV only.

3. The pickwickian syndrome is associated with which of the following?
    I. Central sleep apnea.
    II. Obesity.
    III. Loud snoring.
    IV. Obstructive sleep apnea.
    V. Absence of diaphragmatic excursion.
    a. I only.
    b. IV only.
    c. I and V only.
    d. IV and V only.
    e. II, III, and IV only.

4. During periods of apnea, the patient commonly demonstrates
    I. Systemic hypotension.
    II. Decreased cardiac output.
    III. Increased heart rate.
    IV. Pulmonary hypertension.
    a. I and III only.
    b. II and IV only.
    c. III and IV only.
    d. I, II, and III only.
    e. II, III, and IV only.

5. Periods of severe sleep apnea are commonly associated with
    I. Ventricular tachycardia.
    II. Sinus bradycardia.
    III. Premature ventricular contraction.
    IV. Sinus arrhythmia.
    a. I and IV only.
    b. II and III only.
    c. III and IV only.
    d. II, III, and IV only.
    e. I, II, III, and IV.

6. During REM sleep, there is paralysis of the
    I. Arm muscles.
    II. Upper airway muscles.
    III. Leg muscles.
    IV. Intercostal muscles.

The first thing you do in data cleaning is to define missing values. You have used certain codes to represent the missing information in entering the data into the database file. Before you apply statistical procedures to the data, however, you must let the computer know that these codes are missing values so that they will not be treated as valid values and included in the calculations. The command is easy for accomplishing this task, e.g., MISSING VALUES followed by variable names as well as the codes in a parenthesis in the SPSS (Statistical Package for the Social Sciences) language. Notwithstanding that the step is so simple, you should take extreme care since the results will be seriously distorted if missing values are mistreated as valid values and included in the calculations. In practice, we do not know how many research articles have been rushed into the academic journals with the authors' research assistants having forgotten to define their missing values in performing the data analyses. There is no way for the journal gatekeepers to detect this. Unfortunate indeed, nobody would get to know this kind of tricky thing except those data managers, or maybe in rare cases some others who are determined to replicate the studies and the results. A rule, therefore, is in order: you should never forget the first thing to define your missing values.

Now that you have taken care of that, you need to look carefully at the other values you have got for each of your variables. In theory, these would all be valid values. Yet, in practice, some could be very problematic, and you may want to exclude them from certain statistical analyses by treating them as missing values. For this purpose, you first need to detect the problems and identify what codes are invalid or unusable for a particular analytical purpose.

The examination of your data may begin with browsing and double-checking your computerized data matrix or database file (you can print out a hard copy by using the command LIST VARIABLES in SPSS/PC+). After this important but tedious double-check, you should obtain frequency tables for all your variables. By scrutinizing the frequency distributions, you may find some problems. For example, you know you are studying an elderly sample aged 60 and over. If you find some cases with ages younger than 60 in the frequency table, something must be wrong. It is also questionable if somebody is older than 120 years of age in your sample. If you cannot fix it by going back to the information source, you will have to treat those ages as missing values. Another example is sex. If you have coded 1 as female and 2 as male but you find a case with the value 4 in the frequency table, this must be an error (probably a typo in data entry). You may have to treat this as a missing value if you cannot fix it by checking the original

   V. Diaphragm.
     a. IV only.
     b. V only.
     c. IV and V only.
     d. I, II, III, and IV only.
     e. I, II, III, IV, and V.

7. Normally, REM sleep constitutes about what percentage of the total sleep time?
     a. 5–10.
     b. 10–20.
     c. 20–25.
     d. 25–30.
     e. 35–40.

8. Which of the following therapy modalities are therapeutic for obstructive apnea?
     I. Phrenic pacemaker.
    II. CPAP.
   III. Theophylline.
   IV. Negative-pressure ventilation.
     a. I only.
     b. II only.
     c. III and IV only.
     d. I and IV only.
     e. I, II, III, and IV.

9. Which of the following therapy modalities are therapeutic for central sleep apnea?
     I. Negative-pressure ventilation.
    II. CPAP.
   III. Tracheostomy.
   IV. Endotracheal tube at night.
     a. I only.
     b. II only.
     c. III only.
     d. II and III only.
     e. II, III, and IV only.

10. Normal periods of apnea during REM sleep last for about
     a. 0–5 seconds.
     b. 5–10 seconds.
     c. 10–15 seconds.
     d. 15–20 seconds.
     e. 20–25 seconds.

Answers appear in Appendix XVII.

GENERAL REFERENCES

Anatomy and Physiology

Anthony CP, Thibodeau GA: *Textbook of Anatomy and Physiology*, ed 10. St Louis, CV Mosby Co, 1979.

Clemente CD: *Anatomy: A Regional Atlas of the Human Body*. Philadelphia, Lea & Febiger, 1975.

Crouch JE: *Functional Human Anatomy*, ed 3. Philadelphia, Lea & Febiger, 1978.

Gray H: *Anatomy of the Human Body*, ed 29. Philadelphia, Lea & Febiger, 1973.

Guyton AC: *Anatomy and Physiology*. Philadelphia, WB Saunders Co, 1985.

Guyton AC: *Physiology of the Human Body*. Philadelphia, WB Saunders Co, 1984.

Hole JW: *Essentials of Human Anatomy and Physiology*. Dubuque, Iowa, William C Brown Co, 1982.

Jacob SW, Francone AF, Lossow WJ: *Structure and Function in Man*, ed 5. Philadelphia, WB Saunders Co, 1982.

Luciano DS, Vander AJ, Sherman JH: *Human Anatomy and Physiology—Structure and Function*, ed 2. New York, McGraw-Hill International Book Co, 1982.

McClintic JR: *Basic Anatomy and Physiology of the Human Body*, ed 2. New York, John Wiley & Sons Inc, 1980.

McClintic JR: *Human Anatomy*. St Louis, CV Mosby Co, 1983.

McGinn RMH, Hutchings RT: *Color Atlas of Human Anatomy*. Chicago, Year Book Medical Publishers Inc, 1977.

Montgomery RL: *Basic Anatomy for the Allied Health Professions*. Baltimore, Urban & Schwarzenberg, 1981.

O'Rahilly R: *Basic Human Anatomy*. Philadelphia, WB Saunders Co, 1983.

Snell RS: *Clinical Anatomy for Medical Students*, ed 2. Boston, Little Brown & Co Inc, 1981.

Tortora GJ, Anagnostakos NP: *Principles of Anatomy and Physiology*, ed 2. New York, Harper & Row Publishers Inc, 1978.

Tortora GJ, Ronald EL: *Principles of Human Physiology*, ed 2. New York, Harper & Row Publishers Inc, 1986.

VanDeGraaff KM: *Human Anatomy*. Dubuque, Iowa, William C Brown Co, 1984.

Vander AJ, Sherman JH, Luciano DS: *Human Physiology: The Mechanisms of Body Function*, ed 4. New York, McGraw-Hill International Book Co, 1985.

Woodburne RT: *Essentials of Human Anatomy*, ed 6. Oxford, England, Oxford University Press, 1978.

Cardiopulmonary Anatomy and Physiology

Bouhuys A: *The Physiology of Breathing.* New York, Grune & Stratton, 1977.

Braun HA, Cheney FW Jr, Loehnen CP: *Introduction to Respiratory Physiology,* ed 2. Boston, Little Brown & Co Inc, 1980.

Campbell EJM, Agostoni E, Newsom-Davis JN: *The Respiratory Muscles: Mechanics and Neural Control.* Philadelphia, WB Saunders Co, 1970.

Cherniack RM, Cherniack LC: *Respiration in Health and Disease,* ed 3. Philadelphia, WB Saunders Co, 1983.

Comroe JH: *Physiology of Respiration,* ed 2. Chicago, Year Book Medical Publishers Inc, 1974.

Daily EK, Schroeder JS: *Techniques in Bedside Hemodynamic Monitoring,* ed 3. St Louis, CV Mosby Co, 1987.

Davenport HW: *ABC of Acid-Base Chemistry,* ed 7. Chicago, University of Chicago Press, 1978.

Fraser RG, Pare JAP: *Organ Physiology: Structure and Function of the Lung,* ed 2. Philadelphia, WB Saunders Co, 1977.

Green JF: *Fundamental Cardiovascular and Pulmonary Physiology,* ed 2. Philadelphia, Lea & Febiger, 1987.

Huber GL: *Arterial Blood Gas and Acid-Base Physiology.* A Scope Current Concepts Publication. Kalamazoo, Mich, Upjohn Co, 1978.

Jacquez JA: *Respiratory Physiology.* New York, McGraw-Hill Book International Co, 1979.

Jones NL: *Blood Gases and Acid-Base Physiology.* New York, Thieme-Stratton Inc, 1980.

Levitzky MG: *Pulmonary Physiology.* New York, McGraw-Hill International Book Co, 1982.

McLaughlin AJ: *Essentials of Physiology for Advanced Respiratory Therapy.* St Louis, CV Mosby Co, 1977.

Mines AH: *Respiratory Physiology.* New York, Raven Press, 1981.

Murray JF: *The Normal Lung,* ed 2. Philadelphia, WB Saunders Co, 1986.

Netter FH: *The CIBA Collection of Medical Illustrations,* vol 7, *Respiratory System.* Summit, NJ, CIBA Pharmaceutical Products, 1979, pp 3–43.

Nunn JF: *Applied Respiratory Physiology.* London, Butterworths, 1977.

Pallot DJ: *Control of Respiration.* New York, Oxford University Press, 1983.

Proctor DF: The upper airways. *Am Rev Respir Dis* 1977; 115:97, 315.

Rosendorff C: *Clinical Cardiovascular and Pulmonary Physiology.* New York, Raven Press, 1983.

Schweiss JF: *Continuous Measurement of Blood Oxygen Saturation in the High Risk Patient,* vol 1. San Diego, Beach International, 1983.

Shapiro BA, Harrison RA, Cane RD, et al: *Clinical Application of Blood Gases,* ed 4. Chicago, Year Book Medical Publishers Inc, 1989.

Shapiro BA, Harrison RA, Kacmarek RM, et al: *Clinical Application of Respiratory Care,* ed 2. Chicago, Year Book Medical Publishers Inc, 1985.

Slonim NB, Hamilton LH: *Respiratory Physiology,* ed 5. St Louis, CV Mosby Co, 1987.

West JB: *Respiratory Physiology, The Essentials,* ed 3. Baltimore, Williams & Wilkins, 1985.

West JB: State of the art: Ventilation-perfusion relationships. *Am Rev Respir Dis* 1977; 116:919–943.

West JB: *Ventilation/Blood Flow and Gas Exchange,* ed 3. Oxford, England, Blackwell Scientific Publications, 1977.

Widdicombe JG (ed): *Respiratory Physiology III.* Baltimore, University Park Press, 1981.

Supplementary Respiratory Care

Burton GG, Hodgkin JE: *Respiratory Care: A Guide to Clinical Practice*, ed 2. Philadelphia, JB Lippincott, 1984.

Rau JL: *Respiratory Care Pharmacology*, ed 3. Chicago, Year Book Medical Publishers Inc, 1989.

Ruppel G: *Manual of Pulmonary Function*, ed 3. St Louis, CV Mosby Co, 1982.

Shapiro BA, Harrison RA, Kacmarek RM, et al: *Clinical Application of Respiratory Care*, ed 2. Chicago, Year Book Medical Publishers Inc, 1985.

Spearman CB, Sheldon RL (eds): *Egan's Fundamentals of Respiratory Therapy*, ed 4. St Louis, CV Mosby Co, 1982.

Pulmonary Disorders

Banner AS: *Management of Common Pulmonary Disorders*. Chicago, Year Book Medical Publishers Inc, 1980.

Bates DV, Macklem PT, Christie RV: *Respiratory Function in Disease*. Philadelphia, WB Saunders Co, 1971.

Baum GL, Wolinsky E: *Textbook of Pulmonary Diseases*, ed 3. Boston, Little Brown & Co Inc, 1983.

Bone RC: *Pulmonary Disease Reviews*, vol 1. New York, John Wiley & Sons Inc, 1980.

Bone RC: *Pulmonary Disease Reviews*, vol 2. New York, John Wiley & Sons Inc, 1981.

Bone RC: *Pulmonary Disease Reviews*, vol 3. New York, John Wiley & Sons Inc, 1982.

Brody JS, Snider GL (eds): *Current Topics in the Management of Respiratory Diseases*, vol 1. New York, Churchill Livingstone Inc, 1981.

Burki NK: *Pulmonary Diseases*. New Hyde Park, NY, Medical Examination Publishing Co Inc, 1982.

Burrows B, Knudson RJ; Quan SF, et al: *Respiratory Disorders—A Pathophysiologic Approach*, ed 2. Chicago, Year Book Medical Publishers Inc, 1983.

Campbell EJM: Evaluation of dyspnea: Understanding breathlessness. *Trans Med Soc Lond* 1975; 92:13.

Cherniack RM, Cherniack L, Naimark A: *Respiration in Health Disease*, ed 3. Philadelphia, WB Saunders Co, 1983.

Collins JVA: *A Synopsis of Chest Diseases*. Chicago, Year Book Medical Publishers Inc, 1980.

Comroe JH: Some theories of the mechanisms of dyspnea, in Howell BL, Campbell EJM (eds): *Breathlessness*. Oxford, England, Blackwell Scientific Publications, 1966, p 1.

Crofton SJ, Douglas A: *Respiratory Diseases*, ed 3. Oxford, England, Blackwell Scientific Publications, 1981.

Crompton GK: *Diagnosis and Management of Respiratory Diseases*. Oxford, England, Blackwell Scientific Publications, 1980.

Cumming G, Semple SJ: *Disorders of the Respiratory System*, ed 2. Oxford, England, Blackwell Scientific Publications, 1980.

Farzan S: *A Concise Handbook of Respiratory Diseases*. Reston, Virginia, Reston Publishing Co, 1985.

Fleming PR: Cyanosis, in Hart D (ed): *French's Index of Differential Diagnosis*, ed 11. New York, John Wright & Sons, 1979, pp 194–199.

Fraser RG, Pare JAP: *Diagnosis of Diseases of the Chest*, vol 1, ed 2. Philadelphia, WB Saunders Co, 1977.

Fraser RG, Pare JAP: *Diagnosis of Diseases of the Chest*, vol 2, ed 2. Philadelphia, WB Saunders Co, 1978.

Fraser RG, Pare JAP: *Diagnosis of Diseases of the Chest,* vol 3, ed 2. Philadelphia, WB Saunders Co, 1979.

Fraser RG, Pare JAP: *Diagnosis of Diseases of the Chest,* vol 4, ed 2. Philadelphia, WB Saunders Co, 1979.

George RB, Light RW, Matthay RA: *Chest Medicine.* New York, Churchill Livingstone Inc, 1983.

Glauser FL (ed): *Signs and Symptoms in Pulmonary Medicine.* Philadelphia, JB Lippincott, 1983.

Gracey DR (ed): *Pulmonary Disease in the Adult.* Chicago, Year Book Medical Publishers Inc, 1981.

Guenter CA, Welch M: *Pulmonary Medicine,* ed 2. Philadelphia, JB Lippincott, 1982.

Haas A, Pineda H, Haas F, et al: *Pulmonary Therapy and Rehabilitation: Principles and Practice.* Baltimore, Williams & Wilkins, 1979.

Hinshaw HC: *Diseases of the Chest,* ed. 4. Philadelphia, WB Saunders Co, 1980.

Hodgkin JE (ed): *Chronic Obstructive Pulmonary Disease.* Park Ridge, Ill, American College of Chest Physicians, 1979.

Lapuerta L: *Blood Gases in Clinical Practice.* Springfield, Ill, Charles C Thomas Publishers, 1976.

Leblanc P, Macklem PT, Ross WRD: Breath sounds and the distribution of pulmonary ventilation. *Am Rev Respir Dis* 1970; 102:10–16.

Lukas DS: Cyanosis, in McBryde CM, Blacklow RS (eds): *Signs and Symptoms,* ed 5. Philadelphia, JB Lippincott, 1970.

Mitchell RS, Petty TL: *Synopsis of Clinical Pulmonary Disease,* ed 3. St Louis, CV Mosby Co, 1982.

Murphy RLH, Holford SK: Lung sounds. *Basics Respir Dis* 1980; 8:1–6.

Norton CF: *Microbiology,* ed 2. Reading, Mass, Addison-Wesley Publishing Co Inc, 1986.

Paintal AS: Vagal sensory receptors and the reflex effects. *Physiol Rev* 1973; 53:159.

Porth CM: Pathophysiology, ed 2. Philadelphia, JB Lippincott, 1986.

Rau JL, Douglas JP: *Understanding Chest Radiographs.* St Louis, CV Mosby Co, 1984.

Rochester DF, Braun NT: The respiratory muscles. *Basics Respir Dis* 1978;6.

Schneerson JM: Digital clubbing and hypertrophic osteoarthropathy: The underlying mechanisms. *Br J Dis Chest* 1981; 75:113.

Selecky PA: *Pulmonary Disease.* New York, John Wiley & Sons Inc, 1982.

Senior RN, Lefrak SS, Kleiger RE: The heart in chronic obstructive pulmonary disease: Arrhythmias. *Chest* 1979; 75:1–2.

Sharma OP, Balchum OJ: *Key Facts in Pulmonary Disease.* New York, Churchill Livingstone Inc, 1983.

Spencer H: *Pathology of the Lung,* vol 1, ed 3. Philadelphia, WB Saunders Co, 1977.

Spencer H: *Pathology of the Lung,* vol 2, ed 3. Philadelphia, WB Saunders Co, 1977.

Sproule BJ, Lynne-Davies P, King EG: *Fundamentals of Respiratory Disease.* New York, Churchill Livingstone Inc, 1981.

Thurlbeck WM, Abell MR (eds): *The Lung: Structure, Function and Disease.* Baltimore, Williams & Wilkins, 1978.

West JB: *Pulmonary Pathophysiology: The Essentials.* Baltimore, Williams & Wilkins, 1977.

Williams MH: *Essentials of Pulmonary Medicine.* Philadelphia, WB Saunders Co, 1982.

Neonatal/Pediatric Pulmonary Disorders

Avery ME, Fletcher BD, Williams RG: *The Lung and Its Disorders in the Newborn,* ed. 4. Philadelphia, WB Saunders Co, 1981.

Gerbeaux J, Couvreur J, Tournier G (eds): *Pediatric Respiratory Disease*, ed 2. New York, John Wiley & Sons Inc, 1982.

Levin RM: *Pediatric Respiratory Intensive Care Handbook*. Flushing, NY, Medical Examination Publishing Co, 1976.

Scarpelli EM, Auld PAM, Goldman HS: *Pulmonary Disease of the Fetus, Newborn and Child*. Philadelphia, Lea & Febiger, 1978.

Schaffer AJ: *Diseases of the Newborn*. Philadelphia, WB Saunders Co, 1977.

Thibeault DW, Gregory GA (eds): *Neonatal Pulmonary Care*. Reading, Mass, Addison-Wesley Publishing Co, Inc, 1979.

SELECTED REFERENCES

Chronic Bronchitis and Emphysema

American Thoracic Society, Statement by Committee on Diagnostic Standards for Non-Tuberculous Respiratory Diseases: Definitions and classifications of chronic bronchitis, asthma, and pulmonary emphysema. *Am Rev Respir Dis* 1962; 85:762–768.

Anderson AE, Foraker AG: *Pathology of Disruptive Emphysema.* Springfield, Ill, Charles C Thomas Publishers, 1976.

Ashutosh K: Asynchronous breathing movements in patients with chronic obstructive pulmonary disease. *Chest* 1975; 67:553.

Ayres SM: Bronchial component in chronic obstructive lung disease. *Am J Med* 1974; 57:183.

Bates DV: The fate of the chronic bronchitic: A report of the ten-year follow-up in the Canadian Department of Veterans' Affairs coordinated study of chronic bronchitis. The J Burns Amberson lecture of the American Thoracic Society. *Am Rev Respir Dis* 1973; 108:1043–1065.

Black LF, Kueppers F: Alpha$_1$-antitrypsin deficiency in nonsmokers. *Am Rev Respir Dis* 1978; 117:421.

Boushy SF, Aboumrad MH, North LB, et al: Lung recoil pressure, airway resistance, and forced flows related to morphologic emphysema. *Am Rev Respir Dis* 1971; 104:551.

Burki NK: Breathlessness and mouth occlusion pressure in patients with chronic obstruction of the airways. *Chest* 1979; 76:527.

Burrows B, Knudson RJ, Cline MG, et al: Quantitative relationships between cigarette smoking and ventilatory function. *Am Rev Respir Dis* 1977; 115:195.

Dossman J: The relationship between symptoms and functional abnormalities in clinically healthy cigarette smokers. *Am Rev Respir Dis* 1976; 114:297.

Editorial: The pathogenesis of pulmonary emphysema. *Lancet* 1980; 1:743.

Eichenholz A: Pattern of compensatory response to hypercapnia in patients with chronic obstructive pulmonary disease. *J Lab Clin Med* 1966; 68:265.

Fletcher C, Peto R, Tinker C: Discussion and conclusions, in *The Natural History of Chronic Bronchitis and Emphysema.* Oxford, England, Oxford University Press, 1976.

Gelb AF, Gold WM, Wright RR, et al: Physiologic diagnosis of subclinical emphysema. *Am Rev Respir Dis* 1973; 107:50.

Guenter CA, Welch MH, Russell TR: The pattern of lung disease associated with alpha$_1$-antitrypsin deficiency. *Arch Intern Med* 1968; 122:254–257.

Heard BE, Khatchatourov V, Otto H, et al: The morphology of emphysema, chronic bronchitis, and bronchiectasis: Definition, nomenclature, and classification. *J Clin Pathol* 1979; 32:882–892.

Hugh-Jones P, Whimster W: The etiology and management of disabling emphysema. *Am Rev Respir Dis* 1978; 117:343.

Janoff A, Carp H: Possible mechanisms of emphysema in smokers: Cigarette smoke condensate suppresses protease inhibition in vitro. *Am Rev Respir Dis* 1977; 116:65.

Kilburn KH: New clues for the emphysemas. *Am J Med* 1975; 58:59.

Kueppers F, Black LF: Alpha₁-antitrypsin and its deficiency. *Am Rev Respir Dis* 1974; 110:176.

Langlands J: The dynamics of cough in health and in chronic bronchitis. *Thorax* 1967; 22:88.

Lertzman MM, Cherniack RM: Rehabilitation of patients with chronic obstructive pulmonary disease. *Am Rev Respir Dis* 1976; 114:1145.

Linhartova A, Anderson AE, Foraker AG: Further observations on luminal deformity and stenosis of nonrespiratory bronchioles in pulmonary emphysema. *Thorax* 1977; 32:53–59.

Macklem PT: The pathophysiology of chronic bronchitis and emphysema. *Med Clin North Am* 1973; 57:669.

Mitchell RS: The right ventricle in chronic airways obstruction: A clinicopathologic study. *Am Rev Respir Dis* 1976; 114:147–154.

Naeye RL, Greenberg SD, Valdivia E: Small pulmonary vessels in advanced pulmonary emphysema. *Arch Pathol* 1974; 97:216–220.

Niewoehner DE, Kleinerman J, Rice DB: Pathologic changes in the peripheral airways of young cigarette smokers. *N Engl J Med* 1974; 291:755.

Park SS: Relationship of bronchitis and emphysema to altered pulmonary function. *Am Rev Respir Dis* 1970; 102:927.

Petty TL: Ambulatory care for emphysema and chronic bronchitis. *Chest* 1970; 58:441–448.

Snider GL: The pathogenesis of emphysema—20 years of progress. *Am Rev Respir Dis* 1981; 124:321–324.

Thurlbeck WM: Aspects of chronic airflow obstruction. *Chest* 1977; 72:341.

Thurlbeck WM: *Chronic Airflow Obstruction in Lung Disease*. Philadelphia, WB Saunders Co, 1976.

Bronchiectasis

Anderson WAD, Kissane JM: Bronchiectasis. *Pathology* 1977; 2:.

George RB, Light RW, Mathay RA: Bronchiectasis. *Chest Medicine*. New York, Churchill Livingstone, 1983.

Hodgkin JE: Bronchiectasis, in Conn RB (ed): *Current Diagnosis*. Philadelphia, WB Saunders Book Co, 1985, pp 343–348.

Mazzocco M, Owens GR: Chest percussion and postural drainage on patients with bronchiectasis. *Chest* 1985; 88:360–363.

Smith C: Bronchiectasis in *Core Pathology—Fundamental Concepts and Principles*. Oradell, New Jersey, Medical Economics, 1981.

Asthma

American Thoracic Society: Definitions and classifications of chronic bronchitis, asthma, and pulmonary emphysema. *Am Rev Respir Dis* 1962; 85:762–768.

Austen KF, Orange RP: Bronchial asthma: The possible role of the chemical mediators of immediate hypersensitivity in the pathogenesis of subacute chronic disease. *Am Rev Respir Dis* 1975; 112:423.

Beall GN, Heiner DC, Tashki DP, et al: Asthma: New ideas about an old disease. *Ann Intern Med* 1973; 78:405.

Blair H: Natural history of childhood asthma: 20-year follow-up. *Arch Dis Child* 1977; 52:613.

Cardan DL, Nowak RM, Sarkar D, et al: Vital signs including pulsus paradoxus in the assessment of acute bronchial asthma. *Ann Emerg Med* 1983; 12:80.

Corrao WM, Bramam SS, Irwin RS: Chronic cough as the sole presenting manifestation of bronchial asthma. *N Engl J Med* 1979; 200:633.

Feldman MT, McFadden ER: Asthma therapy old and new. *Med Clin North Am* 1977; 61:1239–1250.

Holmes PW, Campbell AH, Barter CE: Acute changes of lung volumes and lung mechanics in asthma. *Thorax* 1978; 33:394.

Konig P: Conflicting viewpoints about treatment of asthma with cromolyn: A review of the literature. *Ann Allergy* 1979; 43:293.

Leifer KN, Wittig HJ: The beta-2 sympathomimetic aerosols in the treatment of asthma. *Ann Allergy* 1975; 35:69.

Martin AJ: The natural history of childhood asthma to adult life. *Br Med J* 1980; 1:1397.

McCombs RP, Lowell FC, Ohman JL: Myths, morbidity and mortality in asthma. *JAMA* 1979; 242:1521.

McFadden ER, Lyons HA: Arterial blood gas tension in asthma. *N Engl J Med* 1968; 278:1029.

McFadden ER: Asthma: Airway dynamics, cardiac function, and clinical correlates, in Middleton E, Reed CE, Ellis EF (eds): *Allergy: Principles and Practice*, vol 2. St Louis, CV Mosby Co, 1978, pp 687–707.

McFadden ER, Feldman MT: Asthma: Pathophysiology and clinical correlates. *Med Clin North Am* 1977; 61:1229–1238.

Messer JW, Peters GA, Bennett WA: Causes of death and pathological findings in 304 cases of bronchial asthma. *Dis Chest* 1960; 38:616.

Nelson HS: The beta adrenergic theory of bronchial asthma. *Pediatr Clin North Am* 1975; 22:53.

Parker WA: Cromolyn sodium. *Respir Care* 1974; 19:529.

Piafsky KM, Ogilvie RI: Dosage of theophylline in bronchial asthma. *N Engl J Med* 1975; 292:1218.

Rebuck AS, Read J: Assessment and management of severe asthma. *Am J Med* 1971; 51:788.

Reed CE: Epidemiology and natural history, in Stein M (ed): *New Directions in Asthma*. Park Ridge, Ill, American College of Chest Physicians, 1975.

Scoggin CH, Sahn SA, Petty TL: Status asthmaticus, a nine-year experience. *JAMA* 1977; 238:1158.

Shapiro BA: Case study: Status asthmaticus. *Respir Care* 1974; 19:130.

Shim C, Williams NH: Pulsus paradoxus in asthma. *Lancet* 1978; 1:530.

Sibbald B, Turner-Warwick M: Factors influencing the prevalence of asthma among first-degree relatives of extrinsic and intrinsic asthmatics. *Thorax* 1979; 34:332.

Stein M (ed): *New Directions in Asthma*. Park Ridge, Ill, American College of Chest Physicians, 1975.

Szentivanyi A: The beta adrenergic theory of the atropic abnormality in bronchial asthma. *J Allergy* 1968; 42:203–232.

VanArsdel PP, Paul GH: Drug therapy in the management of asthma. *Ann Intern Med* 1977; 87:68–74.

Weiss EB, Segal MS (eds): *Bronchial Asthma: Mechanisms and Therapeutics*. Boston, Little Brown & Co Inc, 1976.

Williams MH: The nature of asthma: Definition and natural history. *Semin Respir Med* 1980; 1:283.

Pneumonia

Alcamo IE: *Study Guide to Accompany Fundamentals of Microbiology.* Reading, Mass, Addison-Wesley Publishing Co Inc, 1983.

Arms R: Aspiration pneumonia. *Chest* 1974; 65:136.

Awe W: The pathophysiology of aspiration pneumonitis. *Surgery* 1966; 60:232.

Balows A, Fraser DE: International symposium on Legionnaires' disease. *Ann Intern Med* 1979; 90:491.

Bartlett JG, Gorbach SL: The triple threat of aspiration pneumonia. *Chest* 1975; 68:560–566.

Brock TD: *Biology of Microorganisms.* Englewood Heights, NJ, Prentice-Hall International Inc, 1979.

Cameron J: Aspiration pneumonia: Magnitude and frequency of the problem. *JAMA* 1972; 219:1194.

Everett ED: *Hemophilus influenzae* pneumonia in adults. *JAMA* 1977; 238:319.

Fraser DW: Legionnaires' disease: Four summers' harvest. *Am J Med* 1980; 68:1.

Fraser DW, Tsai TR, Orenstein W, et al: Legionnaires' disease: Description of an epidemic of pneumonia. *N Engl J Med* 1977; 297:1189.

Frobisher M, Hinsdill RD, Crabtree KT, et al: *Fundamentals of Microbiology.* Philadelphia, WB Saunders Co, 1974.

Fuerst R: *Microbiology in Health and Disease.* Philadelphia, WB Saunders Co, 1978.

Kirby BD, Snyder KM, Meyer RD: Legionnaires' disease: Clinical features of 24 cases. *Ann Intern Med* 1978; 89:297–309.

Levin DC, Schwarz MI, Matthay RA: Bacteremic *Hemophilus influenzae* pneumonia in adults: A report of 24 cases and a review of the literature. *Am J Med* 1977; 62:219–224.

Murray HW, Masur H, Senterfit LB: The protean manifestations of *Mycoplasma pneumoniae* infection in adults. *Am J Med* 1975; 58:229–242.

Musher DM, Franco M: Staphylococcal pneumonia: A new perspective. *Chest* 1981; 79:172.

Nester EW, Roberts CE, Lidstrom ME, et al: *Microbiology.* Philadelphia, WB Saunders Co, 1983.

Norton CF: *Microbiology.* Reading, Mass, Addison-Wesley Publishing Co Inc, 1981.

Pelczar MJ, Reid RD, Chan ECS: *Microbiology,* ed 4. New York, McGraw-Hill International Book Co, 1977.

Pennington JE, Reynolds HY, Carbone PP: *Pseudomonas* pneumonia: A retrospective study of 36 cases. *Am J Med* 1973; 55:155–160.

Ross FC: *Introductory Microbiology.* Columbus, Ohio, Charles E Merrill Publishing Co, 1983.

Sabath LD, Wheeler N, Laverdiere M: A new type of penicillin resistance of *Staphylococcus aureus. Lancet* 1977; 1:443–447.

Smith AL: *Principles of Microbiology.* St Louis, CV Mosby Co, 1981.

Tortora GJ, Funke BR, Case CL: *Microbiology: An Introduction.* Menlo Park, Calif, The Benjamin/Cummings Publishing Co Inc, 1982.

Wallace RJ, Musher DM, Martin RR: *Hemophilus influenzae* pneumonia in adults. *Am J Med* 1978; 64:87–93.

Wilson ME, Mizer HE, Morello JA: *Microbiology in Patient Care.* New York, Macmillan Publishing Co Inc, 1979.

Wistreich GA, Lechtman MD: *Microbiology and Human Disease.* New York, Glencoe Publishing Co Inc, 1976.

Wolfe JE, Bone RC, Ruth WE: Effects of corticosteroids in the treatment of patients with gastric aspiration. *Am J Med* 1977; 63:719–722.

Wynne JW, Modell JH: Respiratory aspiration of stomach contents. *Ann Intern Med* 1977; 87:466–474.

questionnaire.

Now, how to actually turn these erroneous codes into missing values? This is usually done through a procedure called recoding, which is essentially the switching of a code to a different one (either existing or newly created). The simple SPSS language for recoding is "RECODE variable name (old code=new code)." You can put several recodings together. A code in a single command can only be recoded once, however. For example, (5=4) (4=5) in a RECODE command does not mean that you will end up with only one value, that is, 5. Rather, it means the flipping of two values: Old 5 becomes new 4 and old 4 becomes new 5. If you have defined 9 as a missing value for the variable sex, then you can recode the erroneous value 4 in the above example as 9. The SPSS language is "RECODE sex (4=9)."

For the key variables in your research project, you may also want to use the cross-tabulation procedure to find out some potential problems (called "contingency cleaning" in some textbooks). For the number of children that the respondent gave birth to, for instance, the single frequency table may not tell you any potential problem if the codes or numbers are all possible for a woman. By using the CROSSTABS procedure, however, you can immediately detect an error if the person who reported to have given birth to a child is male.

Although you can always exclude all the problematic values from analysis, missing information is never good news for your research purpose. You need to pay attention to the number of missing cases in examining the frequency tables. If information is missing on a significant proportion of the sample, you will face a knotty problem of how to get back some of the information, if possible at all. There are two kinds of missing information in your questionnaire design: the expected and the unexpected. When you use contingency questions — questions relevant only to some respondents, you should expect the information missing for the others. In such cases, there are usually no way and no need to try to eliminate the missing cases unless their identification as the others constitutes a meaningful category in the data analysis. For example, you may first ask every respondent: "Have you ever read this book?" Then you ask those who answered "yes" a further question: "How much do you like it?" Since you do not ask this further question to those who first answered "No," they will be present as missing cases in data analysis. Nevertheless, missing cases may affect your statistical analysis, and you may want to keep those who first answered "No" as a valid category "Never read" rather than missing cases in analyzing the second question. There is an effective approach to the restoration of such information called logical

Yu VL: Legionnaires' disease: New clinical perspective from a prospective pneumonia study. *Am J Med* 1973; 9:357–361.

Pulmonary Edema

Ayres SM: Mechanisms and consequences of pulmonary edema: Cardiac lung, shock lung, and principles of ventilatory therapy in adult respiratory distress syndrome. *Am Heart J* 1982; 103:97–112.

Bo G, Hause A, Waaler BA: Does interstitial lung edema cause changes in lung compliance? *N Engl J Med* 1973; 288:471.

Brigham KL: Factors affecting lung vascular permeability. *Am Rev Respir Dis* 1977; 115:165.

Butler J, Culver BH, Huseby J, et al: The hemodynamics of pulmonary edema. *Am Rev Respir Dis* 1977; 115:173–180.

Carlson RW, Schaeffer RC, Michaels SG, et al: Pulmonary edema following intracranial hemorrhage. *Chest* 1979; 75:731.

Casaburi R, Wasserman K, Effros RM: Detection and measurement of pulmonary edema, in Staub NC (ed): *Lung Water and Solute Exchange.* New York, Marcel Dekker Inc, 1978, pp 323–375.

Daluz PL: Pulmonary edema related to changes in colloid osmotic and PWP in patients after acute myocardial infarction. *Circulation* 1975; 51:350.

Datta SK, Aberman A: Blood gases in pulmonary edema. *Ann Intern Med* 1972; 76:1045–1046.

Figueras J, Weil MM: Increases in plasma oncotic pressure during acute cardiogenic pulmonary edema. *Circulation* 1977; 55:195–199.

Fishman AP: Pulmonary edema: A new dimension. *Circulation* 1972; 46:390.

Gelb AF, Klein E: Hemodynamic and alveolar studies in noncardiogenic edema. *Am Rev Respir Dis* 1976; 114:472–476.

Marland AM, Glauser FL: Hemodynamic and pulmonary edema protein measurements in a case of reexpansion pulmonary edema. *Chest* 1982; 81:250–251.

Marshall BE: Pulmonary edema following injury. *Circ Shock Suppl* 1979; 1:53.

Neumann D, Bailey L: An overview of neurogenic pulmonary edema. *J Neurosurg Nurs* 1980; 12:206–209.

Prichard JS: *Edema of the Lung.* Springfield, Ill, Charles C Thomas Publishers, 1982.

Rackow EC, Fein IA, Leppo J: Colloid osmotic pressure as a prognostic indicator of pulmonary edema and mortality in the critically ill. *Chest* 1977; 72:1709–1713.

Robin ED: Medical progress: Pulmonary edema. Parts 1 & 2. *N Engl J Med* 1973; 288:239.

Smith HC, Gould VF, Cheney FW, et al: Pathogenesis of hemodynamic pulmonary edema in excised dog lungs. *J Appl Physiol* 1974; 37:904–911.

Snashall PD: Pulmonary oedema. *Br J Dis Chest* 1980; 74:1.

Staub NC: Pathogenesis of pulmonary edema. *Am Rev Respir Dis* 1974; 109:358.

Staub NC: Pulmonary edema. *Physiol Rev* 1974; 54:678.

Staub NC: Pulmonary edema—hypoxia and overperfusion. *N Engl J Med* 1980; 302:1085.

Staub NC: Pulmonary edema: Physiologic approaches to management. *Chest* 1978; 74:559.

Staub NC: "State of the art" review: Pathogenesis of pulmonary edema. *Am Rev Respir Dis* 1974; 109:358.

Stein L, Beraud JJ, Morisette M: Pulmonary edema during volume infusion. *Circulation* 1975; 52:483.

Szidon JP, Pietra GG, Fishman AP: The alveolar-capillary membrane and pulmonary edema. *N Engl J Med* 1972; 286:1200.

Theodore J, Robin ED: Speculations on neurogenic pulmonary edema. *Am Rev Respir Dis* 1976; 113:405.

Weil MH, Henning RJ, Puri VK: Colloid oncotic pressure: Clinical significance. *Crit Care Med* 1979; 7:113–116.

Pulmonary Embolism

Andreoli KG, Fowkes VH, Zipes DP, et al (eds): *Comprehensive Cardiac Care*, ed 4. St Louis, CV Mosby Co, 1979.

Barnes RW, Wu KK, Hoak JC: Fallibility of the clinical diagnosis of venous thrombosis. *JAMA* 1975; 234:605.

Bell WR, Meek AG: Guidelines for the use of thrombolytic agents. *N Engl J Med* 1979; 30:1266.

Bell WR, Simon TL, DeMets DL: The clinical features of submassive and massive pulmonary emboli. *Am J Med* 1977; 62:355.

Benator SR, Ferguson AD, Goldschmidt RB: Fat embolism—some clinical observations and a review of controversial aspects. *Q J Med* 1972; 41:85.

Brown AK: Recurrent pulmonary thromboembolism presenting with cardiac arrhythmias. *Thorax* 1979; 34:380.

Bynum LJ, Wilson JE: Characteristics of pleural effusion associated with pulmonary embolism. *Arch Intern Med* 1976; 136:159.

Comroe JH, Van Lingen B, Stroud RC: Reflex and direct cardiopulmonary effects of 5-OH-tryptamine (serotonin): Their possible role in pulmonary embolism and coronary thrombosis. *Am J Physiol* 1953; 173:379–386.

Cooperative study: Urokinase pulmonary embolism trial: A national cooperative study. *Circulation* 1973; 47(suppl 2):1–108.

Dalen JE, Alpert JS: Natural history of pulmonary embolism. *Prog Cardiovasc Dis* 1975; 17:259.

Dalen JE, Brooks HL, Johnson LW: Pulmonary angiography in acute pulmonary embolism: Indications, techniques, and results in 367 patients. *Am Heart J* 1971; 81:175–185.

Daly PO: Surgical management of chronic pulmonary embolism. *J Thorac Cardiovasc Surg* 1980; 79:523.

DeNardo GL, Goodwin DA, Ravasini R: The ventilatory lung scan in the diagnosis of pulmonary embolism. *N Engl J Med* 1970; 282:1334–1336.

Dossey B, Passons JM: Pulmonary embolism: Preventing it, treating it. *Nursing* 1981; 11:26–33.

Evarts CM: The fat embolism syndrome: A review. *Surg Clin North Am* 1970; 50:493.

Ferrer MI: Cor pulmonale (pulmonary heart disease): Present-day status. *Am Heart J* 1975; 89:657–664.

Genton E: Thrombolytic therapy of pulmonary thromboembolism. *Prog Cardiovasc Dis* 1979; 21:333–341.

Gilday DL, Poulose KP, DeLand FH: Accuracy of detection of pulmonary embolism by lung scanning correlated with pulmonary angiography. *AJR* 1972; 115:732.

Goldberger AL, Goldberger E: *Clinical Electrocardiography*, ed 2. St Louis, CV Mosby Co, 1981.

Gregory MG, Clayton EM: Amniotic fluid embolism. *Obstet Gynecol* 1973; 43:236.

Hirsh J: Venous thromboembolism: Diagnosis, treatment, prevention. *Hosp Pract* 1975; 10:53.

Humphries JO, Bell WR, White RI: Criteria for the recognition of pulmonary emboli. *JAMA* 1976; 235:2011.

Kafer ER: Respiratory function in pulmonary thromboembolic disease. *Am J Med* 1969; 47:904–915.

Kakkar VV: Deep vein thrombosis: Detection and prevention. *Circulation* 1975; 51:8–19.

Kernicki T, Weiler W: *Electrocardiography for Nurses: Physiological Correlates.* New York, John Wiley & Sons Inc, 1981.

Martin L: Arterial blood oxygen tension in pulmonary embolism. *Am J Med* 1977; 63:168.

McCarthy B, Mammen E, LeBlanc LP, et al: Subclinical fat embolism: A prospective study of 50 patients with extremity fractures. *J Trauma* 1973; 13:9.

McIntyre KM, Sasahara AA: Determinants of right ventricular function and hemodynamics after pulmonary embolism. *Chest* 1974; 65:534.

McIntyre KM, Sasahara AA: Hemodynamic and ventricular responses to pulmonary embolism. *Prog Cardiovasc Dis* 1974; 17:175–190.

Menzoian JO, Williams LF: Is pulmonary angiography essential for the diagnosis of acute pulmonary embolism? *Am J Surg* 1979; 137:543.

Morris GK, Mitchell JR: Clinical management of venous thromboembolism. *Br Med Bull* 1978; 34:169–175.

Moser KM: Pulmonary embolism. *Am Rev Respir Dis* 1977; 115:829.

Moser KM, Stein M (eds): *Pulmonary Thromboembolism.* Chicago, Year Book Medical Publishers Inc, 1973.

Moses DC, Silver TM, Bookstein JJ: The complementary roles of chest radiography, lung scanning, and selective pulmonary angiography in the diagnosis of pulmonary embolism. *Circulation* 1974; 49:179–188.

Neuhas A: Pulmonary embolism in respiratory failure. *Chest* 1978; 73:4.

Sharma GV: Effect of thrombolytic therapy on pulmonary-capillary blood volume in patients with pulmonary embolism. *N Engl J Med* 1980; 303:842.

Sharma GV, Sasahara AA: Diagnosis and treatment of pulmonary embolism. *Med Clin North Am* 1979; 63:239.

Sherry S, Bell WR, Duckert FH: Thrombolytic therapy in thrombosis: A National Institutes of Health Consensus Development Conference. *Ann Intern Med* 1980; 93:141–144.

Stein PD, Dalen JE, McIntyre KM: The electrocardiogram in acute pulmonary embolism. *Prog Cardiovasc Dis* 1975; 17:247–257.

Thames MD, Alpert JS, Dalen JE: Syncope in patients with pulmonary embolism. *JAMA* 1977; 238:2509.

Thompson DA: *Cardiovascular Assessment.* St Louis, CV Mosby Co, 1981.

Urokinase Pulmonary Embolism Trial: "A National Cooperative Study." *Circulation* 1973; 47(suppl 2):1–108.

Wenger NK: Pulmonary embolism: Recognition and management. *Consultant* 1980; 6:85–98.

Wenger NK, Stein PD, Willis PW: Massive acute pulmonary embolism: The deceiving nonspecific manifestation. *JAMA* 1972; 220:843.

Adult Respiratory Distress Syndrome

Ashbaugh DG, Bigelow DB, Petty TL: Acute respiratory distress in adults. *Lancet* 1967; 2:319.

Balentine J: Pathologic effects of exposure to high oxygen tensions: A review. *N Engl J Med* 1966; 275:1038.

Bone RC: Monitoring respiratory function in the patient with adult respiratory distress syndrome. *Semin Respir Med* 1981; 2:140–150.

Clark JM, Lambertson CJ: Pulmonary oxygen toxicity: A review. *Pharmacol Rev* 1971; 23:37.

Dantzker DR: Ventilation-perfusion distribution in the adult respiratory distress syndrome. *Am Rev Respir Dis* 1979; 120:1039.

Downs JB, Olsen GN: Pulmonary function following adult respiratory distress syndrome. *Chest* 1974; 65:92.

Frank L, Massaro D: Oxygen toxicity. *Am J Med* 1980; 69:117–126.

Hempel F, Lenfant CJM: Current and future research on adult respiratory distress syndrome. *Semin Respir Med* 1981; 2:165–173.

Hopewell PC, Murray JF: The adult respiratory distress syndrome. *Annu Rev Med* 1976; 27:343.

Hudson LD: Ventilatory management of patients with adult respiratory distress syndrome. *Semin Respir Med* 1981; 2:128–139.

Hyers TM: Pathogenesis of adult respiratory distress syndrome: Current concepts. *Semin Respir Med* 1981; 2:104–108.

Kapanci Y, Tosco R, Eggerman J: Oxygen pneumonitis in man. *Chest* 1972; 62:162.

Klein JJ, van Haeringen JR, Sluiter HJ: Pulmonary function after recovery from the adult respiratory distress syndrome. *Chest* 1976; 69:350–355.

Lakshminarayan S, Hudson LD: Pulmonary function following the adult respiratory distress syndrome. *Chest* 1978; 74:489–490.

Lakshminarayan S, Stanford RE, Petty TL: Prognosis after recovery from adult respiratory distress syndrome. *Am Rev Respir Dis* 1976; 113:7.

Lamy M, Fallat RJ, Koeniger E: Pathologic features and mechanisms of hypoxemia in adult respiratory distress syndrome. *Am Rev Respir Dis* 1976; 114:267.

Murray JF: The adult respiratory distress syndrome (may it rest in peace). *Am Rev Respir Dis* 1975; 111:716.

Ostendorf P: Pulmonary radiographic abnormalities in shock. *Radiology* 1975; 115:257.

Petty TL: Abnormalities in lung elastic properties and surfactant function in adult respiratory distress syndrome. *Chest* 1979; 75:571.

Petty TL: Adult respiratory distress syndrome: Historical perspective and definition. *Semin Respir Med* 1981; 2:99–103.

Petty TL, The adult respiratory distress syndrome (confessions of a lumper). *Am Rev Respir Dis* 1975; 111:713.

Petty TL, Ashbaugh DG: The adult respiratory distress syndrome: Clinical features, factors influencing prognosis and principles of management. *Chest* 1971; 60:233.

Petty TL, Reiss OK, Paul GW: Characteristics of pulmonary surfactant in adult respiratory distress syndrome associated with trauma and shock. *Am Rev Respir Dis* 1977; 115:531.

Rinalds JE, Rogers RM: Adult respiratory distress syndrome: Changing concepts of lung injury and repair. *N Engl J Med* 1982; 306:900–909.

Rotman HH: Long term physiologic consequences of the ARDS. *Chest* 1977; 72:190.

Sanders AP, Baylin GJ: A common denominator in the etiology of adult respiratory distress syndrome. *Med. Hypotheses* 1980; 5:951–965.

Shapiro BA, Cane RD, Harrison RA, et al: Changes in intrapulmonary shunting with administration of 100 percent oxygen. *Chest* 1980; 77:138–141.

Shapiro DL: Respiratory distress syndrome. *NY State Med J* 1980; 80:257–259.

Shimada Y, Toshiga I, Tamala K, et al: Evaluation of the progress and prognosis of adult respiratory distress syndrome, simple physiologic measurement. *Chest* 1979; 76:180.

Simpson DL, Goodman M, Spector SL: Long-term follow-up and bronchial reactivity testing in survivors of the adult respiratory distress syndrome. *Am Rev Respir Dis* 1978; 117:449.

Vaisrub S: What's in the cards for ARDS? *JAMA* 1976; 236:960.

Weigelt JA, Mitchell RA, Snyder WH: Early positive end expiratory pressure in the adult respiratory distress syndrome. *Arch Surg* 1979; 114:497–501.

Winter PM, Smith G: The toxicity of oxygen. *Anesthesiology* 1972; 37:210–214.

Yahav J: Pulmonary function following ARDS. *Chest* 1978; 74:247.

Flail Chest

Ashbaugh DG: Chest trauma: Analysis of 685 patients. *Arch Surg* 1967; 95:546.

Blair E: Pulmonary barriers to oxygen transport in chest trauma. *Am Surg* 1976; 42:55–61.

Carpintero JL, Rodriguez DA, Ruiz EMJ, et al: Methods of management of flail chest. *Intensive Care Med* 1980; 6:217–221.

Christensson P, Gisselsson L, Lecerof H, et al: Early and late results of controlled ventilation in flail chest. *Chest* 1979; 75:456–460.

Craven KD, Oppenheimer L, Wood LD: Effects of contusion and flail chest on pulmonary perfusion and oxygen exchange. *J Appl Physiol* 1979; 47:729–737.

Cullen P: Treatment of patients with flail chest by intermittent mandatory ventilation and PEEP. *Crit Care Med* 1975; 3:45.

Duff JH, Goldstein M, McLean APH, et al: Flail chest: A clinical review and physiological study. *J Trauma* 1968; 8:63.

Duffy BL, Kyle JW: The stove-in chest. *Nurs Times* 71:1038–1039.

Enarson DA, Didier EP, Gracey DR: Flail chest as a complication of cardiopulmonary resuscitation. *Heart Lung* 1977; 6:1020–1022.

Garzon AA, Seltzer B, Karlson EI: Physiopathology of crushed chest injuries. *Ann Surg* 1968; 168:128.

Ginsberg RJ, Kostin RF: New approaches to the management of flail chest. *Can Med Assoc J* 1977; 116:613–615.

Hankins JR, Shin B, McAslan TC, et al: Management of flail chest: An analysis of 99 cases. *Am Surg* 1979; 45:176.

Jackson H: Nursing care of patients with chest injuries. *Nursing* 1979; 11:303–309.

Jette NT, Barash PG: Treatment of a flail injury of the chest: A case report with consideration of the evolution of therapy. *Anaesthesia* 1977; 32:475–479.

Maloney JV, Schmutzer KJ, Raschke E: Paradoxical respiration and "pendelluft." *J Thorac Cardiovasc Surg* 1961; 41:291–298.

Ogawa M, Katsurada K, Sugimoto T: Blood gas analysis in management of flail chest injuries. *Jpn J Surg* 1972; 2:117–121.

Paris F, Tarazona V, Blasco E, et al: Surgical stabilization of traumatic flail chest. *Thorax* 1975; 30:521–527.

Relihan M, Litwin MS: Morbidity and mortality associated with flail chest injury: A review of 85 cases. *J Trauma* 1973; 13:663.

Richardson JD, Grover FL, Trinkle JK: Early operative management of isolated sternal fractures. *J Trauma* 1975; 15:156.

Richardson JD, McElvein RB, Trinkle JK: First rib fracture: A hallmark of severe trauma. *Ann Surg* 1975; 181:251.

Sankaran S, Wilson RF: Factors affecting prognosis in patients with flail chest. *J Thorac Cardiovasc Surg* 1970; 60:402.

Schaal MA, Fischer RP, Perry JF: The unchanged mortality of flail chest injuries. *J Trauma* 1979; 19:492–496.

Scott ML, Arens JF, Ochsner JL: Fractured sternum with flail chest and posttraumatic pulmonary insufficiency syndrome: Report of 4 patients. *Ann Thorac Surg* 1973; 15:386–393.

Shackford SR, Virgilio RW, Peters RM: Selective use of ventilator therapy in flail chest injury. *J Thorac Cardiovasc Surg* 1981; 81:194–201.

Sladen A, Aldredge CF, Albarran R: PEEP vs. ZEEP in the treatment of flail chest injuries. *Crit Care Med* 1973; 1:187–191.

Trinkle JK, Glover FL (eds): *Management of Thoracic Trauma Victims.* Philadelphia, JB Lippincott, 1980.

Trinkle JK, Richardson JD, Franz JL, et al: Management of flail chest without mechanical ventilation. *Ann Thorac Surg* 1975; 19:355.

Webb AK: Flail chest: Management and complications. *Br J Hosp Med* 1978; 20:405–411.

Wilson JM, Thomas AN, Goodman PC: Severe chest trauma: Morbidity implication. *Arch Surg* 1978; 113:846.

Wilson RF, Murray C, Antonenko DR: Nonpenetrating thoracic injuries. *Surg Clin North Am* 1977; 57:17–36.

Wiot JF: The radiologic manifestations of blunt chest trauma. *JAMA* 1975; 231:500.

Pneumothorax

Adwers JR, Hodgson PE, Lynch R: Spontaneous pneumomediastinum. *Trauma* 1974; 14:414.

Anthonisen NR: Regional lung function in spontaneous pneumothorax. *Am Rev Respir Dis* 1977; 115:873–876.

Cordice JVW, Cabezon J: Chest trauma with pneumothorax and hemothorax: Review of experience with 502 cases. *J Thorac Cardiovasc Surg* 1965; 50:316.

De Troyer A, Yernault JC, Rodenstein D, et al: Pulmonary function in patients with primary spontaneous pneumothorax. *Bull Eur Physiopathol Respir* 1978; 14:31–39.

Gustman P, Yerser L, Wanner A: Immediate cardiovascular effects of tension pneumothorax. *Am Rev Respir Dis* 1983; 127:171–174.

Lindskog GE, Halasz NA: Spontaneous pneumothorax: A consideration of pathogenesis and management with review of 72 hospitalized cases. *Arch Surg* 1957; 75:693.

Monin P, Vert P: Pneumothorax. *Clin Perinatol* 1978; 5:335–350.

Osata ES, Gregory GA, Kitterman JA, et al: Pneumothorax in the respiratory distress syndrome: Incidence and effect on vital signs, blood gases, and pH. *Pediatrics* 1976; 58:177–183.

Ruckley CV, McCormick RJM: The management of spontaneous pneumothorax. *Thorax* 1966; 21:139.

Yamazaki S, Ogawa J, Shohzu A, et al: Pulmonary blood flow to rapidly reexpanded lung in spontaneous pneumothorax. *Chest* 1982; 81:118–120.

Yeung KY, Bonnet JD: Bronchogenic carcinoma presenting as spontaneous pneumothorax: Case reports with review of literature. *Cancer* 1977; 39:2286–2289.

Pleural Diseases

Brewer PL, Himmelwright JP: Pleural effusion due to infection with *Histoplasma capsulatum. Chest* 1970; 58:76–79.

Brown NE, Zamel N, Aberman A: Changes in pulmonary mechanics and gas exchange following thoracentesis. *Chest* 1978; 74:540–542.

Bynum LJ, Wilson JE III: Characteristics of pleural effusions associated with pulmonary embolism. *Arch Intern Med* 1976; 136:159–162.

Bynum LJ, Wilson JE III: Radiographic features of pleural effusions in pulmonary embolism. *Am Rev Respir Dis* 1978; 117:829–852.

Drutz DJ, Catanzaro A: Coccidioidomycosis. *Am Rev Respir Dis* 1978; 117:727–771.

Eriksson CD, Pickering LK, Salmon GW: Pleural effusion in histoplasmosis. *J Pediatr* 1977; 90:326–327.

Fine NL, Smith LR, Sheedy PF: Frequency of pleural effusions in mycoplasma and viral pneumonias. *N Engl J Med* 1970; 283:790–793.

Hughes RL, et al: The management of chylothorax. *Chest* 1979; 76:212–218.

Light RW: Diseases of the pleura, in Spittell JA Jr (ed): *Clinical Medicine*, vol 5. Hagerstown, Md, Harper & Row, Publishers Inc, 1980, pp 1–61.

Light RW: *Pleural Diseases.* Philadelphia, Lea & Febiger, 1983.

Lowell JR: Pleural Effusions. A Comprehensive Review. Baltimore, University Park Press, 1977.

Moser KM: State of the art: Pulmonary embolism. *Am Rev Respir Dis* 1978; 115:829–852.

Sahn SA: When cancer patients develop pleural effusions. *J Respir Dis* 1981; 2:53–63.

Sarosi GA, Davies SF: Blastomycosis. *Am Rev Respir Dis* 1976; 120:911–938.

Schub HM, Spivey CG Jr, Baird GD: Pleural involvement in histoplasmosis. *Am Rev Respir Dis* 1966; 94:225–232.

Talbot S, Worthington BS, Roebuck EJ: Radiographic signs of pulmonary embolism and pulmonary infarction. *Thorax* 1973; 28:198–203.

Weissbluth M: Pleural effusion in histoplasmosis. *J Pediatr* 1977; 88:894–895.

Kyphoscoliosis

Bergofsky EH: Respiratory failure in disorders of the thoracic cage. *Am Rev Respir Dis* 1979; 119:643–669. Volume 119.

Fulkerson WJ, et al: Life threatening hypoventilation in kyphoscoliosis: Successful treatment with a molded body brace-ventilator. *Am Rev Respir Dis* 1984; 129:185–187.

Guilleminault C, et al: Severe kyphoscoliosis, breathing, and sleep. *Chest* 1981; 79:626–630.

Pneumoconioses

Albeda SM, Epstein DM, Gefter WB, et al: Pleural thickening: Its significance and relationship to asbestos dust and exposure. *Am Rev Respir Dis* 1982; 126:621–624.

Arzt GH: Review of lung function data in 195 patients with asbestosis of the lung. *Int Arch Occup Environ Health* 1980; 45:63–79.

Becklake MR: Asbestos-related diseases of the lung and other organs: Their epidemiology and implications for clinical practice. *Am Rev Respir Dis* 1976; 114:187–227.

Britton MG, Hughes DT, Wever AM: Serial pulmonary function tests in patients with asbestosis. *Thorax* 1977; 32:45–52.

Churg A: Current issues in the pathologic and mineralogic diagnosis of asbestos-induced disease. *Chest* 1983; 84:276–280.

deShazo RD: Current concepts about the pathogenesis of silicosis and asbestosis. *J Allergy Clin Immunol* 1982; 70:41–49.

Heebink DM, Occupational lung disease: An international conference. *Respir Care* 1982; 27:1530–1535.

Krokosky NJ: Black lung and silicosis. *Am J Nurs* 1985; 85:883–886.

Morgan K, Seaton A: *Occupational Lung Disease*, ed 2. Philadelphia, WB Saunders Co, 1984.

Morgan WKC, Lapp NL: Respiratory disease in coal miners. *Am Rev Respir Dis* 1976; 113:531.

Victor LD, Talamonti WJ: Asbestos Lung Disease. Hospital Practice, April 1986, p. 257–268, Volume 21.

Weill H: Asbestos-associated diseases: Science, public policy, and litigation. *Chest* 1983; 84:601–608.

Weill H: Occupational lung diseases. *Hosp Pract* 1981; p. 16:65–80.

Tuberculosis

Perez-Stable EJ, Hopewell P: Chemotherapy of tuberculosis. *Semin Respir Med* 1988; 9:459–469.

Raleigh JW: Disease Due to *Mycobacterium kansasii*. *Semin Respir Med* 1988; 9:498–504.
Rook GA: The role of vitamin D in tuberculosis. *Respir Dis* 1988; 138:768–770.
Smith MJ, Citron KM: Clinical review of pulmonary disease caused by *Mycobacterium*. *Thorax* 1983; 28:197.
Snider DE: Current and future priorities in tuberculosis. *Semin Respir Med* 1988; 9:514–520.
Spires R: Tuberculosis today: The siege isn't over yet. *RN* 1980; 43:43–46.

Fungal Diseases

Bayer MD, Arnold S: Fungal pneumonias: Pulmonary coccidioidal syndromes, parts I & II. *Chest* 1981; 79:575–582, 686–690.
Einstein MD, Hans E: Coccidioidomycosis. *Respir Care* 1981; 26:563–568.
Goodwin RA Jr, Des Prez RM: Histoplasmosis, state of the art. *Am Rev Respir Dis* 1978; 117:929–956.

Cancer of the Lungs

Bone RC, Balk RB: Staging of bronchogenic carcinoma. *Chest* 1982; 82:473–480.
Carr DT: Malignant lung disease. *Hosp Pract* 1981; 16:97–115.
Engelking C: Lung cancer: The language of staging. *Am J Nurs* 1987; 87:1434–1437.
Filderman AE, Matthay RA: Update on lung cancer. *Respir Ther* 1985; 15:21–31.
Greco FA, Oldham RK: Current concepts in cancer: Small-cell lung cancer. *N Engl J Med* 1979; 301:355–357.
Hande KR, Des Prez RM: Current perspectives in small cell lung cancer. *Chest* 1984; 85:669–677.
Tisi GM, et al: Clinical staging of primary lung cancer. New York, American Thoracic Society, November 1981.

Idiopathic Respiratory Distress Syndrome

Ashbaugh T, Bigelow DB, Petty TL, et al: Acute respiratory distress in adults. *Lancet* 1967; 2:319–323.
Avery ME: In pursuit of understanding the first breath. *Am Rev Respir Dis* 1969; 100:295.
Avery ME: *The Lung and Its Disorders in the Newborn Infant*. Philadelphia, WB Saunders Co, 1974.
Barrie H: Simple method of applying continuous positive airway pressure in respiratory distress syndrome. *Lancet* 1972; 1:776.
Belani KG, Gilmour IJ, Liao JC, et al: Respiratory failure in newborns, infants and children. *Indian J Pediatr* 1981; 48:21–36.
Carlo WA, Martin RJ, Versteesh FG, et al: The effect of respiratory distress syndrome on chest wall movements and respiratory pauses in preterm infants. *Am Rev Respir Dis* 1982; 126:103–107.
Chu J: The pulmonary hypoperfusion syndrome. *Pediatrics* 1975; 35:733.
Farrell PM, Avery ME: Hyaline membrane disease. *Am Rev Respir Dis* 1975; 111:657–688.
Fawcett WA, Gluck L: Respiratory distress syndrome in the tiny baby. *Clin Perinatol* 1977; 4:411–423.

Gerhardt T, Bancalari E, Cohen H, et al: Respiratory depression at birth: Value of Apgar score and ventilatory measurements in its detection. *J Pediatr* 1977; 90:971–975.

Gregory GA: Treatment of idiopathic respiratory-distress syndrome with continuous positive airway pressure. *N Engl J Med* 1971; 284:1333.

Hack M: Neonatal respiratory distress following electric delivery: A preventable disease? *Am J Obstet Gynecol* 1976; 126:43.

Hallman M, Teramo K, Kankaanpaa K: Prevention of respiratory distress syndrome: Current view of fetal lung maturity studies. *Ann Clin Res* 1980; 12:36–44.

Croup and Epiglottitis

Ashcraft CK, Russell WS: Epiglottitis: A pediatric emergency. *J Respir Dis* 1988; 7:48–60.

Barker GA: Current management of croup and epiglottitis. *Pediatr Clin North Am* 1979; 26:565.

Cherry JD: The treatment of croup: Continued controversy due to failure of recognition of historic, ecologic, etiological, and clinical perspectives. *J Pediatr* 1979; 94:352.

Denny FW: Croup: An 11-tear study in a pediatric practice. *Pediatrics* 1983; 71:871.

Eigen H: Croup or epiglottitis: Differential diagnosis and treatment. *Respir Care* 1975; 20:1158–1163.

Fried MP: Controversies in the management of supraglottitis and croup. *Pediatr Clin North Am* 1979; 26:931.

Mayo-Smith MF, Hirsch PJ, Wodzinski SF, et al: An eight-year experience in the state of Rhode Island. *N Engl J Med* 1986; 314:1133–1139.

Simkins R: Croup and epiglottitis. *Am J Nurs* 1981; 81:519–520.

Thomas DO: Are you sure it's only croup? *RN* 1984; 47:40–43.

Vernon DD, Ashok PS: Acute epiglottitis in children: A conservative approach to diagnosis and management. *Crit Care Med* 1986; 14:1.

Cystic Fibrosis

Barker R, Levison H: Effects of ultrasonically nebulized distilled water on airway dynamics in children with cystic fibrosis and asthma. *J Pediatr* 1972; 80:396.

Berry HK: Dietary supplement and nutrition in children with cystic fibrosis. *Am J Dis Child* 1975; 129:165.

Bowling SA: Case study: Cystic fibrosis. *Am J Med Technol* 1982; 1:25–27.

Davis PB, di Sant'Agnese PA: A review: Cystic fibrosis at forty—quo vadis? *Pediatr Res* 1980; 14:83–87.

Dietzsch HJ: Cystic fibrosis: Comparison of two mucolytic drugs for inhalation treatment (acetylcysteine and arginine hydrochloride). *Pediatrics* 1975; 55:96.

di Sant'Agnese PA, Davis PB: Cystic fibrosis in adults: 75 cases and a review of 232 cases in the literature. *Am J Med* 1979; 66:121.

Fink RJ, Doershuk CF, Tucker AS: Pulmonary function and morbidity in 40 adult patients with cystic fibrosis. *Chest* 1978; 74:643.

Fowler RS, Rappaport H, Cunningham K, et al: Cor pulmonale in cystic fibrosis. *J Electrocardiol* 1981; 14:319–324.

Gayton WF, Friedman SB: Psychosocial aspects of cystic fibrosis: A review of the literature. *Am J Dis Child* 1973; 126:856.

Hen J, Dolan TF, Touloukian RJ: Meconium plug syndrome associated with cystic fibrosis and Hirschsprung's disease. *Pediatrics* 1980; 66:466–468.

Hilman BC: Cystic fibrosis: Not just a pediatric disease. *J Respir Dis* 1981; 2:83–97.

Holsclaw DS: Cystic fibrosis: Overview and pulmonary aspects in young adults. *Clin. Chest Med* 1980; 1:407.

Landau LI, Phelan PD: The spectrum of cystic fibrosis: A study of pulmonary mechanics in 46 patients. *Am Rev Respir Dis* 1973; 108:593.

Larter N: Cystic fibrosis. *Am J Nurs* 1981; 81:527–532.

Ledger S: Nursing care study: A young patient with cystic fibrosis. *Nurs Times* 1981; 77:1291–1294.

Marks MI: The pathogenesis and treatment of pulmonary infections in patients with cystic fibrosis. *J Pediatr* 1981; 98:173–179.

Maxwell M: Review of literature of physiotherapy in cystic fibrosis. *Physiotherapy* 1980; 66:245–246.

Moss AJ: The cardiovascular system in cystic fibrosis. *Pediatrics* 1982; 70:728–741.

Oppenheimer EH: Similarity of the tracheobronchial mucous glands and epithelium in infants with and without cystic fibrosis. *Hum Pathol* 1981; 12:36–48.

Rosenstein BJ: Incidence of meconium abnormalities in newborn infants with cystic fibrosis. *Am J Dis Child* 1980; 134:72–73.

Rossman CM, Waldes R, Sampson D, et al: Effect of chest physiotherapy on the removal of mucus in patients with cystic fibrosis. *Am Rev Respir Dis* 1982; 126:131–135.

Russell NJ, Bagg LR, Hughes DT, et al: Lung function in young adults with cystic fibrosis. *Br J Dis Chest* 1982; 76:35–43.

Scalin TF: Cystic fibrosis: Current trends in research. *Clin Chest Med* 1980; 1:423–427.

Stephan U: Cystic fibrosis detection by means of a test strip. *Pediatrics* 1975; 55:35.

Svenonius E, Arborelius M, Kautto R, et al: Lung function in cystic fibrosis: Acute effect of salbutamol. *Respiration* 1980; 40:226–232.

Taussig LM: *Cystic Fibrosis.* New York, Thieme-Stratton Inc, 1982.

Taussig LM, Lemen RJ: Chronic obstructive lung disease. *Adv Pediatr* 1979; 26:343–416.

Tecklin J, Holsclaw D: Evaluation of bronchial drainage in patients with cystic fibrosis. *Phys Ther* 1975; 55:1081.

Vawter GF, Shwachman H: Cystic fibrosis in adults: An autopsy study. *Pathol Annu* 1979; 14:357–382.

Webster HL, Barlow WK: New approach to cystic fibrosis diagnosis by use of an improved sweat-induction/collection system and osmometry. *Clin Chem* 1981; 27:385–387.

Weller PH, Bush E, Preece MA, et al: Short-term effects of chest physiotherapy on pulmonary function in children with cystic fibrosis. *Respiration* 1980; 40:53–56.

Williams RF: Infection of the respiratory tract and lungs in cystic fibrosis. *Nurs Times* 1980; 76:517–520.

Wood RE: Cystic fibrosis: Diagnosis, treatment, and prognosis. *South Med J* 1979; 72:189.

Wood RE, Boat TF, Doershuk CF: Cystic fibrosis. *Am Rev Respir Dis* 1976; 113:833.

Zach M, Oberwaldner B, Hausler F: Cystic fibrosis: Physical exercise versus chest physiotherapy. *Arch Dis Child* 1982; 57:587–589.

Myasthenia Gravis

Barry L: The patient with myasthenia gravis really needs you. *Nursing* 1982; 12:50–53.

Gracey D, Divertie M, Howard F: Mechanical ventilation for respiratory failure in myasthenia gravis. *Mayo Clin Proc* 1983; 58:597–602.

Lisak R: Myasthenia gravis: Mechanisms and management. *Hosp Pract* 1983; 18:101–109.

Wyngaarden JB, Smith LH (eds) *Cecil: Textbook of Medicine.* Philadelphia, WB Saunders Co, 1988.

control. In SPSS language, you may use the "IF" command to accomplish this task. Translated in plain English, it is "if the respondent has never read the book, then restore the missing value to another valid code." By applying the logical control, you have a new valid category "Never read" in addition to those who read and like the book "Very much," "Much," "Somewhat," "Little," and "Not at all." And now you have only those cases missing who said they have read the book but for some reason did not give you the information as to how much they like it. The number of missing cases is thus significantly reduced.

For those unexpected missing cases, it may also be possible to restore some of the information since the presence of other questions may provide more or less logical control. Sometimes this could be problematic and debatable, though. For example, if a lot of respondents skipped the question as to how many children they have, you may get the hunch that some of them probably have no children at all. To add a bit logical control, you may want to make use of the marital status variable. The logical reasoning is that if the respondent is single (never married), then the number of his children would be zero. But people may argue that an unmarried person may also have children, especially in our society. From this case you can see that research is not a straightforward business. Since these kinds of subtle and "trivial" issues almost never get exposed, the research results seem always to contain some uncertainty. This is true especially when you have conflicting information in a study. In questionnaire design, you are taught to arrange for some logical check against false and inaccurate answers. But if a contradiction does exist you might simply get a dilemma in data management, since you hardly know which answer is correct that you should go for. The decision could be rather arbitrary. Note that logical control applied in such cases is not just for restoring missing information but also for changing valid (non-missing) yet questionable values to more "reasonable" ones.

Another task in data cleaning is labeling, which is simple but can also be very time-consuming. Depending on the number of variables you have and how many values of each variable need be labeled, your computer program could run into many hundred of lines. Labels are helpful but not required. Generally speaking, you use two kinds of languages in doing research. One is ordinary language (e.g., standard English), and the other is computer-operated statistical jargon that is a highly abbreviated form of English. For example, the questions listed on the questionnaire are written in ordinary language (e.g., English). You have to abbreviate the sentence to a variable when talking about statistical analysis, and the variable can have a name of no more than 8 characters long when being

Guillain-Barré Syndrome

Asbury AK: Diagnostic considerations in Guillain-Barré syndrome. *Ann Neurol* 1981.
Guillain-Barré Syndrome Study Group: Plasmapheresis and acute Guillain-Barré syndrome. *Neurology* 1985; 35:1096–1104.
Koski CL, Khurana R, Mayer RF: Guillain-Barré syndrome. *Am Fam Physician* 1986; 34(3):198–210.
Schonberger LB, Bregman DJ, Sullivan-Bolyai JZ, et al: Guillain-Barré syndrome following vaccination in the National Influenza Immunization Program, United States, 1976–1977. *Am J Epidemiol* 1979; 110:105–123.

Sleep Apnea

Becker K, Cummiskey J: Managing sleep apnea: What are today's options? *J Respir Dis* 1985; 50–71.
Cherniack NS: Breathing disorders during sleep. *Hosp Pract* 1986; 21(2):81–104.
Douglas NJ: Breathing during sleep in patients with respiratory disease. *Semin Respir Med* 1988; 9:586–593.
George C, Kryger M: Management of sleep apnea. *Semin Respir Med* 1988; 9:569–576.
Guilleminault C, Partinen M, et al: Determinants of daytime sleepiness in obstructive sleep apnea. *Chest* 1988; 94:32–37.
Jiang H, et al: Mortality and apnea index in obstructive sleep apnea. *Chest* 1988; 94:9–14.
Lugaresi E, et al: Snoring: Pathophysiology and clinical consequences. *Semin Respir Med* 1988; 9:577–585.
Oesting HH, Manza RJ: Sleep apnea. *Geriatr Nurs* 1988; 9:232–233.
Onal E: Central sleep apnea. *Semin Respir Med* 1988; 9:547–553.
Partinen M, Jamieson A, Guilleminault C: Long-term outcome for obstructive sleep apnea syndrome patients: Mortality. *Chest* 1988; 94:1200–1204.
Roth T, Roehrs TA, Conway WA: Behavioral morbidity of apnea. *Semin Respir Med* 1988; 9:554–559.
Shepard JW Jr: Pathophysiology and medical therapy of sleep apnea. *Ear Nose Throat J* 1984; 63:24–48.
Shepard JW Jr: Physiologic and clinical consequences of sleep apnea. *Semin Respir Med* 1988; 9:560–568.
Smith PL: Evaluation of patients with sleep disorders. *Semin Respir Med* 1988; 9:534–539.
Stauffer JL, et al: Pharyngeal size and resistance in obstructive sleep apnea. *Am J Respir Dis* 1987; 136:623–627.
White DP: Disorders of breathing during sleep: Introduction, epidemiology, and incidence. *Semin Respir Med* 1988; 9:529–533.
Wiegand L, Zwillich CW: Pathogenesis of obstructive sleep Apnea: Role of the pharynx. *Semin Respir Med* 1988; 9:540–546.

GLOSSARY

Abscess   Localized collection of pus in any part of the body that results from disintegration or displacement of tissue.

Acetylcholine   A neurotransmitter substance widely distributed in body tissue with a primary function of mediating synaptic activity of the nervous system.

Acidemia   Decreased pH or an increased hydrogen ion concentration of the blood.

Acidosis   Pathologic condition resulting from accumulation of acid or loss of base from the body.

Acinus   Smallest division of a gland; a group of secretory cells surrounding a cavity; the functional part of an organ. (The respiratory acinus includes respiratory bronchioles, alveolar ducts, alveoli, and all other structures therein.)

Acute   Sharp, severe; of rapid onset and characterized by severe symptoms and a short course; not chronic.

Adhesion   Fibrous band that holds together parts that are normally separated.

Adrenergic   Term applied to nerve fibers that, when stimulated, release epinephrine at their endings. Includes nearly all sympathetic postganglionic fibers except those innervating sweat glands.

Adrenocorticotropic hormone (ACTH)   A hormone secreted by the anterior pituitary. It is regulated by the corticotropin-releasing factor (CRF) from the hypothalamus and is essential to growth, development and continued function of the adrenal cortex.

Aerosol   Gaseous suspension of fine solid or liquid particles.

Afebrile   Without fever.

Afferent   Carrying impulses toward a center.

Afferent nerves   Nerves that transmit impulses from the peripheral to the central nervous system.

Air trapping   Trapping of alveolar gas during exhalation.

Albumin   One of a group of simple proteins widely distributed in plant and animal tissues. It is found in the blood as serum albumin, in milk as lactalbumin, and in the white of an egg as ovalbumin.

Alkalemia   Increased pH or decreased hydrogen ion concentration of the blood.

Allele   One of two or more different genes containing specific inheritable characteristics that occupy corresponding positions on paired chromosomes.

Allergen   Any substance that causes manifestations of allergy. It may or may not be a protein.

Allergy   Acquired hypersensitivity to a substance (allergen) that normally does not cause a reaction. An allergic reaction is essentially an antibody-antigen reaction, but in some cases the antibody cannot be demonstrated. The reaction is caused by the release of histamine or histamine-like substances from injured cells.

α_1-Antitrypsin   Inhibitor of trypsin that may be deficient in persons with emphysema.

α-Receptor   Site in the autonomic nerve pathways where excitatory responses occur when adrenergic agents such as norepinephrine and epinephrine are released.

Anaerobic   Metabolic pathway that does not require oxygen; this process usually produces lactic acid.

Anaphylaxis   Allergic hypersensitivity reaction of the body to a foreign protein or drug.

Anemia   Condition in which there is a reduction in the number of circulating red blood cells per cubic millimeter, the amount of hemoglobin per 100 mL, or the volume of packed red cells per 100 mL of blood.

Aneurysm   Localized dilation of a blood vessel, usually an artery.

Angiogram   Serial roentgenograms of a blood vessel taken in rapid sequence following injection of a radiopaque substance into the vessel.

Angiography   Roentgenography of blood vessels after injection of a radiopaque substance.

Anoxia   Deficiency of oxygen.

Anterolateral   In front and to one side.

Antibody   Protein substance that develops in response to and interacts with an antigen. The antigen-antibody reaction forms the basis of immunity. Antibodies are produced by plasma cells in lymphoid tissue. Antibodies may be present due to previous infection, vaccination, or transfer from the mother to the fetus in utero or may occur without known antigenic stimulus, usually as a result of unknown, accidental exposure.

Antigen Substance that induces the formation of antibodies that interact specifically with it. The antigen-antibody reaction forms the basis for immunity. An antigen may be introduced into the body or may be formed within the body.

Aortic valve Valve between the left ventricle and the ascending aorta that prevents regurgitation of blood into the left ventricle.

Aperture Opening or orifice.

Apex Top, end, or tip of a structure.

Apnea Complete absence of spontaneous ventilation. This causes the $P_{A_{O_2}}$ and Pa_{O_2} to rapidly decrease and the $P_{A_{CO_2}}$ and Pa_{CO_2} to increase. Death will ensue in minutes.

Aponeurosis Flat, fibrous sheet of connective tissue that attaches muscle to bone or other tissues. May sometimes serve as a fascia.

Arrhythmia Irregularity or loss of rhythm, especially of the heartbeat.

Arteriole Minute artery, especially one that, at its distal end, leads into a capillary.

Arthralgia Any pain that affects a joint.

Arthropod Any member of a large group of animals that possess a hard external skeleton and jointed legs and other appendages. Many arthropods are of medical importance (e.g., mites, ticks, and insects).

Asepsis The absence of germs; sterile.

Asphyxia Condition caused by an insufficient uptake of oxygen.

Aspiration Inhalation of pharyngeal contents into the pulmonary tree.

Asymmetric Unequal correspondence in shape, size, and relative position of parts on opposite sides of the body.

Asystole Absence of contractions of the heart.

Atelectasis Collapsed or airless lung. May be caused by obstruction by foreign bodies, mucous plugs, or excessive secretions or by compression from without, as by tumors, aneurysms, or enlarged lymph nodes.

Atmospheric pressure In physics, pressure of the air on the earth at mean sea level, approximately 14.7 pounds to the square inch (760 mm Hg).

Atopic Of or pertaining to a hereditary tendency to develop immediate allergic reactions because of the presence of an antibody in the skin and sometimes the blood stream.

Atrial fibrillation Irregular and rapid randomized contractions of the atria working independently of the ventricles.

Atrial flutter Extremely rapid (200–400/min) contractions of the atrium. In pure flutter, a regular rhythm is maintained; in impure flutter, the rhythm is irregular.

Atrophy A wasting or decrease in size of an organ or tissue.

Atropine Highly poisonous salt of an alkaloid obtained from belladonna. It is a parasympatholytic agent and counteracts the effects of parasympathetic stimulation. It stimulates circulatory actions.

Autosomal recessive trait Pattern of inheritance in which the transmission of a recessive gene on an autosome results in a carrier state if the person is heterozygous for the trait and in an affected state if the person is homozygous for the trait. Males and females are affected with equal frequency. Affected individuals have unaffected parents who are heterozygous for the trait.

Bacillus Any rod-shaped bacterium.

Bacteria Unicellular, ovoid, or rod-shaped organisms existing in free-living or parasitic forms. They display a wide range of biochemical and pathogenic properties.

Bedsonia Former genus name for *Chlamydia*, now used as a common term denoting species of *Chlamydia* (e.g., bedsonias, *Bedsonia* organisms, bedsonial agents).

Benign Not recurrent or progressive.

β-Receptor Site in autonomic nerve pathways wherein inhibitory responses occur when adrenergic agents such as norepinephrine and epinephrine are released.

Bicarbonate Any salt containing the HCO_3^- anion.

Bifurcation A separation into two branches; the point of forking.

Biopsy Excision of a small piece of living tissue for microscopic examination; usually performed to establish a diagnosis.

Bleb Blister or bulla. Blebs may vary in size from that of a bean to that of a goose egg and may contain serous, seropurulent, or bloody fluid.

Blood-brain barrier Membrane between circulating blood and the brain that prevents certain substances from reaching brain tissue and cerebrospinal fluid.

Bradykinin Kinin composed of a chain of nine amino acids liberated by the action of trypsin or of certain snake venoms on a globulin of blood plasma.

Bronchoconstriction Constriction of the bronchial tubes.

Bronchodilation Dilation of a bronchus.

Bronchograms Film of the bronchi after a radiopaque substance has been injected into them.

Bronchoscopy   A visual examination of the tracheobronchial tree with the use of a bronchoscope.

Bronchospasm   Involuntary sudden movement or convulsive contraction of the muscular coats of the bronchus.

Bulla   Blister or skin vesicle filled with fluid; a bleb.

Calcification   Process in which organic tissue becomes hardened by the deposition of lime salts in tissue.

Cannulation   Placement of a tube or sheath enclosing a trocar to allow the escape of fluid after the trocar is withdrawn from the body.

Capillary stasis   Stagnation of the normal flow of fluids or blood in capillaries.

Carbon dioxide (CO_2)   Colorless, odorless, incombustible gas formed during respiration and combustion; normally constitutes only 0.03% of the atmosphere. Quantities up to 5% in inspired air stimulate respiration.

Carcinoma   New growth or malignant tumor that occurs in epithelial tissue. These neoplasms tend to infiltrate and give rise to metastases.

Cardiogenic   Originating in the heart.

Cardiotonic drugs   Drugs that increase the tonicity of the heart.

Carotid sinus baroreceptors   Sensory nerve endings located in the carotid sinus, a dilated area at the bifurcation of the common carotid artery. Changes in pressure stimulate the nerve endings.

Cartilage   Dense, firm, compact connective tissue capable of withstanding considerable pressure and tension; located in all true joints, the outer ear, bronchi, and movable sections of the ribs.

Catecholamines   Biologically active amines that behave as epinephrine and norepinephrine. Catecholamines have marked effects on the nervous and cardiovascular systems, metabolic rate, temperature, and smooth muscle.

Cavitation   The formation of cavities or hollow spaces within the body, as those formed in the lung by tuberculosis.

Central venous pressure (CVP)   Pressure within the superior vena cava. It reflects the pressure under which the blood is returned to the right atrium.

Cerebrospinal fluid (CSF)   Water cushion protecting the brain and spinal cord from shock.

Chemoreceptor   Sense organ or sensory nerve ending that is stimulated by and reacts to chemical stimuli and that is located outside the central nervous system. Chemoreceptors are found in the large arteries of the thorax and neck (carotid and aortic bodies), the taste buds, and the olfactory cells of the nose.

Chemotactic Attraction and repulsion of living protoplasm to a chemical stimulus.

Chlamydia Genus of viruslike microorganisms that cause disease in humans and birds. Some *Chlamydia* infections of birds can be transmitted to humans (ornithosis, parrot disease). The organisms resemble bacteria but are of similar size to viruses and are obligate parasites.

Chronic Denoting a process that shows little change and slow progression and is of long duration.

Cilia Small hairlike projections on the surface of epithelial cells. In the bronchi, they propel mucus and foreign particles in a whiplike movement toward the throat.

Clinical manifestations Symptoms or signs demonstrated by a patient; may be subjective or objective in nature.

Coagulation Process of clotting. Coagulation requires the presence of several substances, the most important of which are prothrombin, thrombin, thromboplastin, calcium in ionic form, and fibrinogen. Prothrombin is converted to thrombin by the action of thromboplastin and calcium ions. Thrombin then converts fibrinogen to fibrin. The fibrin forms a meshwork of fibers in which the corpuscles of blood become entangled and form a clot.

Coalesce To fuse, run, or grow together.

Coccobacillus Short, thick bacterial rod in the shape of an oval or slightly elongated coccus.

Coccus Bacterium with a spherical shape.

Collagen Fibrous insoluble protein found in connective tissue, including skin, bone, ligaments, and cartilage. Collagen represents about 30% of the total body protein.

Colloid Type of solution; a gluelike substance such as protein or starch whose particles (molecules or aggregates of molecules), when dispersed in a solvent to the greatest degree, remain uniformly distributed and fail to form a true solution.

Compromise A blending of the qualities of two different things; an unfavorable change.

Congenital Existing at and usually before birth; referring to conditions that are present at birth, regardless of their cause.

Congestion Excessive amount of blood or tissue fluid in an organ or in tissue.

Consolidation The process of becoming solid; a mass that has solidified.

Contusion Injury in which the skin is not broken; a bruise. Symptoms are pain, swelling, and discoloration.

Convex Having a rounded, somewhat elevated surface resembling a segment of the external surface of a sphere.

Cor pulmonale Hypertrophy or failure of the right ventricle resulting from disorders of the lungs, pulmonary vessels, or chest wall.

Corticosteroids Any of a number of hormonal steroid substances obtained from the cortex of the adrenal gland.

Costophrenic angle The junction of the rib cage and the diaphragm.

Cuirass A chest covering; breastplate.

Cyclic adenosine monophosphate (cAMP) Cyclic nucleotide participating in the activities of many hormones, including catecholamines, adrenocorticotropin, and vasopressin. It is synthesized from adenosine triphosphate and is stimulated by the enzyme adenylate cyclase. cAMP is important in a wide variety of metabolic responses to cell stimuli.

Cyst Closed pouch or sac with a definite wall that contains fluid, semifluid, or solid material. It is usually an abnormal structure that results from developmental anomalies, obstruction of ducts, or parasitic infection.

Cytoplasm Protoplasm of a cell exclusive of the nucleus.

Decubitus radiograph An x-ray film taken with the patient in a recumbent or horizontal position.

Demarcate To set or mark boundaries or limits.

Demyelination The destruction or removal of the myelin sheath from a nerve or nerve fiber.

Density Mass of a substance per unit of volume; the relative weight of a substance compared with a reference standard.

Deoxyribonucleic acid (DNA) Type of nucleic acid containing deoxyribose as the sugar component and found principally in the nuclei of animal and vegetable cells, usually loosely bound to protein (hence termed deoxyribonucleoprotein). DNA is considered to be the autoreproducing component of chromosomes and of many viruses and the repository of hereditary characteristics.

Depolarize To reduce to a nonpolarized condition. To reduce the amount of electrical charge between oppositely charged particles (ions).

Desensitization Prevention of anaphylaxis.

Diabetes mellitus Chronic disease of pancreatic origin that is characterized by insulin deficiency and a subsequent inability to utilize carbohydrates. This condition results in excess sugar in the blood and urine; excessive thirst, hunger, urination, weakness, and emaciation; and imperfect combustion of fats. If untreated, diabetes mellitus leads to acidosis, coma, and death.

Diagnostic Pertaining to the use of scientific and skillful methods to establish the cause and nature of a sick person's disease.

Diastole   Normal period in the heart cycle during which the muscle fibers lengthen, the heart dilates, and the cavities fill with blood.

Dilation   Expansion of an organ, orifice, or vessel.

Dimorphic fungus   A condition where the organism has two distinct types of fungus.

Dimorphism   The quality of existing in two distinct forms.

Disseminate   Scatter or distribute over a considerable area; when applied to disease organisms, scattered throughout an organ or the body.

Distal   Farthest from the center, from a medial line, or from the trunk.

Driving pressure   Pressure difference between two areas of the pulmonary vascular bed.

Ductus arteriosus   Vessel between the pulmonary artery and the aorta. It bypasses the lungs in the fetus.

Dynamometer   An instrument for measuring the force of muscular contractions. For example, a squeeze dynamometer is one by which the grip of the hand is measured.

Dysplasia   Abnormal development of organ tissues or cells.

Dyspnea   Air hunger resulting in labored or difficult breathing, sometimes accompanied by pain. Symptoms include audible labored breathing, distressed anxious expression, dilated nostrils, protrusion of the abdomen with an expanded chest, and gasping.

Edema   A local or generalized condition in which the body tissues contain an excessive amount of tissue fluid.

Efferent   Carrying away from a central organ or section. Efferent nerves conduct impulses from the brain or spinal cord to the periphery.

Efferent nerves   Nerves that carry impulses having the following effects: motor, causing contraction of the muscles; secretory, causing glands to secrete; and inhibitory, causing some organs to become quiescent.

Effusion   Seeping of serous, purulent, or bloody fluid into a cavity; the result of such a seeping.

Elastase   Enzyme that dissolves elastin.

Electrocardiogram (ECG)   Record of the electrical activity of the heart.

Electrodiagnostic   Use of electric and electronic devices for diagnostic purposes.

Electrolyte   Substance that, in solution, conducts an electrical current and is decomposed by the passage of an electrical current. Acids, bases, and salts are common electrolytes.

Electromyogram A graphic record of the contraction of a muscle as a result of electrical stimulation.

Electrophoresis Movement of charged colloidal particles through the medium in which they are dispersed as a result of changes in electrical potential.

Embolus Mass of undissolved matter present in blood or lymphatic vessels to which it has been brought by the blood or lymph current. Emboli may be solid, liquid, or gaseous. Some consist of bits of tissue, tumor cells, globules of fat, air bubbles, clumps of bacteria, and foreign bodies. Emboli may arise within the body or may gain entrance from without.

Empyema Pus in a body cavity, especially in the pleural cavity; usually the result of a primary infection in the lungs.

Encapsulated Enclosed in a fibrous or membranous sheath.

Encephalitis Inflammation of the brain.

Endemic A disease that occurs continuously in a particular population but has low mortality, such as measles.

Endocarditis Inflammation of the endocardium, the lining membrane of the heart. It may involve only the membrane covering the valves or the general lining of the chambers of the heart.

Endothelium The layer of epithelial cells that lines the cavities of the heart, blood and lymph vessels, and the serous cavities of the body; originating from the mesoderm.

Enuresis Involuntary discharge of urine, usually referring to involuntary discharge of urine during sleep at night; bed-wetting beyond the age when bladder control should have been achieved.

Enzyme Complex protein capable of inducing chemical changes in other substances without being changed itself. Enzymes speed chemical reactions.

Eosinophil Cell or cellular structure that stains readily with the acid stain eosin. Specifically refers to a granular leukocyte.

Epidemiology Science concerned with defining and explaining the interrelationships of factors that determine disease frequency and distribution.

Epinephrine Hormone secreted by the adrenal medulla in response to splanchnic stimulation. Epinephrine and norepinephrine are the two active hormones produced by the adrenal medulla.

Epithelium Covering of the internal and the external organs of the body, including the lining of vessels. It consists of cells bound together by connective material and varies in the number of layers and the kinds of cells.

Erythema multiforme A hypersensitivity syndrome characterized by polymorphous eruptions of the skin and mucous membranes.

computerized. You must also reduce the answers to some simple codes. In research practice you need to commute or translate frequently between the two kinds of languages. To reduce the mental burden on yourself and others, you can give a variable or a code a label as close as possible to the original language used. This will greatly facilitate your conversion between the variables and the questions as well as between the values and the answers. In SPSS, the task is accomplished by using these two commands, "VARIABLE LABELS" and "VALUE LABELS."

The importance of data cleaning to the quality of research can hardly be overstated. A person who does not understand the issues involved and the amount of work required can hardly appreciate the effort to accomplish quality work. Rather, they would easily be fooled by poor research results.

A cleaned data set, however, does not mean that it is ready for all kinds of analysis. The data need be further processed, or manipulated, for the possibility and convenience of various particular analytic procedures in order to achieve specific research objectives.

Data manipulation is not used here in a negative sense. Rather, it is considered a faithful treatment of information. It changes the form of data in order to facilitate data analysis. This includes various kinds of data conversion. Note that information acquired can be condensed by means of categorization and combination, but by no means can it be expanded or enlarged. It is advisable, therefore, to use the most detailed form needed for collecting the data and recording the information. For instance, unless you are sure that you will never need or get the detailed information of age by individual years, you should not use any kind of aggregate age group to collect and record the information. You can always "collapse" the individual years into any kind of age groups or categories, but you can never stretch the aggregated age categories to the detail of individual years. Since different forms of information have different uses in data analysis, you do not want to lose your choice through simple ignorance.

Collapsing detailed raw data into different gross categories takes a large share of the work of data manipulation. This can be done by the procedure of recoding. If the categorization is determined by some other conditions, then you will have to use the "IF" command instead of the simple recoding procedure. The specific language can be found in the manual or on-line instructions of each computer statistical package.

Before you make any decision on categorization, you should look at the frequency distribution tables again. You can collapse the original variable into

Erythropoiesis Formation of red blood cells.

Etiology Cause of disease.

Exocrine gland Gland whose secretion reaches an epithelial surface either directly or through a duct.

Expectoration To clear out the chest and lungs by coughing up and spitting out matter.

Extravascular Outside a vessel.

Exudate Accumulation of a fluid in a cavity; matter that penetrates through vessel walls into adjoining tissue.

Fascia Fibrous membrane covering, supporting, and separating muscles.

Febrile Pertaining to a fever.

Fibrin Whitish, filamentous protein formed by the action of prothrombin on fibrinogen. The conversion of fibrinogen into fibrin is the basis for blood clotting. Fibrin is deposited as fine interlacing filaments in which are entangled red and white blood cells and platelets, the whole forming a coagulum or clot.

Fibrinolytic Pertaining to the splitting up of fibrin.

Fibroelastic Composed of fibrous and elastic tissue.

Fibrosis Formation of scar tissue in the connective tissue framework of the lungs.

Fissure Cleft or groove on the surface of an organ, often marking division of the organ into parts, as the lobes of the lung.

Fistula Abnormal passage or communication, usually between two internal organs or leading from an internal organ to the surface of the body; frequently designated according to the organs or parts with which it communicates.

Flaccid paralysis Paralysis in which there is loss of muscle tone, loss or reduction of tendon reflexes, atrophy and degeneration of muscles, and reaction of degeneration.

Flare Flush or spreading area of redness that surrounds a line made by drawing a pointed instrument across the skin. It is the second reaction in the triple response of skin to injury and is due to dilation of the arterioles.

Fluorescent antibody microscopy Microscopic examination of antibodies tagged with fluorescent material for the diagnosis of infections.

Foramen ovale Opening between the atria of the heart in the fetus. This opening normally closes shortly after birth.

Fossa Hollow or depression, especially on the surface of the end of a bone.

Galactosemia Presence of galactose in the blood.

Gastric juice Juice of the gastric glands of the stomach. It contains pepsin, hydrochloric acid, mucin, small quantities of inorganic salts, and the intrinsic antianemic principle. Gastric juice is strongly acid, having a pH of 0.9–1.5. Its total acidity is equivalent to 10–50 mL of 0.1N (10%) hydrochloric acid.

Genus In natural history classification, the division between the family or tribe and the species; a group of species alike in the broad features of their organization but different in detail.

Globulin One of a group of simple proteins insoluble in pure water but soluble in neutral solutions of salts of strong acids. It is found in the blood as serum globulin, the fraction of the blood serum with which antibodies are associated.

Glossopharyngeal nerve Ninth cranial nerve. Function: special sensory (taste), visceral sensory, and motor. Origin: by several roots from the medulla oblongata. Distribution: pharynx, ear, meninges, posterior third of the tongue, and parotid gland. Branches: carotid, tympanic, pharyngeal, lingual, tonsillar, and sinus nerve of Hering.

Glycolysis Breakdown of sugar by enzymes in the body. This occurs without oxygen.

Glycoprotein Any of a class of conjugated proteins consisting of a compound of protein with a carbohydrate group.

Hematocrit Volume of erythrocytes packed by centrifugation in a given volume of blood. Hematocrit is expressed as a percentage of the total blood volume that consists of erythrocytes or as the volume in cubic centimeters of erythrocytes packed by centrifugation of the blood.

Hematopoietic Pertaining to the production and development of blood cells.

Hemoptysis Expectoration of blood.

Hemorrhage Abnormal internal or external discharge of blood; may be venous, arterial, or capillary from blood vessels into tissues or from the body. Venous blood is dark red; flow is continuous. Arterial blood is bright red; flow is in jets. Capillary blood is of a reddish color and exudes from tissue.

Heparin Polysaccharide that has been isolated from the liver, lung, and other tissues. It is produced by the mast cells of the liver and by basophil leukocytes. It inhibits coagulation by preventing conversion of prothrombin to thrombin through the formation an antithrombin and by preventing the liberation of thromboplastin from blood platelets.

Hepatosplenomegaly Enlargement of both the liver and spleen.

Heterozygote Individual with different alleles for a given characteristic.

Hilus Root of the lungs at the level of the fourth and fifth dorsal vertebrae.

Histamine Substance normally present in the body; it exerts a pharmacologic action when released from injured cells. The red flush of a burn is due to the local production of histamine. It is produced from the amino acid histidine.

Homozygote Individual developing from gametes with similar alleles and thus possessing like pairs of genes for a given hereditary characteristic.

Hormone Substance originating in an organ or gland that is conveyed through the blood to another part of the body where by chemical action, it stimulates increased functional activity and increased secretion.

Humoral Pertaining to body fluids or substances contained in them.

Hydrostatic Pertaining to the pressure of liquids in equilibrium and that exerted on liquids.

Hydrous Containing water, usually chemically combined.

Hypercarbia, hypercapnea Excess carbon dioxide in the blood; indicated by an elevated P_{CO_2}.

Hypercoagulation Greater-than-normal clotting.

Hyperinflation Distension of a part by air, gas, or liquid.

Hyperplasia Excessive proliferation of normal cells in the normal tissue arrangement of an organ.

Hyperpnea Increased depth (volume) of breathing with or without an increased frequency.

Hypersecretions Substance or fluid separated and elaborated by cells or glands in an excessive amount or more than normal.

Hypersensitivity Abnormal sensitivity to a stimulus of any kind.

Hypertension Higher-than-normal blood pressure; greater-than-normal tension or tonus.

Hypertrophy Increase in size of an organ or structure that does not involve tumor formation.

Hyperventilation Increased rate and depth of breathing.

Hypoperfusion Deficiency of blood coursing through the vessels of the circulatory system.

Hypoproteinemia Decrease in the amount of protein in the blood.

Hypoventilation Reduced rate and depth of breathing.

Hypoxemia Below-normal oxygen content in blood.

Hypoxia Tissue oxygen deficiency.

Iatrogenic Any adverse mental or physical condition induced in a patient by the effects of treatment by a physician or surgeon.

Idiopathic Disease or condition without a recognizable cause.

Ileocecal valve Valve between the ileum of the small intestine and the cecum of the large intestine. It consists of two flaps that project into the lumen of the large intestine just above the vermiform appendix; this allows the contents of the intestine to pass only in a forward direction.

Immunoglobulin One of a family of closely related but not identical proteins that are capable of acting as antibodies. Five major types of immunoglobulins are normally present in the human adult: IgG, IgA, IgM, IgD, and IgE.

Immunoglobulin α E (IgE) An α-globulin produced by cells of the lining of the respiratory and intestinal tract. IgE is important in forming reagin antibodies.

Immunologic mechanism Reaction of the body to substances that are foreign or are interpreted as foreign.

Immunotherapy Production or enhancement of immunity.

Incubation period Development of an infection from the time of entry into an organism up to the time of the first appearance of signs or symptoms.

Infarction Necrosis of tissue following cessation of blood supply.

Inferior vena cava (IVC) Venous trunk for the lower extremities and for the pelvic and abdominal viscera. It begins at the level of the fifth lumbar vertebra by union of the common iliac veins, passes upward on the right of the aorta, and empties into the right atrium of the heart.

Inflammation Localized heat, redness, swelling, and pain as a result of irritation, injury, or infection.

Inotropic (positive) Increasing myocardial contractibility.

Insertion Manner or place of attachment of a muscle to the bone so that it moves.

Intercostal retraction Also known as retraction of the chest. Visible sinking-in of the soft tissues of the chest between and around the firmer tissue of the cartilaginous and bony ribs, such as occurs with increased inspiratory effort.

Interstitial Placed or lying between; pertaining to interstices or spaces within an organ or tissue.

Intrapleural pressure Pressure within the pleural cavity.

Iodine Nonmetallic element belonging to the halogen group.

Ion Atom, group of atoms, or molecule that has acquired a net electrical charge by gaining or losing electrons.

Ischemia Local and temporary deficiency of blood supply due to obstruction of the circulation to a part.

Isotope One of a series of chemical elements that have nearly identical chemical properties but differ in their atomic weights and electrical charge. Many isotopes are radioactive.

Kerley lines Thickening of the interlobular septa as seen in chest roentgenography; may be due to cellular infiltration or edema associated with pulmonary vein hypertension.

Kinetic Pertaining to or consisting of motion.

Kulchitsky cell A cell containing serotonin-secreting granules that stain readily with silver and chromium parts; also known as an argentaffin cell.

Lactic acid Acid formed in muscles during activity by the breakdown of sugar without oxygen.

Latency State of being concealed, hidden, inactive, or inapparent.

Lesions A wound, injury, or pathologic change in body tissue.

Lethargy The state or quality of being indifferent, apathetic, or sluggish; stupor.

Leukocytes White blood corpuscles, including cells both with and without granules within their cytoplasm.

Leukopenia An abnormal decrease in the number of white blood cells to fewer than 5,000 cells/mm^3.

Ligamentum nuchae Upward continuation of the supraspinous ligament, extending from the seventh cervical vertebra to the occipital bone.

Linea alba White line of connective tissue in the middle of the abdomen from sternum to pubis.

Lipid Any of numerous fats generally insoluble in water that constitute one of the principal structural materials of cells.

Longitudinal Parallel to the long axis of the body or part.

Lubricant Agent, usually a liquid oil, that reduces friction between parts that brush against each other as they move. Joints are lubricated by synovial fluid.

Lumen Inner open space of a tubular organ such as a blood vessel or intestine.

Lymph Alkaline fluid found in the lymphatic vessels and the cisterna chyli. It is usually a clear, transparent, colorless fluid. It differs from blood in that red blood corpuscles are absent and its protein content is lower. Cells present are principally lymphocytes, which are formed in lymph nodes and other lymphatic organs. Lymph passes through lymph nodes, which filter it. This action frees the lymph of foreign particulate matter, especially bacteria.

Lymphangitis carcinomatosa The condition of having widespread dissemination of carcinoma in lymphatic channels or vessels.

Lymphatic vessels   Thin-walled vessels conveying lymph from the tissues. Like veins, they possess valves ensuring one-way flow and eventually empty into the venous system at the junction of the internal jugular and subclavian veins.

Lymph node   Rounded body consisting of accumulations of lymphatic tissue found at intervals in the course of lymphatic vessels.

Macrophage   Cell whose major function is phagocytosis of foreign matter.

Malaise   A vague feeling of body weakness or discomfort that often marks the onset of disease.

Mast cell   Connective tissue cells that contain heparin and histamine in their granules; important in cellular defense mechanisms, including blood coagulation; needed during injury or infection.

Mechanoreceptor   Receptor that receives mechanical stimuli such as pressure from sound or touch.

Meconium ileus   Obstruction of the small intestine in the newborn that is caused by impaction of thick, dry, tenacious meconium, usually at or near the ileocecal valve. The condition results from a deficiency in pancreatic enzymes and is the earliest manifestation of cystic fibrosis.

Meningitis   Any infection or inflammation of the membranes covering the brain and spinal cord.

Mesotheliomas   A rare, malignant tumor of the mesothelium of the pleura or peritoneum; associated with earlier exposure to asbestos.

Metabolism   Sum of all physical and chemical changes that take place within an organism; all energy and material transformations that occur within living cells.

Metaplasia   Conversion of one kind of tissue into a form that is not normal for that tissue.

Methylxanthine   Methylated xanthine. A nitrogenous extraction contained in muscle tissue, liver, spleen, pancreas, other organs, and urine; formed during the metabolism of nucleoproteins. The three methylated xanthines are caffeine, theophylline, and theobromine.

Microvilli   Minute cylindrical processes on the free surface of a cell, especially cells of the proximal convoluted renal tubule and of the intestinal epithelium, they increase the surface size of the cell.

Mitosis   A type of cell division of somatic cells where each daughter cell contains the same number of chromosomes as the parent cell.

Mitral valve   Bicuspid valve between the left atrium and left ventricle.

Mononucleosis   Presence of an abnormally high number of mononuclear leukocytes in the blood.

Motile   Having the power to move spontaneously.

Mucociliary clearing action   In the large airways, a continuous blanket of mucus covering the tracheobronchial tree epithelium that is mobilized by the forward motion of cilia. The ciliary action causes the mucous blanket to be mobilized in a continuous motion toward the hilus of the lung, eventually moving to the larynx where the mucus is moved into the pharynx and swallowed or expectorated.

Mucous   Pertaining to or resembling mucus; also secreting mucus.

Mucus   The free slime of the mucous membranes. It is composed of secretions of the glands along with various inorganic salts, desquamated cells, and leukocytes.

Myelin   Insulating material covering the axons of many neurons; increases the velocity of the nerve impulse along the axon.

Myeloma   Tumor originating in cells of the hematopoietic (blood cell–producing) portion of bone marrow.

Myocardial infarction   Development of an infarct in the myocardium, usually the result of myocardial ischemia following occlusion of a coronary artery.

Myocarditis   Inflammation of the myocardium.

Myocardium   Middle layer of the walls of the heart, composed of cardiac muscle.

Myopathy   An abnormal condition of skeletal muscle characterized by muscle weakness, wasting, and histologic changes within muscle tissue, as seen in any of the muscular dystrophies.

Necrosis   Death of areas of tissue or bone surrounded by healthy parts.

Neoplasm   New and abnormal formation of tissue, such as a tumor or growth. It serves no useful function but grows at the expense of the healthy organism.

Nephritis   Inflammation of the kidney. The glomeruli, tubules, and interstitial tissue may be affected.

Neuroendocrine   Pertaining to the nervous and endocrine systems as an integrated functioning mechanism.

Neuromuscular junction   The area of contact between the ends of a large myelinated nerve fiber and a fiber of skeletal muscle.

Nitrogen oxides   Automotive air pollutant. Depending on concentration, these gases cause respiratory irritation, bronchitis, and pneumonitis. Concentrations over 100 ppm usually cause pulmonary edema and result in death.

Nocturnal   Pertaining to or occurring in the night.

Nodule   A small aggregation of cells; a small node.

Nomogram Graph consisting of three lines or curves (usually parallel) graduated for different variables in such a way that a straight line cutting the three lines gives the related values of the three variables.

Norepinephrine Hormone produced by the adrenal medulla, similar in chemical and pharmacologic properties to epinephrine. It is chiefly a vasoconstrictor and has little effect on cardiac output.

Normal flora Naturally occurring bacteria found in specific bodily areas. Normal flora has no detrimental effect.

Occlude To close, obstruct, or join together.

Olfactory Pertaining to the sense of smell.

Oncotic pressure Osmotic pressure due to the presence of colloids in a solution.

Opacity Opaque spot or area; the condition of being opaque.

Opaque Impervious to light rays or, by extension, to roentgen rays or other electromagnetic vibrations; neither transparent nor translucent.

Orbicularis oculi The muscular body of the eyelid composed of the palpebral, orbital, and lacrimal muscles.

Orifice Mouth, entrance, or outlet to any aperture.

Origin The more fixed attachment of a muscle.

Orthopnea Respiratory condition in which there is discomfort in any but an erect sitting or standing position.

Osmotic pressure Pressure that develops when two solutions are separated by a semipermeable membrane.

Osteoporosis Increased softening of bone seen most often in the elderly.

Oxygen content Total oxygen in blood.

Ozone Formed by the action of sunlight on oxygen in which three atoms form the molecule O_3. Ozone corrodes organic matter, and more than 1 ppm is considered hazardous. It is an irritant to the respiratory tract.

Palatine arches Vault-shaped muscular structures forming the soft palate between the mouth and the nasopharynx.

Pancreas Fish-shaped, grayish pink gland that stretches transversely across the posterior abdominal wall in the epigastric region of the body. It secretes various substances such as digestive enzymes, insulin, and glucagon.

Pancreatic juice Clear alkaline pancreatic secretion that contains at least three different enzymes (trypsin, amylopsin, and lipase). It is poured into the duodenum where, mixed with bile and intestinal juices, it furthers the digestion of foodstuffs already partly broken down by salivary and gastric enzymes.

Paracentesis A procedure in which fluid is withdrawn from a cavity of the body as in pleural effusion of ascites.

Paradoxical Occurring at variance with the normal rule.

Paramyxovirus Subgroup of viruses including parainfluenza, measles, mumps, German measles, and respiratory syncytial viruses.

Parasite Any organism that grows, feeds, and is sheltered on or in a different organism while contributing nothing to the survival of the host.

Parenchyma Essential parts of an organ that are concerned with its function in contradistinction to its framework.

Paroxysmal Concerning the sudden, periodic attack or recurrence of symptoms of a disease.

Particulate Made up of particles.

Patent ductus Open, narrow, tubular channel.

Pathogen Any agent causing disease, especially a microorganism.

Pendelluft Shunting of air from one lung to another.

Perforation Hole made through a substance or part.

Peribronchial Located around the bronchi.

Peripheral airways Small bronchi on the outer sections of the lung where most gas transfer takes place.

Peritoneal dialysis Removal of toxic substances from the body by perfusing specific warm sterile chemical solutions through the peritoneal cavity.

Perivascular Located around a vessel, especially a blood vessel.

Permeability The quality of being permeable; that which may be transversed.

Permeable Capable of allowing the passage of fluids or substances in solution.

pH Symbol for the logarithm of the reciprocal of the hydrogen ion concentration. A solution with a pH of 7.00 is neutral, one with a pH above 7.00 is alkaline, one with a pH lower than 7.00 is acid.

Phagocytosis Envelopment and digestion of bacteria or other foreign bodies by cells.

Phalanges Bones of the fingers or toes.

Phenotype   Physical makeup of an individual. Some phenotypes, such as the blood groups, are completely determined by heredity, while others such as stature are readily altered by environmental agents.

Phenylketonuria   Abnormal presence of phenylketone in the urine.

Phlegmasia alba dolens   Acute edema, especially of the leg, from venous obstruction, usually a thrombosis.

Phosgene   Carbonyl chloride ($COCl_2$), a poisonous gas causing nausea and suffocation when inhaled.

Phosphodiesterase   Enzyme that catalyzes the breakdown of the second messenger cyclic adenosine monophosphate to adenosine monophosphate.

Plaque   Patch on the skin or on a mucous surface.

Pleomorphic   Multiform; occurring in more than one morphological form.

Pleurisy   Inflammation of the pleura.

Pleuritis   Inflammation of the pleura.

Polyarteritis nodosa   Necrosis and inflammation of small and medium-sized arteries and subsequent involvement of tissue supplied by these arteries.

Polycythemia   Excess of red blood cells.

Polymorphonuclear leukocyte   Subclass of white blood cells, including neutrophils, eosinophils, and basophils.

Polyneuritis   Inflammation of two or more nerves at once.

Polyneuropathy   Term applied to any disorder of peripheral nerves, but preferably to those of a noninflammatory nature.

Polyradiculitis   Inflammation of nerve roots, especially those of spinal nerves as found in Guillain-Barré syndrome.

Polyradiculoneuropathy   Guillain-Barré syndrome.

Postpartum   Occurring after childbirth.

Postural drainage   Drainage of secretions from the bronchi or a cavity in the lung by positioning the patient so that gravity will allow drainage of the particular lobe or lobes of the lung involved.

Pressure   In physics, the quotient obtained by dividing a force by the area of the surface on which it acts.

Prognostic   Related to prediction of the outcome of a disease.

How to Prepare for Your Own Research

Once you have entered a doctoral, master's, or undergraduate honors program, you have got the opportunity to prepare for your own research in a most academic way. Yet a good many students, especially the doctoral candidates, would find themselves stuck at some point of their project (*The Chronicle of Higher Education*, December 6, 1989, pp. A13-16). Perhaps most of the students are native speakers of the language they use to prepare their thesis or dissertation (e.g., English for most American students). And my observation over the years is that most of the students are so good at writing and expression that they should otherwise be really admired for their versatile and imaginative pens. The problem, in my view, is not or not mainly because they do not know how to communicate. In other words, you cannot simply *write* a thesis or dissertation. You have to know how to prepare for and eventually be able to carry out the *research*.

The enterprise of research is full of challenges and pitfalls. If you have not yet demonstrated your strength in research, you should carefully prepare for it by equipping yourself with needed skills, insights, and experience. The preparation should be oriented toward your thesis/dissertation. It does not mean, however, that you should not include any activity that does not directly relate to your thesis or dissertation project. As a matter of fact, you can get started in a very generic way. For example, while you are in school, always try to get your work typed, and saved in a computer file. Not only are typing skills important for any kind of job you are likely to find after graduation, but they are especially important for doing research. The rest of your life, indeed, will probably be tied to the computer keyboard (as long as the input technology stays that way).

more than one categorized variables, and each decision is based on both the distribution patterns and your particular research needs. For instance, if the original variable age goes by individual years, you need to keep it for such analyses as correlation and regression. However, you also need variables of age that go by 5-year, 10-year, or some special groups so that you can present the data in such forms as cross-tabulation or "contingency" tables. It may even be necessary to dichotomize a continuous variable if you want to perform such analyses as T-Tests or logistic regression. Another frequently seen case is the marital status variable. Although researchers tend to use such detailed categories as single, married, widowed, divorced, separated, and etc. in asking the question, in certain analyses they often need to reclassify the variable into married vs. non-married. Generally speaking, dichotomization has special significance in statistical manipulation since dichotomous variables can be used at an measurement level, especially when coded as dummy variables. Dichotomization also brings extreme convenience to cross-tabulation.

Although the categorization of a variable or the grouping of its values may result in some other related variables, the creation of new variables for the purpose of data analysis is a general task that takes another major share of work in data manipulation. New variables can be created in a variety of ways, one of which is to use the command COMPUTE in SPSS language.

In questionnaire design, you do not want to include too many questions; otherwise the quality of your research will be sacrificed. In data analysis, in contrast, the more variables you have, the more freedom you will enjoy in constructing various analytical models. A guideline in resolving these contradictory requirements is that in questionnaire design, you should reduce the number of or eliminate those questions whose answers can be calculated from the answers to other questions. For example, if you have asked a teenager how many parents, siblings, and others are in her household, you do not need to ask her what is her household size since you can always figure it out from the information you already asked. Methodologists might argue that a repetitive question would serve the function of a logical check. This may reassure you if consistency of the answers is found. But if there is any inconsistency it would only put you in a dilemma in data analysis, since you hardly know which part of the contradictory information is more valid. As a matter of fact, if you do know that some answers (usually those to more detailed questions) are more valid than the others (usually those to more general questions), then why do you use those questions that will yield less valid results in the first place? Instead of adding to the burden of asking

Proliferation Increasing or spreading at a rapid rate; the process or results of rapid reproduction.

Prophylactic Any agent or regimen that contributes to the prevention of infection and disease.

Propranolol Drug used in treating cardiac arrhythmias, particularly supraventricular tachycardia.

Prostaglandin F One of a group of fatty acid derivatives present in many tissues, including the prostate gland, menstrual fluid, brain, lung, kidney, thymus, seminal fluid, and pancreas. Prostaglandin F is believed to cause bronchoconstriction and vasoconstriction.

Prostration A condition of extreme exhaustion.

Proteolytic Hastening the hydrolysis of proteins.

Proximal Nearest the point of attachment, center of the body, or point of reference.

Pulmonary Concerning or involving the lungs.

Pulmonary blood vessels Vessels that transport blood from the heart to the lungs and then back to the heart. Blood from the right ventricle passes into the pulmonary artery, which divides into two branches, one going to each lung. Oxygenated blood returns to the left heart by way of the four pulmonary veins, two from each lung.

Pulmonary capillary wedge pressure (PCWP) Pressure measured in the pulmonary artery at its capillary end. The pressure is determined during cardiac catheterization by pushing the catheter from the right atrium into the pulmonary artery. This provides an indication of left ventricular pressure at the end of diastole and the average pressure in the left atrium.

Pulmonary circulation Passage of blood from the heart to the lungs and back again for purification. The blood flows from the right ventricle to the lungs, where it is oxygenated, and then back to the left atrium.

Pulmonary vascular resistance (PVR) Pressure loss, per unit of blood flow, from the pulmonary artery to the left ventricle.

Pulsus paradoxus An exaggeration of the normal variation in the pulse volume with respiration. The pulse becomes weaker with inspiration and stronger with expiration. Pulsus paradoxus is characteristic of constrictive pericarditis and pericardial effusion. The changes are independent of changes in pulse rate.

Purulent Containing or forming pus.

Radiopaque Impenetrable to x-irradiation or other forms of radiation.

Recumbent Lying down or leaning backward.

Refractory   Resistant to ordinary treatment; obstinate, stubborn.

Remission   Lessening of severity or abatement of symptoms; the period during which symptoms abate.

Reticular formation   Located at the brain stem, it acts as a filter from sense organs to the conscious brain. It analyzes incoming information for importance and influences alertness, waking, sleeping, and some reflexes.

Ribonucleic acid (RNA)   Nucleic acid occurring in the nucleus and cytoplasm of cells that is involved in the synthesis of proteins. The RNA molecule is a single strand made up of units called nucleotides.

Roentgenogram   Film produced by roentgenography.

Roentgenography   Process of obtaining pictures by the use of roentgen rays.

Scintillation camera   Camera used to photograph the emissions that come from radioactive substances injected into the body; used to determine the outline and function of organs and tissues in which the radioactive substance collects or is secreted.

Semilunar valves   Valves separating the heart and aorta and heart and pulmonary artery.

Semipermeable   Permitting diffusion or flow of some liquids or particles but preventing the transmission of others, usually in reference to a membrane.

Septicemia   Systemic disease caused by pathogenic organisms or toxins in the blood; may be a late development of any purulent infections.

Septum   Wall dividing two cavities.

Serotonin   Chemical present in platelets, gastrointestinal mucosa, mast cells, and carcinoid tumors. Serotonin is a potent vasoconstrictor.

Serum   Clear, watery fluid, especially that moistening surfaces of serous membranes or exuded in inflammation of any of those membranes; the fluid portion of the blood obtained after removal of the fibrin clot and blood cells, sometimes used as a synonym for antiserum.

Sibilant   Hissing or whistling; applied to sounds heard in a certain rale.

Sign   Any objective evidence of manifestation of an illness or disordered function of the body. Signs are more or less definitive, obvious, and apart from the patient's impressions, in contrast to symptoms, which are subjective.

Silicate   Salt of silicic acid.

Sinus tachycardia   Uncomplicated tachycardia when sinus rhythm is faster than 100 beats per minute, e.g., that due to exercise. Causes other than exercise include hyperthermia, thyrotoxicosis, hemorrhage, anoxia, infections, cardiac failure, and certain drugs such as atropine, epinephrine, and nicotine.

Smooth muscle Muscle tissue that lacks cross-striations on its fibers; involuntary in action and found principally in visceral organs.

Somatic nerve Nerve that innervates somatic structures, i.e., those constituting the body wall and extremities.

Spasm Involuntary sudden movement or convulsive muscular contraction. Spasms may be clonic or tonic and may involve either visceral or skeletal muscle. Asthma is considered to be due to spasm of bronchial smooth muscle.

Sphygmomanometer Instrument for determining arterial blood pressure indirectly.

Sputum Substance expelled by coughing or clearing the throat. It may contain a variety of material from the respiratory tract, including one or more of the following: cellular debris, mucus, blood, pus, caseous material and microorganisms.

Stasis Stagnation of the normal flow of fluids, as of the blood, urine, or intestinal mechanism.

Status asthmaticus Persistent and intractable asthma.

Streptokinase Enzyme produced by certain strains of streptococci that is capable of converting plasminogen to plasmin.

Stroke volume Amount of blood ejected by the ventricle at each beat.

Subarachnoid space Space occupied by cerebrospinal fluid beneath the arachnoid membrane surrounding the brain and spinal cord. This is the space from which a sample of cerebrospinal fluid is collected.

Subcutaneous Beneath the skin.

Sulfur dioxide Common industrial air pollutant. Particulate matter absorbs sulfur dioxide, which gets into the small air passages and causes spasms and cell destruction.

Superficial Confined to the surface.

Superior vena cava Venous trunk draining blood from the head, neck, upper extremities, and chest. It begins by union of the two brachiocephalic veins, passes directly downward, and empties into the right atrium of the heart.

Surface tension Condition at the surface of a liquid in contact with a gas or another liquid that causes its surface to act as a stretched rubber membrane. It is the result of the mutual attraction of molecules to produce a cohesive state, which causes liquids to assume a shape presenting the smallest surface area to the surrounding medium. This accounts for the spherical shape assumed by fluids such as drops of oil or water.

Surfactant Phospholipoid substance important in controlling the surface tension of the air-liquid emulsion in the lungs; an agent that lowers the surface tension.

Swan-Ganz catheter   Soft, flexible catheter that contains a balloon near its tip. The sterile catheter is passed through the vein to the right heart, being carried along by the blood returning to the heart. The balloon then helps, without the use of fluoroscopy, to guide the catheter to the pulmonary artery. Once in the pulmonary artery, the balloon is inflated sufficiently to block the flow of blood from the right heart to the lung. This allows the backpressure in the pulmonary artery distal to the balloon to be recorded. This pressure reflects the pressure transmitted back from the left atrium to the heart.

Symmetric   Equal correspondence in shape, size, and relative position of parts on opposite sides of the body.

Sympathomimetic   Producing effects resembling those resulting from stimulation of the sympathetic nervous system, such as the effects following the injection of epinephrine.

Symptom   Any perceptible change in the body or its functions that indicates disease or the kind or phases of a disease. Symptoms may be classified as objective, subjective, cardinal, and sometimes constitutional. However, another classification considers all symptoms as being subjective, with objective indications being called signs.

Syncope   Transient loss of consciousness due to inadequate blood flow to the brain.

Syncytial   Group of cells in which the protoplasm of one cell is continuous with that of adjoining cells.

Systemic   Pertaining to the whole body rather than to one of its parts.

Systemic reaction   Whole-body response to a stimulus.

Systole   Part of the heart cycle in which the heart is in contraction.

Systolic pressure   Maximum blood pressure; occurs during contraction of the ventricle.

Tachycardia   Abnormal rapidity of heart action, usually defined as a heart rate over 100 beats per minute.

Tachypnea   A rapid breathing rate.

Technetium 99m   Radioisotope of technetium that emits α-rays; used in determining blood flow to certain organs by use of a scanning technique. It has a half-life of 6 hours.

Tenacious   Adhering to; adhesive, retentive.

Tension of gases   Gas pressure measured in millimeters of mercury (mm Hg).

Thoracentesis   Surgical puncture of the chest wall for removal of fluids, usually done by using a large-bore needle.

Thrombocytopenia   Abnormal decrease in the number of blood platelets.

Thromboembolic   Blood clot caused by an embolus obstructing a vessel.

Thrombophlebitis   Inflammation of a vein in conjunction with the formation of a thrombus; usually occurs in an extremity, most frequently a leg.

Thrombus   Blood clot that obstructs a blood vessel or a cavity of the heart.

Thymectomy   Surgical removal of the thymus gland.

Thymus   Ductless, glandlike body situated in the anterior mediastinal cavity that reaches maximum development during early childhood and then undergoes involution. It usually has two longitudinal lobes joined across a median plane. Once considered an endocrine gland, the thymus is now thought to be a lymphoid body. It is a site of lymphopoiesis and plays a role in immunologic competence.

Titer   A measurement of the concentration of a substance in a solution.

Tone   That state of a body or any of its organs or parts in which the functions are healthy and normal. In a more restricted sense, it is the resistance of muscles to passive elongation or stretch; normal tension or responsiveness to stimuli, as of arteries or muscles, seen particularly in involuntary muscle.

Toxemia   The condition resulting from the spread of bacterial products via the blood stream; toxemic condition resulting from metabolic disturbances.

Toxin   Poisonous substance of animal or plant origin.

Trachea   Fibroelastic tube found at the level of the sixth cervical vertebra to the fifth thoracic vertebra; carries air to and from the lungs. At a point called the carina it divides into two bronchi, one leading to each lung. The trachea is lined with mucous membrane, and its inner surface is lined with ciliated epithelium.

Tracheobronchial clearance   Mechanism by which the airways are cleared of foreign substances; the act of clearing the airways by mucociliary action, coughing, macrophages, etc.

Tracheostomy   Operation entailing cutting into the trachea through the neck, usually for insertion of a tube to overcome upper airway obstruction.

Tracheotomy   Incision of the skin, muscles, and trachea.

Transfusion   Injection of blood or a blood component into the blood stream; transfer of the blood of one person into the blood vessels of another.

Translucent   Transmitting light, but diffusing it so that objects beyond are not clearly distinguishable.

Transmission   Transference of disease or infection.

Transpulmonary pressure   The pressure difference between the mouth and intrapleural pressure.

Transverse Describing the state of something that is lying across or at right angles to something else; lying at right angles to the long axis of the body.

Trauma Physical injury or wound caused by external forces or violence.

Tricuspid valve Right atrioventricular valve separating the right atrium from the right ventricle.

Trypsin Proteolytic enzyme of pancreatic secretion.

Tuberculosis Infectious disease caused by the tubercle bacillus *Mycobacterium tuberculosis* and characterized pathologically by inflammatory infiltrations, formations of tubercles, caseation, necrosis, abscesses, fibrosis, and calcification. It most commonly affects the respiratory system.

T wave Portion of the electrocardiogram that is due to repolarization of the ventricles. The wave may be positive or negative, depending on the lead involved in recording the ECG and whether or not the electrical activity of the heart is within normal limits.

Ulcerate To produce or become affected with an open sore or lesion of the skin.

Underventilation Reduced rate and depth of breathing.

Uremia Toxic condition associated with renal insufficiency that is produced by retention in the blood of nitrogenous substances normally excreted by the kidney. It is a result of the disturbed kidney function seen in nephritis and is due to suppression or deficient excretion of urine from any cause.

Urokinase Enzyme obtained from human urine and used experimentally for dissolving intravascular clots. It is administered intravenously.

Vaccinia A contagious disease of cattle that is produced in humans by inoculation with cowpox virus to confer immunity against smallpox.

Vagus Pneumogastric or tenth cranial nerve. It is a mixed nerve, having motor and sensory functions and a wider distribution than any of the other cranial nerves. Paralysis of the main trunk on one side causes hoarseness and difficulty in swallowing and talking.

Variola An acute contagious febrile disease with skin eruptions. It is also known as smallpox and is considered to have been eradicated.

Vasoconstriction Constriction of the blood vessels.

Venous stasis Stagnation of the normal flow of blood; caused by venous congestion.

Ventilation Mechanical movement of air into and out of the lungs in a cyclic fashion. The activity is both autonomic and voluntary and has two components—an inward flow of air, called inhalation or inspiration, and an outward flow, called exhalation or expiration.

Ventricle Either of the two lower chambers of the heart that, when filled with blood, contract to propel it into arteries. The right ventricles forces blood into the pulmonary artery and thence into the lungs; the left, through the aorta.

Vernix Protective fatty deposit covering the fetus.

Visceral pleura Pleura that invests the lungs and enters into and lines the interlobar fissures. It is loose at the base and at the sternal and vertebral borders to allow lung expansion.

Viscosity Stickiness or gumminess; resistance offered by a fluid to change of form or relative position of its particles due to the attraction of molecules to each other.

Viscous Sticky, gummy, gelatinous.

Viscus Any internal organ enclosed within a cavity such as the thorax or abdomen.

Volume percent (vol%) The number of cubic centimeters (millimeters) of a substance contained in 100 cc (or mL) of another substance.

Wheal More or less round and evanescent elevation of the skin, white in the center, with a pale red periphery. It is accompanied by itching and is seen in urticaria, insect bites, anaphylaxis, and angioneurotic edema.

Xenon 133 Radioactive isotope of xenon used in photoscanning studies of the lung.

APPENDIXES

APPENDIX I: SYMBOLS AND ABBREVIATIONS COMMONLY USED IN RESPIRATORY PHYSIOLOGY

PRIMARY SYMBOLS

GAS SYMBOLS
P   Pressure
V   Gas volume
$\dot{V}$ Gas volume per unit of time, or flow
F   Fractional concentration of gas

BLOOD SYMBOLS
Q   Blood volume
$\dot{Q}$ Blood flow
C   Content in blood
S   Saturation

SECONDARY SYMBOLS

GAS SYMBOLS
I   Inspired
E   Expired
A   Alveolar
T   Tidal
D   Deadspace

BLOOD SYMBOLS
a   Arterial
c   Capillary
v   Venous
$\bar{v}$ Mixed venous

ABBREVIATIONS

Lung volume

VC	Vital capacity
IC	Inspiratory capacity
IRV	Inspiratory reserve volume
ERV	Expiratory reserve volume
FRC	Functional residual capacity
RV	Residual volume
TLC	Total lung capacity
RV/TLC (%)	Residual volume-to-total lung capacity ratio, expressed as a percentage
V_T	Tidal volume
V_A	Alveolar ventilation
V_D	Dead-space ventilation
V_L	Actual lung volume

Spirometry

FVC	Forced vital capacity with maximally forced expiratory effort
FEV_T	Forced expiratory volume, timed
$FEF_{200-1,200}$	Average rate of airflow between 200 and 1,200 mL of the FVC
$FEF_{25\%-75\%}$	Forced expiratory flow during the middle half of the FVC (formerly called the maximal midexpiratory flow [MMF])
PEFR	Maximum flow rate that can be achieved
$V_{max\ x}$	Forced expiratory flow related to the actual volume of the lungs as denoted by the subscript x, which refers to the amount of lung volume remaining when measurement is made
MVV	Maximal voluntary ventilation as the volume of air expired in a specified interval

Mechanics

C_L	Lung compliance, volume change per unit of pressure change
R_{aw}	Airway resistance, pressure per unit of flow

Diffusion

DL_{CO}	Diffusing capacity of carbon monoxide

Blood Gases

$P_{A_{O_2}}$	Alveolar oxygen tension
Pc_{O_2}	Pulmonary capillary oxygen tension
Pa_{O_2}	Arterial oxygen tension
$P\bar{v}_{O_2}$	Mixed venous oxygen tension
$P_{A_{CO_2}}$	Alveolar carbon dioxide tension
Pc_{CO_2}	Pulmonary capillary carbon dioxide tension
Pa_{CO_2}	Arterial carbon dioxide tension
Sa_{O_2}	Arterial oxygen saturation
$S\bar{v}_{O_2}$	Mixed venous oxygen saturation
pH	Negative logarithm of the H^+ concentration used as a positive number
HCO_3^-	Plasma bicarbonate concentration
mEq/L	The number of grams of solute dissolved in a normal solution
Ca_{O_2}	Oxygen content of arterial blood
Cc_{O_2}	Oxygen content of capillary blood
$C\bar{v}_{O_2}$	Oxygen content of mixed venous blood
$\dot{V}/\dot{Q}$	Ventilation-perfusion ratio
Qs/Qt	Shunt
QT	Total cardiac output

APPENDIX II: SYMPATHOMIMETIC AGENTS

Sympathomimetic agents are used to offset bronchial smooth muscle constractions.

Generic Name	Trade Name
Epinephrine	Adrenalin
Racemic epinephrine	MicroNefrin
	Vaponefrin
	AsthmaNefrin

Generic Name	Trade name
Isoproterenol	Isuprel
	Mistometer
Isoetharine	Bronkosol
	Bronkometer
Metaproterenol	Alupent
	Metaprel
Terbutaline	Brethine
	Brethaire
Albuterol	Proventil
	Ventolin

APPENDIX III: PARASYMPATHOLYTIC (ANTICHOLINERGIC) AGENTS

Parasympatholytic agents are used to offset bronchial smooth muscle constriction.

Generic Name	Trade Name
Atropine sulfate	Dey-Dose Atropine Sulfate
Ipratropium bromide	Atrovent

APPENDIX IV: XANTHINE BRONCHODILATORS

Xanthine bronchodilators are used to enhance bronchial smooth muscle relaxation.

Generic Name	Trade Name
Theophylline	Bronkodyl
	Elixophyllin
	Somophyllin-T
	Slo-Phyllin
	Theolair
	Theo-Dur
	Theo-Dur Sprinkle
	Constant-T
	Quibron-T/SR
	Respbid
Theophylline sodium glycinate	Synophylate
Oxtriphylline (choline theophyllinate)	Choledyl
Aminophylline (theophylline ethylenediamine)	Aminophyllin Phyllocontin
Dyphylline	Lufyllin

questions and to the dilemma of dealing with contradictory answers, a better approach to quality control seems to be working out the most appropriate and necessary questions and carefully handling the interview process or self-administering situations.

From the above you may have understood better why it is important to have your core hypotheses or major models of data analysis in mind when designing your questions. The bottom line is that you must provide all the needed information to test your research ideas, hypotheses, and models. But you do not need to directly ask all the questions. In real terms, deviating from the variables in your hypotheses and models to some other questions may leave more room for your new ideas in future analysis, which can be embodied in new variables created by such a command as COMPUTE in SPSS. You must make sure, however, that there is a logical connection by which you can still calculate those variables to directly test your original hypotheses and hypothetical models.

Sometimes the logic is simple. For example, instead of asking the respondent whether he went to high school or college, you may record the total number of years of formal schooling he has received. This may be advantageous since the educational system in today's world is complicated and not uniform, especially viewed from interregional and international perspectives. Later you can categorize this variable by choosing a single standard, which, for example, takes elementary school as the equivalent of 1-6 years of education, high school as the equivalent of 7-12 years of education, and college and above, 13 years or more. This logic could also be problematic, however. Some would argue that the education level cannot be assigned this way since some students may be making extraordinary advances while some others are repeating the classes.

Occasionally the logical connection between the original variable(s) and the derived variable is complex and complicated. This is especially the case of multi-item scale development. If the variable is a theoretical construct, it usually cannot be well measured by simply making up a general question and asking the respondent about it. For example, you usually cannot directly ask a respondent, "How is your social support?" since even experts often get confused about what the term "social support" means. In some other cases, you may directly ask about the variable but one question is just not enough to yield a good measure. For instance, although you may ask the respondent "Do you feel depressed?" you usually cannot stop right there since measuring depression requires you to know more about the life of the respondent. In such multi-item measurement, the issue of the logical connection between the questions asked and the original variable

APPENDIX V: CORTICOSTEROIDS

Aerosolized corticosteroids are used to suppress bronchial inflammation and bronchial edema. They are also used for their ability to enchance the responsiveness of B_2 receptor sites to sympathomimetic agents.

Generic Name	Trade Name
Dexamethasone	Decadron
Beclomethasone	Vanceril
	Beclovent
Triamcinolone acetonide	Aristocort
Flunisolide	AeroBid

APPENDIX VI: MUCUS-CONTROLLING AGENTS

The following agents are used to enhance the mobilization of bronchial secretions:

Generic Name	Trade Name
Acetylcysteine	Mucomyst
Sodium Bicarbonate	2% solution

APPENDIX VII: EXPECTORANTS

Expectorants are agents used to increase bronchial secretion production, which in turn decreases mucus viscosity. This facilitates the mobilization and expectoration of bronchial secretions.

Generic Name	Trade Name
Ammonium chloride	—
Potassium iodide	SSKI
Guaifenesin (glyceryl guaiacolate)	Anti-tuss
Citrates	Sodium citrate
Bromhexine	Bisolvon

APPENDIX VIII: ANTIBIOTIC AGENTS

Agent	Therapeutic Uses

Penicillins
  Penicillin G
  Penicillin V
  Oxacillin (Prostaphilin)
  Cloxacillin (Tegopen)
  Methicillin (Staphcillin)
  Ampicillin (Omnipren)
  Amoxicillin (Polymox)
  Carbenicillin (Geopen)
  Ticarcillin (Ticar)
	Used in treating streptococcal species, staphylococcal species, *Haemophilus influenzae*. Also used in treating aspiration pneumonia

Cephalosporins
  First generation
    Cefaclor (Ceclor)
    Cephalexin (Keflex)
    Cefadroxil (Duricef)
    Cephalothin (Keflin)
  Second generation
    Cephamandole (Mandol)
    Cefoxitin (Mefoxin)
    Cefonicid (Monocid)
  Third generation
    Cefoperazone (Cefobid)
    Cefotaxime (Claforan)
    Ceftizoxime (Cefizox)
	Important for their broad-spectrum activity against common gram-positive cocci (primarily the first generation) and some gram-negative organisms (primarily the second and third generations). Also active against *Klebsiella* species, but lack efficacy against *Pseudomonas aeruginosa* and *Haemophilus influenzae*

Aminoglycosides
  Streptomycin
  Gentamicin (Garamycin)
  Netilmicin (Netromycin)
  Amikacin (Amikin)
  Kanamycin (Kantrex)
  Neomycin (Neosporin)
	Used for treating gram-negative organisms. Commonly used to treat *Pseudomonas* in cystic fibrosis. Streptomycin is also used in treating *M. tuberculosis*

Tetracyclines
  Tetracycline (Achromycin)
  Oxytetracycline (Terramycin)
  Demeclocycline (Declomycin)
  Methacycline (Rondomycin)
  Doxycycline (Vibramycin)
  Minocycline (Minocin)
	Used in treating mycoplasmal and other atypical pneumonias and acute infections superimposed on chronic bronchitis

Other antibiotic agents Vancomycin (Vancocin)	Used in treating staphyloccal infections
Chloramphenicol (Chloromycetin)	Used in treating penicillinase-producing *Staphylococcus*, *Klebsiella*, *Haemophilus influenzae*
Erythromycin (Erythrocin, Ilotycin)	Used in treating penicillin-allergic patients with pneumococcal pneumonia

Polymyxins
    Polymyxin B
    Polymyxin E
	Used in treating *Pseudomonas* and other gram-negative organisms

Clindamycin (Cleocin) and Lincomycin (Linococin)	Used in treating aspiration pneumonia
Metronidazole (Flagyl, Metizol)	Active against anaerobic infections
Quinolones	Used in treating *H influenzae*, *Legionella pneumophillia*, *M. pneumoniae*, *P. aeruginosa*
Pentamidine, isethionate (Pentam)	Used in treating the protozoan *Pneumocystis carinii* in AIDS patients

APPENDIX IX: POSITIVE INOTROPIC AGENTS

The following positive inotropic agents are used to increase cardiac output.

Generic Name	Trade Name
Digitalis	—
Deslanoside	Cedilanid-D
Digoxin	Lanoxin
Digitoxin	Crystodigin
Amrinone	Inocor
Dobutamine	Dobutrex
Dopamine	Intropin
Epinephrine	—
Isoproterenol	Isoprel

APPENDIX X: DIURETICS

Diuretics are drugs used to increase urine output.

Generic Name	Trade Name
Furosemide	Lasix
Ethacrynic acid	Edecrin
Bumetanide	Bumex
Hydrochlorthiazide	Esidrix
Spironolactone	Aldactone

APPENDIX XI: TECHNIQUES USED TO MOBILIZE BRONCHIAL SECRETIONS

The following respiratory therapy modalities are used to enhance the mobilization of bronchial secretions:

- Ultrasonic nebulization
- Increased fluid intake (6–10 glasses of water daily)
- Chest physical therapy
- Postural drainage
- Percussion and vibration with postural drainage
- Deep breathing and coughing
  - Intermittent positive-pressure breathing (IPPB)
  - Incentive spirometry
- Suctioning

APPENDIX XII: HYPERINFLATION TECHNIQUES

Hyperinflation techniques are often used to offset alveolar consolidation and atelectasis. Common techniques include the following:

- Cough and deep breathing
- Incentive spirometry

- Intermittent positive-pressure breathing (IPPB)
- Continuous positive airway pressure (CPAP)
- Positive end-expiratory pressure (PEEP)

APPENDIX XIII: THE IDEAL ALVEOLAR GAS EQUATION

Clinically, the alveolar oxygen tension can be computed from the ideal alveolar gas equation. A useful clinical approximation of the ideal alveolar gas equation is as follows:

$$P_{A_{O_2}} = [P_B - P_{H_2O}]\, F_{I_{O_2}} - P_{a_{CO_2}}\,(1.25)$$

where P_B is barometric pressure, $P_{A_{O_2}}$ is the partial pressure of oxygen within the alveoli, P_{H_2O} is the partial pressure of water vapor in the alveoli (at body temperature and at sea level P_{H_2O} in the alveoli is 47 mm Hg), $F_{I_{O_2}}$ is the fractional concentration of inspired oxygen, and $P_{a_{CO_2}}$ is the partial pressure of arterial carbon dioxide. The number 1.25 is a factor that adjusts for alterations in oxygen tension due to variations in the respiratory exchange ratio. The respiratory exchange ratio indicates that less carbon dioxide is transferred into the alveoli (about 200 cc/min) than the amount of oxygen that moves into the pulmonary capillary blood (about 250 mL/min). This ratio is normally about 0.8.

Therefore, if a patient is receiving an $F_{I_{O_2}}$ of 40% on a day when the barometric pressure is 755 mm Hg and if the $P_{a_{CO_2}}$ is 55 mm Hg the patient's alveolar oxygen tension ($P_{A_{O_2}}$) can be calculated as follows:

$$
\begin{aligned}
P_{A_{O_2}} &= (P_B - P_{H_2O})\, F_{I_{O_2}} - P_{a_{CO_2}}\,(1.25) \\
&= (755 - 47)\,.40 - 55\,(1.25) \\
&= (708)\,.40 - 68.75 \\
&= (283.2) - 68.75 \\
&= 214.45
\end{aligned}
$$

The ideal alveolar gas equation is part of the clinical information needed to calculate the degree of pulmonary shunting.

APPENDIX XIV: PHYSIOLOGIC DEAD-SPACE CALCULATION

The amount of physiologic dead space (V_D) in the tidal volume (V_T) can be estimated by using the dead space-to-tidal volume ratio (V_D/V_T) equation. The equation is arranged as follows:

$$
\begin{aligned}
V_D/V_T &= \frac{P_{a_{CO_2}} - P_{\bar{E}_{CO_2}}}{P_{a_{CO_2}}} \\
&= \frac{40 - 28}{40} \\
&= \frac{12}{40} \\
&= .3
\end{aligned}
$$

In this case, approximately 30% of the patient's ventilation is dead-space ventilation. This is within the normal range.

APPENDIX XV: UNITS OF MEASUREMENT

Metric Weight

Grams	Centigrams	Milligrams	Micrograms	Nanograms
1	100	1000	1,000,000	1,000,000,000
.01	1	10	10,000	10,000,000
.001	.1	1	1000	1,000,000
.000001	.0001	.001	1	1000
.000000001	.0000001	.000001	.001	1

Weight

Metric	Approximate Apothecary Equivalents
Grams	*Grains*
.0002	1/300
.0003	1/200
.0004	1/150
.0005	1/120
.0006	1/100
.001	1/60
.002	1/30
.005	1/12
.010	1/6
.015	1/4
.025	3/8
.030	1/2
.050	3/4
.060	1
.100	1½
.120	2
.200	3
.300	5
.500	7½
.600	10
1	15
2	30
4	60

Liquid Measure

Metric	Approximate Apothecary Equivalents
Milliliters	
1,000	1 quart
750	1½ pints
500	1 pint
250	8 fluid ounces
200	7 fluid ounces
100	3½ fluid ounces
50	1¾ fluid ounces
30	1 fluid ounce
15	4 fluid drams
10	2½ fluid drams
8	2 fluid drams
5	1¼ fluid drams
4	1 fluid dram
3	45 minims
2	30 minims
1	15 minims
0.75	12 minims
0.6	10 minims
0.5	8 minims
0.3	5 minims
0.25	4 minims
0.2	3 minims
0.1	1½ minims
0.06	1 minim
0.05	3/4 minim
0.03	1/2 minim

Metric Liquid

Liter	Centiliter	Milliliter	Microliter	Nanoliter
1	100	1000	1,000,000	1,000,000,000
.01	1	10	10,000	10,000,000
.001	.1	1	1000	1,000,000
.000001	.0001	.001	1	1000
.000000001	.0000001	.000001	.001	1

Metric Length

Meter	Centimeter	Millimeter	Micrometer	Nanometer
1	100	1000	1,000,000	1,000,000,000
.01	1	10	10,000	10,000,000
.001	.1	1	1000	1,000,000
.000001	.0001	.001	1	1000
.000000001	.0000001	.000001	.001	1

Weight Conversions (Metric and Avoirdupois)

Grams	Kilograms	Ounces	Pounds
1	.001	.0353	.0022
1000	1	35.3	2.2
28.35	.02835	1	$\frac{1}{16}$
454.5	.4545	16	1

Weight Conversions (Metric and Apothecary)

Grams	Milligrams	Grains	Drams	Ounces	Pounds
1	1000	15.4	.2577	.0322	.00268
.001	1	.0154	.00026	.0000322	.00000268
.0648	64.8	1	$\frac{1}{60}$	$\frac{1}{480}$	$\frac{1}{5760}$
3.888	3888	60	1	$\frac{1}{8}$	$\frac{1}{96}$
31.1	31104	480	8	1	$\frac{1}{12}$
363.25	373248	5760	96	12	1

Approximate Household Measurement Equivalents (volume)

	1 tsp =	5 mL
1 tbsp = 3 tsp =	15 mL
1 fl oz = 2 tbsp = 6 tsp =	30 mL
1 cup = 8 fl oz	= 240 mL
1 pt = 2 cups = 16 fl oz	= 480 mL
1 qt = 2 pt = 4 cups = 32 fl oz	= 960 mL
1 gal = 4 qt = 8 pt = 16 cups = 128 fl oz	= 3840 mL

Volume Conversions (Metric and Apothecary)

Milliliters	Minims	Fluid Drams	Fluid Ounces	Pints	Liters	Gallons	Quarts	Fluid Ounces	Pints
1	16.2	.27	.0333	.0021	1	.2642	1.057	33.824	2.114
.0616	1	$\frac{1}{60}$	$\frac{1}{480}$	$\frac{1}{7680}$	3.785	1	4	128	8
3.697	60	1	$\frac{1}{8}$	$\frac{1}{128}$	.946	$\frac{1}{4}$	1	32	2
29.58	480	8	1	$\frac{1}{16}$	.473	$\frac{1}{8}$	$\frac{1}{2}$	16	1
473.2	7680	128	16	1	.0296	$\frac{1}{128}$	$\frac{1}{32}$	1	$\frac{1}{16}$

Length Conversions (Metric and English System)

	Millimeters	Centimeters	Inches	Feet	Yards	Meters
1 A =	$\dfrac{1}{10{,}000{,}000}$	$\dfrac{1}{100{,}000{,}000}$	$\dfrac{1}{254{,}000{,}000}$	$\dfrac{1}{3{,}050{,}000{,}000}$	$\dfrac{1}{9{,}140{,}000{,}000}$	$\dfrac{1}{10{,}000{,}000{,}000}$
1 nm =	$\dfrac{1}{1{,}000{,}000}$	$\dfrac{1}{10{,}000{,}000}$	$\dfrac{1}{25{,}400{,}000}$	$\dfrac{1}{305{,}000{,}000}$	$\dfrac{1}{914{,}000{,}000}$	$\dfrac{1}{1{,}000{,}000{,}000}$
1 µm =	$\dfrac{1}{1{,}000}$	$\dfrac{1}{10{,}000}$	$\dfrac{1}{25{,}400}$	$\dfrac{1}{305{,}000}$	$\dfrac{1}{914{,}000}$	$\dfrac{1}{1{,}000{,}000}$
1 mm =	1.0	0.1	0.03937	0.00328	0.0011	0.001
1 cm =	10.0	1.0	0.3937	0.03281	0.0109	0.01
1 in =	25.4	2.54	1.0	0.0833	0.0278	0.0254
1 ft =	304.8	30.48	12.0	1.0	0.333	0.3048
1 yd =	914.40	91.44	36.0	3.0	1.0	0.9144
1 m =	1000.0	100.0	39.37	3.2808	1.0936	1.0

APPENDIX XVI: MATHEMATICS

Poiseuille's Law for Flow Rearranged to a Simple Proportionality

$$\dot{V} \simeq \Delta P r^4, \text{ or rewritten as } \frac{\dot{V}}{r^4} \simeq \Delta P.$$

When ΔP remains constant, then

$$\frac{\dot{V}_1}{r_1^{\,4}} \simeq \frac{\dot{V}_2}{r_2^{\,4}}$$

Example 1.—If the radius (r_1) is decreased to half its previous radius ($r_2 = \frac{1}{2}\, r_1$), then

$$\frac{\dot{V}_1}{r_1^{\,4}} \simeq \frac{\dot{V}_2}{(\frac{1}{2}\, r_1)^4}$$

$$\frac{\dot{V}_1}{r_1^{\,4}} \simeq \frac{\dot{V}_2}{(\frac{1}{16})r_1^{\,4}}$$

$$(r_1^{\,4}) \frac{\dot{V}_1}{r_1^{\,4}} \simeq (r_1^{\,4}) \frac{\dot{V}_2}{(\frac{1}{16})\, r_1^{\,4}}$$

$$\dot{V}_1 \simeq \frac{\dot{V}_2}{\frac{1}{16}}$$

$$(\frac{1}{16})\, \dot{V}_1 \simeq (\frac{1}{16}) \frac{\dot{V}_2}{\frac{1}{16}}$$

$$(\frac{1}{16})\, \dot{V}_1 \simeq \dot{V}_2$$

The gas flow ($\dot{V}_1$) is reduced to $\frac{1}{16}$ its original flow rate [$\dot{V}_2 \simeq (\frac{1}{16})\, \dot{V}_1$].

Example 2.—If the radius (r_1) is decreased by 16% ($r_2 = r_1 - 0.16\, r_1 = 0.84 r_1$), then

$$\frac{\dot{V}_1}{r_1^{\,4}} \simeq \frac{\dot{V}_2}{r_2^{\,4}}$$

$$\frac{\dot{V}_1}{r_1^{\,4}} \simeq \frac{\dot{V}_2}{(0.84r_1)^4}$$

$$\dot{V}_2 \simeq \frac{(0.84r_1)^4\,\dot{V}_1}{r_1^{\,4}}$$

$$\dot{V}_2 \simeq \frac{0.4979\,\cancel{r_1^{\,4}}\,\dot{V}_1}{\cancel{r_1^{\,4}}}$$

$$\dot{V}_2 \simeq \tfrac{1}{2}\,\dot{V}_1$$

The flow rate ($\dot{V}_1$) would decrease to half the original flow rate ($\dot{V}_2 \simeq \frac{1}{2}\,\dot{V}_1$).

Poiseuille's Law for Pressure Rearranged to a Simple Proportionality

$$P \simeq \frac{\dot{V}}{r^4}, \text{ or rewritten as } P \cdot r^4 \simeq \dot{V}$$

When $\dot{V}$ remains constant, then

$$P_1 \cdot r_1^{\,4} \simeq P_2 \cdot r_2^{\,4}$$

Example 1.—If the radius (r_1) is reduced to half its original radius [$r_2 = (\frac{1}{2})\,r_1$], then

$$P_1 \cdot r_1^{\,4} \simeq P_2 \cdot r_2^{\,4}$$
$$P_1 \cdot r_1^{\,4} \simeq P_2[(\tfrac{1}{2})\,r_1]^4$$
$$P_1 \cdot r_1^{\,4} \simeq P_2 \cdot (\tfrac{1}{16})\,r_1^{\,4}$$
$$\frac{P_1 \cdot \cancel{r_1^{\,4}}}{\cancel{r_1^{\,4}}} \simeq \frac{P_2 \cdot (\tfrac{1}{16})\,\cancel{r_1^{\,4}}}{\cancel{r_1^{\,4}}}$$
$$P_1 \simeq P_2 \cdot (\tfrac{1}{16})$$
$$16\,P_1 \simeq \cancel{16} \cdot P_2 \cdot (\cancel{\tfrac{1}{16}})$$
$$16\,P_1 \simeq P_2$$

The pressure (P_1) will increase to 16 times its original level ($P_2 \simeq 16 \cdot P_1$).

Example 2.— If the radius (r_1) is decreased by 16% ($r_2 = r_1 - 0.16\,r_1 = 0.84\,r_1$), then

$$P_1 \cdot r_1^{\,4} \simeq P_2 \cdot r_2^{\,4}$$
$$P_1 \cdot r_1^{\,4} \simeq P_2\,(0.4979)r_1^{\,4}$$
$$\frac{P_1\cancel{r_1^{\,4}}}{(0.4979r_1)^{\cancel{4}}} = P_2$$
$$2\,P_1 = P_2$$

The pressure (P_1) would increase to twice its original pressure ($P_2 \simeq 2 \cdot P_1$).

APPENDIX XVII: SELF-ASSESSMENT ANSWERS

Chapter 1

Multiple Choice

1. d	6. c	11. d	16. d	21. b	26. e
2. e	7. e	12. b	17. b	22. e	
3. c	8. a	13. b	18. e	23. a	
4. b	9. d	14. c	19. d	24. c	
5. d	10. b	15. e	20. c	25. e	

True or False

1. False	6. True
2. True	7. False
3. True	8. True
4. True	9. True
5. False	10. False

Clinical Application of the Ideal Alveolar Gas Equation

$$P_{A_{O_2}} = [PB - P_{H_2O}] \, F_{I_{O_2}} - P_{a_{CO_2}} (1.25)$$
$$[745 - 47] \, .55 - 50 \, (1.25)$$
$$[698] \, .55 - 62.5$$
$$[383.9] - 62.5$$
$$321.4$$

Clinical Application of the Shunt Equation

1. $P_{A_{O_2}} = (PB - (P_{H_2O}) \, F_{I_{O_2}} - P_{a_{CO_2}} (1.25)$
   $= (745 - 47) \, .70 - 46 \, (1.25)$
   $= (698) \, .70 - 57.5$
   $= (488.6) - 57.5$
   $= 431.1$
   Answer: 431.1

2. $C_{c_{O_2}} = (Hb \times 1.34) + (P_{A_{O_2}} \times 0.003)$
   $= (11 \times 1.34) + (431.1 \times 0.003)$
   $= (14.74) + (1.293)$
   $= 16.033$
   Answer: 16.033

3. $C_{a_{O_2}} = (Hb \times 1.34 \times S_{a_{O_2}}) + (P_{a_{O_2}} \times 0.003)$
   $= (11 \times 1.34 \times .90) + (60 \times 0.003)$
   $= (13.266) + (.18)$
   $= 13.446$
   Answer: 13.446

4. $C_{\bar{v}_{O_2}} = (Hb \times 1.34 \times S_{\bar{v}_{O_2}}) + (P_{\bar{v}_{O_2}} \times 0.003)$
   $= (11 \times 1.34 \times .75) + (38 \times 0.003)$
   $= (11.055) + (.114)$
   $= 11.169$
   Answer: 11.169

5. $\dfrac{\dot{Q}s}{\dot{Q}T} = \dfrac{Cc_{O_2} - Ca_{O_2}}{Cc_{O_2} - C\bar{v}_{O_2}}$

$= \dfrac{16.033 - 13.446}{16.033 - 11.169}$

$= \dfrac{2.587}{4.864}$

$= .531$

Answer: 53%

Matching

1. c
2. d
3. a
4. b

Chapter 2

Multiple Choice

1. b   6. c
2. e   7. e
3. d   8. c
4. e   9. d
5. a   10. e

Chapter 3

Multiple Choice

1. c   6. e
2. a   7. b
3. b   8. b
4. b   9. b
5. a   10. d

True or False

1. True   4b. False   5b. False
2. False   4c. False   6a. False
3. False   4d. False   6b. True
4a. True   5a. True

Fill in the blank

1. Cigarette smoking
2. Dynamic
3. Equal pressure point

as designed or final variable as tested becomes the methodological crux of how to combine the items into a general scale. This is an important and complicated topic that requires special treatment in a research methods book. Chapter twelve of this volume is devoted to related issues. Here we need only to remember that the requirement for scale development may involve a tremendous amount of work in data manipulation and management.

Computer files

Your data can be entered into a computer file with a program chosen from a variety of software packages. For example, you can make use of the data entry function of a statistical program such as SPSS for Windows to directly create a system file, which contains not only the raw data but also their definitions, or a "dictionary," including variable names, specifications of variable types and lengths, missing values, and variable and value labels. Alternatively, you may choose to use a separate data management system such as dBASE to establish a database file, which not only accommodates the raw data, but also provides variable names as well as type and length specifications. A dBASE file, however, does not contain variable and value labels nor definition of missing values. These must be added later when using a statistical package to analyze the data. Finally, you may even use a word processor to set up a raw data file, which supplies nothing else but a matrix of codes (usually only numbers). Again, a detailed "dictionary" need be added when using a statistical package to analyze the data. All these computer files serve as different means for computerizing your data.

To clean and transform the data, you need to compose a program or command file by using a particular statistical language such as SPSS or SAS. In SPSS, this is actually the only program file that you must write to carry out all the data management tasks, including data entry, data cleaning, and data transformation. You do not even have to create a separate data file since SPSS allows you to directly put a data matrix in the data management program (between the commands BEGIN DATA and END DATA). In such a case, you are considered using "in stream" data and you need to use the command DATA LIST to define the variables corresponding to the columns of the data matrix. It would make your data management program file much easier to handle, however, when you put your data in a separate file. What you need to do first in your data management program depends on what kind of raw data file you have. If you have placed the data in a file created by a word processor, you can use the

Chapter 4

Multiple Choice
1. e   6. a
2. b   7. d
3. b   8. d
4. b   9. e
5. d   10. b

Chapter 5

Multiple Choice
1. b   6. c
2. c   7. c
3. d   8. e
4. c   9. e
5. d

True or False
1. True   5. True
2. False   6. True
3. True
4. True

Matching
1. e   6. e
2. c   7. a
3. b   8. c
4. i   9. g
5. g   10. a

Chapter 6

Multiple Choice
1. d   6. e
2. b   7. a
3. d   8. b
4. b   9. b
5. d

True or False
1. True   6. True
2. False   7. False
3. True   8. True
4. True   9. True
5. True 10. False

Chapter 7

Multiple Choice
1. e   6. c
2. b   7. a
3. e   8. b
4. a
5. e

True or False
1. True   4. True
2. True   5. False
3. False

Fill in the blank
1. albumin

Chapter 8

Multiple Choice
1. c   6. b
2. d   7. c
3. c   8. d
4. e   9. b
5. c   10. a

Chapter 9

Multiple Choice
1. d
2. b
3. a
4. b

True or False
1. True   4. False
2. False   5. False
3. False

Chapter 10

Multiple Choice
1. c   5. d
2. d   6. c
3. b   7. a
4. d

True or False
1. True   4. True
2. True   5. True
3. False

Chapter 11

Multiple Choice
1. e   6. d
2. c   7. e
3. e   8. b
4. d   9. d
5. a

True or False
1. True   4. False
2. True   5. True
3. False

Chapter 12

Multiple Choice
1. e
2. b
3. d
4. c
5. d

True or False
1. True
2. False
3. True
4. True
5. True

Chapter 13

Multiple Choice
1. a
2. c
3. c
4. a
5. e

True or False
1. True
2. False
3. True
4. False
5. False

Chapter 14

Multiple Choice
1. e
2. d
3. c
4. b
5. e

True or False
1. True
2. True
3. True
4. False
5. False

Chapter 15

Multiple Choice
1. e
2. d
3. e
4. c
5. c

True or False
1. True
2. False
3. True
4. True
5. False

Chapter 16

Multiple Choice
1. b
2. a
3. d
4. d
5. b

True or False
1. True
2. False
3. False
4. True
5. True

Chapter 17

Multiple Choice
1. a
2. b
3. c
4. b
5. e

True or False
1. True
2. True
3. True
4. False
5. True

Chapter 18

Multiple Choice

1. e		6. d
2. b		7. d
3. e		8. b
4. a		9. e
5. a		10. e

True or False
1. True
2. True
3. False
4. False
5. False

Fill in the blank
1. 2.5 kg

Chapter 19

True or False

1. False		6. False
2. True		7. True
3. False		8. False
4. True		9. False
5. True		10. False

Chapter 20

Multiple Choice
1. d   6. d
2. c   7. b
3. a   8. b
4. e   9. a
5. d   10. c

True or False
1. False
2. True
3. False
4. False
5. True

Chapter 21

Multiple Choice
1. e
2. d
3. c
4. e
5. e

True or False
1. True
2. False
3. False
4. True
5. True

Chapter 22

True or False
1. False   6. False
2. True   7. True
3. False   8. True
4. True   9. False
5. False   10. True

Chapter 23

Multiple Choice
1. d   6. d
2. c   7. c
3. e   8. b
4. b   9. a
5. e   10. d

INDEX

A

Abbreviations, 343–344
  for blood gases, 344
  for lung volume, 343
  in spirometry, 344
Abscess: lung, with pleural
    effusion, 192
Accessory muscles (see
    Muscles, accessory)
Acetylcholine, 317
  in myasthenia gravis, 278
Acidemia, 317
Acidosis, 317
  lactic, 57
Acinus, 317
ACTH, 317
  in myasthenia gravis, 282
Adenocarcinoma: lung, 230,
    232
Adenosine monophosphate:
    cyclic, 323
Adenovirus
  in laryngotracheobronchitis,
    254
  pneumonia due to, 127
Adrenergic, 317
Adrenocorticotropic hormone,
    317
  in myasthenia gravis, 282
Aerosol mist: cool, in
    laryngotracheobronchitis
    and epiglottitis, 257
Air trapping, 317
  in lung disease, obstructive, 13
Airway
  bronchial
    dynamic compression,
      40–42
    Poiseuille's law for flow
      and, 44
    Poiseuille's law for
      pressure and, 45–46
  obstruction in croup, 252
  peripheral, 334
  resistance
    equation in lung disease,
      obstructive, 46
    increase, in ventilatory
      frequency and tidal
      volume, 26

  in ventilatory patterns,
    24–27
  upper, anatomic alterations
    in croup syndrome,
    253–254
Albumin, 318
  in pulmonary edema, 141
Alcohol: in pulmonary edema,
    141
Aldinamide: in tuberculosis,
    218
Alkalemia, 318
Allele, 318
Allergic asthma, 111–113
Allergy, 318
Alpha$_1$-antitrypsin, 318
  deficiency in emphysema,
    92–93
Alveoli, 60
  compression, schematic
    illustration, 69
  consolidation
    chemoreceptors in,
      peripheral, stimulation,
      49
    in dull percussion note, 9
    in pneumonia, 122
    in respiratory distress
      syndrome, idiopathic,
      240
    venous admixture in, 49
  dead space, 19
  in flail chest, 166
  gas equation, ideal, 349
Histoplasmosis capsulatum
    spores in, 220
  hyperinflation
    in cystic fibrosis, 260
    in hyperresonant
      percussion note, 10
    with hypoxemia in
      asthma, 115
    in lung disease,
      obstructive, 13
  hyperventilation with
      hypoxemia, 48–57
    in bronchiectasis, 104
    in bronchitis, chronic, 83
    in cancer of lung, 234
    in cystic fibrosis, 263
    in emphysema, 94

  in epiglottitis, 255
  in flail chest, 169
  in fungal diseases, 224
  in kyphoscoliosis, 198
  in laryngotracheobronchi-
    tis, 255
  in pneumoconiosis, 207
  in pneumonia, 129
  in pneumothorax, 179
  in pulmonary edema, 138
  in pulmonary embolism,
    148
  in respiratory distress
    syndrome, adult, 161
  in tuberculosis, 216
  hyperventilation in pleural
    effusion, 190
  hypoventilation, 54
  hypoxia causing
    vasoconstriction in
      pulmonary embolism,
      149
  in pneumothorax, 174
Aminoglycoside, 347
Analgesics: in pneumonia,
    131
Anaphylaxis, 318
Anatomic dead space, 19
Anatomic shunt, 18
Anatomy: references for,
    297–298
Anemia, 318
Aneurysm, 318
Angiography, 318
  in pulmonary embolism,
    152, 154
Anomalies: chest, lung
    compression with
    atelectasis in, 196
Anoxia, 318
Antibiotics, 347
  in bronchiectasis, 107
  in bronchitis, chronic, 86
  in cystic fibrosis, 266
  in emphysema, 97
  in epiglottitis, 257
  in laryngotracheobronchitis,
    257
  in pneumonia, 131
  in respiratory distress
    syndrome, adult, 163

Antibody(ies), 318
    circulating, in myasthenia
        gravis, 278
    complement-activating, in
        Guillain-Barré
        syndrome, 272
    fluorescent antibody
        microscopy, 326
    in myasthenia gravis,
        278
Anticholinergic agents (see
    Parasympatholytic
    agents)
Antifungal agents: in fungal
    diseases, 225–226
Antigen, 319
α_1-Antitrypsin, 318
    deficiency in emphysema,
        92–93
Anxiety, 30
Aortic
    baroreceptors, 29
        reflexes from, 30
        sinus, 29
    chemosensitive cells, 29
    valve, 319
Apnea, 319
    sleep (see Sleep apnea)
Apneustic center, 27
Aponeurosis, 319
Apothecary volume, 351
Apothecary weight, 351
ARDS (see Respiratory distress
    syndrome, adult)
Arrhythmia, 319
    in sleep apnea, 291
Arteries
    bronchial, 60
    carotid, chemosensitive cells
        and baroreceptors on,
        29
    pulmonary, chemosensitive
        cells and baroreceptors
        on, 29
Arthralgia, 319
Arthritis: "desert," 223
Arthropod, 319
Asbestosis, 202
    discussion of, 204
    x-ray in, chest, 209
Asepsis, 319
Asphyxia, 319
Aspiration, 319
Asthma, 110–121
    accessory muscles in, 114
    allergic, 111–113
    alveolar hyperventilation
        with hypoxemia in, 115
    anatomic alterations of lungs
        in, 111
    atopic, 111–113
    barrel chest increase in,
        114
    blood gases in, 115
    blood pressure decrease in,
        115

blood pressure increase in,
    114, 115–116
bronchial secretion
    mobilization in, 117
bronchodilators in, xanthine,
    117
chest assessment in, 115
clinical manifestations,
    cardiopulmonary,
    overview, 114–116
corticosteroids in, 117
cough in, 115
cyanosis in, 115
environmental control in,
    116–117
etiology, 111–113
expiratory maneuver in,
    114
extrinsic, 111–113
heart output increase in,
    114
heart rate increase in, 114
immunologic mechanism in,
    112–113
intrinsic, 111, 113
    beta$_2$-blockade theory of,
        113
intrinsic factors triggering,
    113
lung capacity in, 114
lung function in, 114
lung volume in, 114
management, general,
    116–117
medications in, 117
monitoring in, 117
oxygen in, supplemental,
    117
parasympatholytic agents in,
    117
pulsus paradoxus in,
    115–116
pursed-lip breathing in, 114
references for, 303–304
respiratory rate increase in,
    114
rhonchi in, 13
sputum production in, 115
sympathomimetics in, 117
ventilation in, mechanical,
    117
ventilatory failure with
    hypoxemia in, 115
wheezing in, 13
x-ray in, chest, 116
Asystole, 319
Atelectasis, 319
    in cystic fibrosis, 260
    with lung compression in
        chest anomalies, 196
    in respiratory distress
        syndrome, idiopathic,
        240
Atmospheric pollutants: in
    bronchitis, chronic,
    81–82

Atmospheric pressure, 319
Atopic, 319
Atopic asthma, 111–113
Atrial
    fibrillation, 319
    flutter, 320
Atrophy, 320
Atropine, 320
Auscultation, 8–10
    breath sounds
        bronchial, in lung
            consolidation, 12
        vesicular, 11
    path of, 10
    whispered voice sounds, 14
        in lung consolidation, 15
Automobile accident victim:
    and venous admixture,
    22–23
Autonomic nervous system:
    dysfunction in
    Guillain-Barré
    syndrome, 274
Autosomal recessive trait,
    320
Avoirdupois, 351

B

Bacillus, 320
    diagram of, 125
    Friedländer's, 124
    pyocyaneus, 125
Bacteria, 320
    pneumonia due to (see
        Pneumonia, bacteria
        causing)
Baroreceptors
    aortic, reflexes from, 30,
        148
    aortic sinus, 29
        reflexes from, in
            pulmonary embolism,
            148
    carotid sinus (see Carotid
        sinus baroreceptors)
Barrel chest, 67, 68
    diameter increase in
        bronchitis, chronic, 83
    in emphysema, 94
    increase
        in asthma, 114
        in bronchiectasis, 104
        in cystic fibrosis, 263
Basement membrane, 60
Bedsonia, 320
    pneumonia due to, 127
Behavioral management
    in bronchitis, chronic, 86
    in emphysema, 96
Bernoulli's principle
    dynamic compression
        mechanism in
        obstructive lung disease
        and, 42
    illustration of, 42

Berylliosis: discussion of, 206
Beta-receptor, 320
Beta₂-blockade theory: of
        intrinsic asthma, 113
Bicarbonate, 320
    concentration (*see* HCO₃⁻)
Bifurcation, 320
Biopsy, 320
Black lung, 205
Black phthisis, 205
Blastomyces dermatitidis, 223
Blastomycosis, 223
Bleb, 320
Blood
  -brain barrier, 320
  gases
    abbreviations for, 344
    abnormal, 48–57
    in asthma, 115
    in bronchiectasis, 104
    in bronchitis, chronic, 83
    in cancer of lung, 234
    in cystic fibrosis, 263
    in emphysema, 94
    in epiglottitis, 255
    in flail chest, 169
    in fungal diseases, 224
    in Guillain-Barré
        syndrome, 273
    in kyphoscoliosis, 198
    in laryngotracheobronchi-
        tis, 255
    in myasthenia gravis, 281
    normal, 48
    in pleural effusion, 190
    in pneumoconiosis, 207
    in pneumonia, 129
    in pneumothorax, 179–180
    in pulmonary edema, 138
    in pulmonary embolism,
        148
    in respiratory distress
        syndrome, adult, 161
    in respiratory distress
        syndrome, idiopathic,
        245–247
    in sleep apnea, 290
    in tuberculosis, 216
  pressure
    decrease in asthma, 115
    increase in asthma, 114,
        115–116
    increase in bronchiectasis,
        104
    increase in bronchitis,
        chronic, 82
    increase in cancer of lung,
        234
    increase in cystic fibrosis,
        263
    increase in emphysema,
        94
    increase in epiglottitis,
        255

increase in flail chest, 169
increase in fungal
    diseases, 224
increase in kyphoscoliosis,
    198
increase in
    laryngotracheobronchitis,
    255
increase in pleural
    effusion, 190
increase in
    pneumoconiosis, 207
increase in pneumonia, 129
increase in pneumothorax,
    179
increase in respiratory
    distress syndrome,
    adult, 161
increase in respiratory
    distress syndrome,
    idiopathic, 243
increase in tuberculosis,
    216
in lung disease, 57
systemic, decrease in flail
    chest, 169
systemic, decrease in
    pleural effusion, 190
systemic, decrease in
    pneumothorax, 179
systemic, in lung disease,
    57
symbols for, 343
Bracing: in kyphoscoliosis, 199
Bradykinin, 320
Brain
  -blood barrier, 320
  stem, lower, respiratory
      components of, 27
Breath
  sounds
    abnormal, 11–14
    bronchial, 11–12
    bronchial, auscultation in
        lung consolidation, 12
    diminished, 12
    diminished, in obstructive
        lung disease, 13
    in intrapleural space, 183
    normal, 10–11
    vesicular, auscultation of,
        11
Breathing
  pursed-lip (*see* Pursed-lip
      breathing)
  work of, relationship to lung
      compliance decrease,
      24–27
Bronchi
  airway (*see* Airway,
      bronchial)
  breath sounds, 11–12
    auscultation in lung
        consolidation, 12

carcinoma of lung projecting
    into bronchus, 230
obstruction in
    bronchiectasis, 102
secretion mobilization
    in asthma, 117
    in bronchiectasis, 106
    in bronchitis, chronic, 86
    in cancer of lung, 237
    in cystic fibrosis, 265
    in emphysema, 96
    in Guillain-Barré
        syndrome, 275
    in kyphoscoliosis, 200
    in myasthenia gravis, 283
    techniques, 348
tracheobronchial (*see*
    Tracheobronchial)
Bronchial artery, 60
Bronchial glands, 60
Bronchial vein, 60
Bronchiectasis, 100–109
  accessory muscles in, 104
  acquired, 102
  alveolar hyperventilation
      with hypoxemia in, 104
  anatomic alterations of lungs
      in, 101
  antibiotics in, 107
  barrel chest diameter
      increase in, 104
  blood gases in, 104
  blood pressure increase in,
      104
  bronchial obstruction in, 102
  bronchial secretion
      mobilization in, 106
  bronchodilators in, xanthine,
      107
  bronchography in, 106
  chest assessment in,
      104–105
  clinical manifestations,
      cardiopulmonary,
      overview, 103–106
  congenital, 102
  cor pulmonale in, 104
  cough in, 105
  cyanosis in, 104
  cylindrical, 100, 101
  cystic, 101
  with cystic fibrosis, 102
  digital clubbing in, 104
  etiology, 102
  expectorants in, 107
  expiratory maneuver in, 103
  fusiform, 101
  heart output increase in,
      104
  heart rate increase in, 104
  hemoptysis in, 105
  hypogammaglobulinemia
      and, 102
  infection in, 102

inotropic agents in, positive,
    107
lung capacity in, 103
lung function in, 103
lung volume in, 103
management, general,
    106–107
medications in, 106–107
mucolytic agents in, 106
obstructive, 103, 104
oxygen in, supplemental,
    107
parasympatholytic agents in,
    106
polycythemia in, 104
pursed-lip breathing in, 104
references for, 303
respiratory rate increase in,
    103
restrictive, 103–104, 105
saccular, 100, 101–102
sputum production in, 105
sympathomimetics in, 106
tuberculosis in, pulmonary,
    102
tubular, 101
varicose, 100, 101
ventilatory failure with
    hypoxemia in, 104
x-ray in, chest, 105
Bronchioles, 60
Bronchitis
    chronic, 80–89
        accessory muscles in, 83
        alveolar hyperventilation
            with hypoxemia in, 83
        anatomic alterations of
            lungs in, 81
        antibiotics in, 86
        atmospheric pollutants in,
            81–82
        barrel chest diameter
            increase in, 83
        behavioral management,
            86
        blood gases in, 83
        bronchial secretion
            mobilization in, 86
        bronchodilators in,
            xanthine, 86
        chest assessment in, 83
        cigarette smoking in, 81
        cigarette smoking
            avoidance in, 86
        clinical manifestations,
            cardiopulmonary,
            overview, 82–85
        cor pulmonale in, 83
        cough in, 83
        cyanosis in, 83
        education of patient and
            family in, 85
        etiology, 81–82
        expectorants in, 86

expiratory maneuver in, 82
heart output increase in,
    82
heart rate increase in, 82
infection in, 82, 86
inhaled irritant avoidance
    in, 86
inotropic agents in,
    positive, 86
lung capacity in, 82
lung function in, 82
lung volume in, 82
management, general,
    85–86
medications in, 86
mucolytic agents in, 86
oxygen in, supplemental,
    86
parasympatholytic agents
    in, 86
polycythemia in, 83
pursed-lip breathing in,
    83
references for, 302–303
Reid index increase in,
    84–85
respiratory rate increase
    in, 82
sputum production in, 83
sympathomimetics in, 86
ventilatory failure with
    hypoxemia in, 83
    laryngotracheobronchitis (see
        Laryngotracheobronchi-
        tis)
Bronchoconstriction, 320
Bronchodilation, 320
Bronchodilators, xanthine, 345
    in asthma, 117
    in bronchiectasis, 107
    in bronchitis, chronic, 86
    in cystic fibrosis, 266
    in emphysema, 96
Bronchography, 320
    in bronchiectasis, 106
Bronchoscopy, 321
Bronchospasm, 321
Bulla, 321

C

Camera: scintillation, 337
cAMP, 323
Cancer of lung, 230–238
    (See also Carcinoma of lung)
    alveolar hyperventilation
        with hypoxemia in, 234
    anatomic alterations of lungs
        in, 231–232
    blood gases in, 234
    blood pressure increase in,
        234
    bronchial secretion
        mobilization in, 237

chemotherapy in, 236
chest assessment in, 234
chest expansion decrease in,
    234
clinical manifestations
    cardiopulmonary,
        overview, 233–236
    common nonrespiratory,
        235–236
cough in, 234
cyanosis in, 234
etiology, 232–233
expiratory maneuver in, 233
heart output increase in,
    234
heart rate increase in, 234
hemoptysis in, 234
hyperinflation techniques in,
    237
immunotherapy in, 236
interferon in, 236
lung capacities in, 233–234
lung function in, 233–234
lung volumes in, 233–234
management, general,
    236–237
oxygen in, supplemental,
    237
pain in, chest, 234
radiation in, 236
references for, 313
respiratory care in, 237
respiratory rate increase in,
    233
sputum production in, 234
surgery in, 236
ventilatory failure with
    hypoxemia in, 234
x-ray in, chest, 234–236
Cannulation, 321
Capacity(ies)
    closing, 36
    diffusion
        of carbon monoxide, 37
        decrease in emphysema,
            93
    functional residual (see
        Functional residual
        capacity)
    inspiratory, definition, 31
    lung
        in asthma, 114
        in bronchiectasis, 103
        in bronchitis, chronic, 82
        in cancer of lung,
            233–234
        in cystic fibrosis, 263
        definitions, 31
        in emphysema, 93
        in flail chest, 168
        in fungal diseases, 224
        in Guillain-Barré
            syndrome, 273
        in kyphoscoliosis, 198

command "DATA LIST FILE= file name" in your data management program to call up the raw data file. Since this kind of file only contains a matrix of codes, you need to start by defining and labeling the variables and values in your data management program file. If you have used dBASE or some similar system to create your database file, you can use the command "TRANSLATE FROM FILE= file name" to include the already defined variables. But you still need to define the missing values and add all the labels in your programming. If you have used an SPSS data entry function, you will have a system file ready for use that contains a complete dictionary. You simply use the command "GET FILE= file name" and immediately begin data cleaning and manipulation programming. In all the above commands, "file name" should be replaced with the real name you have given to your data file.

At the end of data management programming, you need to ask the computer to save the cleaned and transformed data in a system file in place of the original data file, no matter what the type is, for the ultimate purpose of data analysis. What you do is to use the command "SAVE OUTFILE= file name" and run through the entire program. You can use a different file name here to avoid overriding the original data file. Although you can write data analysis procedures in the same program, it is advisable to separate the task of data management from the task of data analysis. Each stage may involve more than one program, but it is helpful to put all the data management commands together by compiling and updating a master program.

It should be noted that although you are composing an SPSS or SAS file, you do not have to use the program's editor. As a matter of fact, a word processor like WordPerfect has by far the better editing function. If you do not rely on SPSS/PC+'s menu selection to compile your program, you can always use a word processor to edit your program and then run it on SPSS. Generally speaking, any program or data matrix (other than a dBASE file or a SPSS system file) can be created by a word processor. You must, however, save it in a special type (i.e., ASCII or DOS file) instead of an ordinary text file for it to be executable (in other words, for the computer to be able to read the commands and execute them).

All in all, it is possible for you to have a raw data file created by one of the software programs that is compatible with the statistical package you use (e.g., an ASCII text file, a dBASE file, or an EXCEL file for SPSS/PC+). You must compose a data management program file to contain all the data cleaning and manipulation commands. And you need to save the defined, labeled, cleaned, and

Capacity(ies) (cont.)
    in lung disease,
        obstructive, 47–48
    in lung disease,
        restrictive, 37–38, 39
    in myasthenia gravis, 281
    normal, overview of,
        31–32
    in pleural effusion, 190
    in pneumoconiosis, 206
    in pneumonia, 128
    in pneumothorax, 179
    in pulmonary edema, 138
    in respiratory distress
        syndrome, adult, 161
    in respiratory distress
        syndrome, idiopathic,
        243
    total (see Total lung
        capacity)
    in tuberculosis, 215–216
    vital (see Vital capacity)
Capillary
    -juxtapulmonary receptors,
        30
    permeability increase in
        pulmonary edema, 136
    shunt, 18
Carbon
    dioxide, 321
        tension (see Pa$_{CO_2}$)
        transportation as HCO$_3^-$,
            51
    monoxide, diffusion capacity
        of, 37
Carbonic anhydrase, 51, 52
Carcinoma, 321
Carcinoma of lung, 230–238
    (See also Cancer of lung)
    epidermoid, 230, 232
    large cell, 230, 233
    oat cell, 230, 232
    projecting into bronchus,
        230
    small cell, 230, 232
    squamous cell, 230, 232
Cardiac (see Heart)
Cardiogenic, 321
    pulmonary edema, 135–136
Cardiotonic medications, 321
Care: respiratory (see
        Respiratory care)
Carotid arteries:
        chemosensitive cells
        and baroreceptors on, 29
Carotid sinus baroreceptors,
        321
    on carotid artery, 29
    reflexes, 30
        in pulmonary embolism,
            148
Cartilage: tracheobronchial
        tree, 60
Catecholamines, 321

Catheter: Swan-Ganz, 339
Cavitation, 321
Cell(s)
    goblet, 60
    Kulchitsky, 330
    mast, 331
Central nervous system:
        stimulants in sleep
        apnea, 292
Central venous pressure, 57,
        321
    increase
        in flail chest, 169
        in pleural effusion, 190
        in pneumothorax, 179
Cephalosporin, 347
Cerebrospinal fluid, 321
Chemoreceptor(s), 321
    central, stimulation of,
        27–28
        by hydrogen ions, 28
    peripheral, stimulation of,
        28–30
        in alveolar consolidation,
            49
        in flail chest, 167–168
        in pneumothorax,
            178–179
        in pulmonary embolism,
            146–148
Chemotactic, 322
Chemotherapy: in cancer of
        lung, 236
Chest
    anomalies, lung compression
        with atelectasis in, 196
    assessment, 3–78
        in asthma, 115
        in bronchiectasis,
            104–105
        in bronchitis, chronic, 83
        in cancer of lung, 234
        in cystic fibrosis, 264
        discussion of, 3–16
        in emphysema, 94
        in epiglottitis, 256
        in fungal diseases, 224
        in Guillain-Barré
            syndrome, 273
        in kyphoscoliosis,
            198–199
        in laryngotracheobronchi-
            tis, 256
        in myasthenia gravis, 281
        in pleural effusion, 190
        in pneumoconiosis,
            207–208
        in pneumonia, 129
        in pneumothorax, 182
        in pulmonary edema, 138
        in pulmonary embolism,
            148
        in respiratory distress
            syndrome, adult, 162

        in respiratory distress
            syndrome, idiopathic,
            248
        in tuberculosis, 216
    barrel (see Barrel chest)
    diameter
        anteroposterior (see Barrel
            chest)
        increase in pnemothorax,
            180
        expansion decrease, 70–72
            in cancer of lung, 234
            in fungal diseases, 224
            in pneumoconiosis, 207
            in pneumonia, 130
            in tuberculosis, 216
    flail (see Flail chest)
    landmarks, external, 5
    pain (see Pain, chest)
    vertical lines of, imaginary,
        6
    wall
        parodoxical movement in
            flail chest, 170
        percussion, 7–8
        percussion dull note in
            alveolar consolidation, 9
        percussion of normal
            lung, 9
        percussion, path of, 8
        percussion technique, 7
    x-ray (see X-ray, chest)
Chickenpox: causing
        pneumonia, 128
Children: lung disease,
        references for, 300–301
Chlamydia, 322
    in Guillain-Barré syndrome,
        272
    in pneumonia, 127
Chloramphenicol, 347
Chloride: elevation in sweat in
        cystic fibrosis, 265
Chylothorax: pleural
        separation due to,
        parietal, 189
Cigarette smoking
    avoidance
        in bronchitis, chronic, 86
        in emphysema, 96
    in bronchitis, chronic, 81
    in emphysema, 91–92
Cilia, 322
Circulation
    fetal
        persistent, 247
        in respiratory distress
            syndrome, idiopathic,
            246
    pulmonary, 336
Clavicle, 5
Clindamycin, 347
Clinical manifestations, 3–78,
        322

Closing capacity, 36
Closing volume (CV), 36
  decrease in bronchiectasis,
    103
  increase
    in asthma, 114
    in bronchitis, chronic, 82
    in cystic fibrosis, 263
    in emphysema, 93
    in lung disease,
      obstructive, 47
Clubbing (see Digital clubbing)
CO_2 (see Carbon dioxide)
Coagulation, 322
Coal macules, 205
Coal miner's lung, 205
Coal worker's pneumoconiosis
    (see Pneumoconiosis,
    coal worker's)
Coccidioides immitis, 222
Coccidioidomycosis, 222–223
Coccobacillus, 322
Coccus, 322
Collagen, 322
  vascular disease causing
    pleural effusion, 189
Colloid, 322
Complement-activating
    antibodies: in
    Guillain-Barré
    syndrome, 272
Compliance (see Lung,
    compliance)
Compression
  dynamic, 40–42
  mechanism, dynamic, 41
    activation of, 40–46
    Bernoulli's principle and,
      42
Confusion: in pulmonary
    embolism, 149
Congenital, 322
Continuous positive airway
    pressure: in sleep
    apnea, 293
Contusion, 322
Cor pulmonale, 67–69, 323
  in bronchiectasis, 104
  in bronchitis, chronic, 83
  in cystic fibrosis, 263
  definition, 67
  in emphysema, 94
  in kyphoscoliosis, 198
  in pneumoconiosis, 207
Corticosteroids, 323, 346
  in asthma, 117
  in myasthenia gravis, 282
  in respiratory distress
    syndrome, adult, 163
Costophrenic angle, 323
Cough, 58
  in asthma, 115
  in bronchiectasis, 105
  in bronchitis, chronic, 83

in cancer of lung, 234
in cystic fibrosis, 263
dry, in pleural effusion, 190
in fungal diseases, 224
in kyphoscoliosis, 198
nonproductive, in pleural
    effusion, 190
in pleural effusion, 190
in pneumoconiosis, 207
in pneumonia, 129
in pulmonary edema, 138
in pulmonary embolism, 151
in tuberculosis, 216
Crackles, 12–13
Croup, 252–259
  anatomic alterations of upper
    airway in, 253–254
  definition, 253
  references for, 314
  subglottic (see
    Laryngotracheobronchitis)
  supraglottic (see Epiglottitis,
    acute)
  syndrome, 253–259
CSF (see Cerebrospinal fluid)
Cuirass, 323
CV (see Closing volume)
CVP (see Central venous
    pressure)
Cyanosis, 16–19
  in asthma, 115
  in bronchiectasis, 104
  in bronchitis, chronic, 83
  in cancer of lung, 234
  in cystic fibrosis, 263
  in emphysema, 94
  in epiglottitis, 256
  in flail chest, 170
  in fungal diseases, 224
  in Guillain-Barré syndrome,
    273
  hemoglobin in, 17
  in kyphoscoliosis, 198
  in laryngotracheobronchitis,
    256
  in myasthenia gravis, 281
  in pleural effusion, 190
  in pneumoconiosis, 207
  in pnemonia, 129
  in pneumothorax, 180
  in pulmonary edema, 138
  in pulmonary embolism, 148
  in respiratory distress
    syndrome
    adult, 162
    idiopathic, 248
    in sleep apnea, 290
  in tuberculosis, 216
Cyst, 323
Cystic bronchiectasis, 101
Cystic fibrosis, 260–269
  accessory muscles in, 263
  alveolar hyperventilation
    with hypoxemia in, 263

anatomic alterations of lungs
    in, 261
antibiotics in, 266
barrel chest increase in, 263
blood gases in, 263
blood pressure increase in,
    263
body development in, poor,
    265
bronchial secretion
    mobilization in, 265
  with bronchiectasis, 102
bronchodilators in, xanthine,
    266
chest assessment in, 264
chloride elevation in sweat
    in, 265
clinical manifestations
  cardiopulmonary,
    overview, 262–265
  common nonrespiratory,
    265
cor pulmonale in, 263
cough in, 263
cyanosis in, 263
digital clubbing in, 264
etiology, 261–262
expectorants in, 266
expiratory maneuver in,
    262–263
heart output increase in,
    263
heart rate increase in, 263
lung capacities in, 263
lung function in, 262–263
lung volumes in, 263
malnutrition in, 265
management, general,
    265–266
meconium ileus in, 265
medications in, 265–266
mendelian pattern in,
    standard, 262
mucolytic agents in, 265
oxygen in, supplemental,
    266
pancreatic enzymes in, 266
parasympatholytic agents in,
    265
polycythemia in, 263
pursed-lip breathing in,
    263
references for, 314–315
respiratory rate increase in,
    262
salt in, 266
sodium elevation in sweat
    in, 265
sputum production in, 263
sympathomimetics in, 265
ventilatory failure with
    hypoxemia in, 263
x-ray in, chest, 264
Cytoplasm, 323

D

Dead space
  alveolar, 19
  anatomic, 19
  physiologic, 19
    calculation, 349
  ventilation, 19
Decubitus x-ray, 323
Deflation reflex, 30
Deformities (*see* Anomalies)
Demyelination, 323
Deoxyribonucleic acid, 323
"Desert arthritis," 223
"Desert bumps," 223
"Desert rheumatism," 223
Diabetes mellitus, 323
Dialysis, peritoneal, 334
  causing pleural effusion, 188
Diastole, 324
Diffusion capacity (*see*
    Capacity, diffusion)
Digital clubbing, 70
  in bronchiectasis, 104
  in cystic fibrosis, 264
  in emphysema, 94
  in pneumoconiosis, 207
Dilator naris: in idiopathic
    respiratory distress
    syndrome, 244
Dimorphism, 324
Diplococcus pneumoniae:
    causing pneumonia, 123
Diuretics, 348
  in pulmonary edema, 141
  in respiratory distress
    syndrome, adult, 163
DNA, 323
Driving pressure, 324
Drugs (*see* Medications)
Ductus arteriosus, 324
Dynamic compression (*see*
    Compression, dynamic)
Dynamometer, 324
Dysplasia, 324
Dyspnea, 324
  paroxysmal nocturnal, in
    pulmonary edema,
    138–139

E

Edema, 324
Edema, pulmonary, 134–143
  albumin in, 141
  alcohol in, 141
  alveolar hyperventilation
    with hypoxemia in, 138
  anatomic alterations of lungs
    in, 135
  blood gases in, 138
  capillary permeability
    increase in, 136
  cardiogenic, 135–136, 139
  chest assessment in, 138

clinical manifestations,
    cardiopulmonary,
    overview, 137–139
  cough in, 138
  cyanosis in, 138
  diuretics in, 141
  dyspnea in, paroxysmal
    nocturnal, 138–139
  etiology, 135–137
  frothy, 134
  with heart failure, 140
  hydrostatic pressure
    increase in, 136
  hydrostatic pressure in,
    methods for decreasing,
    141
  hyperinflation techniques in,
    139
  inotropic agents in, positive,
    141
  interstitial, 134
  intrapleural pressure
    decrease in, 137
  lung capacities in, 138
  lung function in, 138
  lung volumes in, 138
  lymphatic insufficiency in,
    136
  management, general,
    139–141
  medications for, 141
  morphine sulfate in, 141
  noncardiogenic, 136–137,
    139
  oncotic pressure decrease
    in, 137
  oxygen in, supplemental,
    139–141
  pleural effusion in, 138
  pulmonary wedge pressure
    increase in, 139
  references for, 306–307
  respiratory rate increase in,
    137
  sputum in, frothy, 138
  sympathomimetics in, 141
  ventilatory failure with
    hypoxemia in, 138
  x-ray in, chest, 139
Effusion, 324
  pleural (*see* Pleural effusion)
Elastase, 324
  in emphysema, 92
Electrical stimulation: in
    kyphoscoliosis, 200
Electrocardiography, 324
  abnormalities in pulmonary
    embolism, 150
Electrolyte, 324
Electromyography, 325
Electrophoresis, 325
Embolectomy: pulmonary,
    154
Embolism, 325

Embolism, pulmonary,
    144–157
  alveolar hyperventilation
    with hypoxemia in, 148
  anatomic alterations of lungs
    in, 145
  angiography of, pulmonary,
    152, 154
  aortic sinus baroreceptor
    reflexes in, 148
  blood gases in, 148
  carotid sinus baroreceptor
    reflexes in, 148
  chemoreceptor stimulation
    in, peripheral, 146–148
  chest assessment in, 148
  clinical manifestations,
    cardiopulmonary,
    overview, 146–153
  confusion in, 149
  cough in, 151
  cyanosis in, 148
  ECG abnormalities in, 150
  etiology, 145–146
  heart rate increase in,
    149–150
  heart sound abnormalities
    in, 150–151
  hemoptysis in, 151
  hypertension in, pulmonary,
    148–149
  hypotension in, systemic, 149
  light-headedness in, 149
  lung imaging abnormalities
    in, 152
  management, 153–154
  pain in, chest, 152
  pleural effusion in, 148, 188
  preventive measures, 153
  pulmonary vascular system
    in, 149
  references for, 307–308
  respiratory rate increase in,
    146–148
  S_2 split in, 16
  syncope in, 149
  thrombolytics in, 154
  vasoconstriction in
    alveolar hypoxia causing,
    149
    humoral agents causing,
    149
  venous admixture in, 147
  ventilatory failure with
    hypoxemia in, 148
  ventricle in, right, 151
  ventricular gallop in, 151
  x-ray in, chest, 152
Emphysema, 91–99
  accessory muscles in, 94
  alpha$_1$-antitrypsin deficiency
    in, 92–93
  alveolar hyperventilation
    with hypoxemia in, 94

anatomic alterations of lungs in, 91
antibiotics in, 97
barrel chest in, 94
behavioral management in, 96
blood gases in, 94
blood pressure increase in, 94
bronchial secretion mobilization in, 96
bronchodilators in, xanthine, 96
centrilobular, 91, 92
chest assessment in, 94
cigarette smoking in, 91–92
    avoidance of, 96
clinical manifestations, cardiopulmonary, overview, 93–95
cor pulmonale in, 94
cyanosis in, 94
diffusion capacity decrease in, 93
digital clubbing in, 94
education of patient and family in, 95–96
elastase in, 92
etiology, 91–93
expectorants in, 97
expiratory maneuver in, 93
focal, in coal worker's pneumoconiosis, 205
heart output increase in, 94
heart rate increase in, 94
infection in, 93, 96
inhaled irritants in, 93
    avoidance of, 96
inotropic agents in, positive, 97
lung capacity in, 93
lung function in, 93
lung volume in, 93
management, general, 95–97
medications in, 96–97
nutrition in, proper, 96
oxygen in, supplemental, 97
panlobular, 90, 91
parasympatholytic agents in, 96
polycythemia in, 94
pursed-lip breathing in, 94
references for, 302–303
respiratory rate increase in, 93
sympathomimetics in, 96
ventilatory failure with hypoxemia in, 94
x-ray in, chest, 94–95
Empyema, 325
    pleural separation due to, 189
Encephalitis, 325

Endocarditis, 325
Endothelium, 325
Endotracheal intubation
    in epiglottitis, 257
    in laryngotracheobronchitis, 257
English system length conversions, 352
Enuresis, 325
Environmental control: in asthma, 116–117
Enzyme, 325
Eosinophil, 325
Epidemiology, 325
Epiglottitis, 252–259
    accessory muscles in, 256
    acute, 253–259
        anatomic alterations of upper airway in, 254
        etiology, 254–255
    aerosol mist in, cool, 257
    alveolar hyperventilation with hypoxemia in, 255
    antibiotics in, 257
    blood gases in, 255
    blood pressure increase in, 255
    chest assessment in, 256
    clinical manifestations, overview, 255–256
    cyanosis in, 256
    edematous, classic "thumb sign" in, 257
    endotracheal intubation in, 257
    heart output increase in, 255
    heart rate increase in, 255
    history, 255
    management, general, 256–257
    oxygen in, supplemental, 256
    physical findings, 255
    references for, 314
    respiratory rate increase in, 255
    sternal intercostal retractions in, 256
    stridor in, inspiratory, 256
    ventilatory failure with hypoxemia in, 255
    x-ray in, neck, 256
Epinephrine, 325
    racemic, in laryngotracheobronchitis and epiglottitis, 257
Epithelium, 325
Equal-pressure point, 40
Equation
    airway resistance, in obstructive lung disease, 46
    gas, alveolar, ideal, 349
    shunt, 21
        classic, 21

ERV (see Expiratory reserve volume)
Erythema multiforme, 325
Erythromycin, 347
Erythropoiesis, 326
Ethambutol: in tuberculosis, 218
Ethanol: in pulmonary edema, 141
Ethyl alcohol: in pulmonary edema, 141
Exocrine gland, 326
Expectorants, 346
    in bronchiectasis, 107
    in bronchitis, chronic, 86
    in cystic fibrosis, 266
    in emphysema, 97
Expectoration, 326
Expiration: muscles during, accessory, 64–67, 68
Expiratory flow
    forced (see Forced expiratory flow)
    peak rate (see Peak expiratory flow rate)
    rate measurements, overview of, 32–37
Expiratory grunting: in idiopathic respiratory distress syndrome, 244–245
Expiratory maneuver, 38–47
    in asthma, 114
    in bronchiectasis, 103
    in bronchitis, chronic, 82
    in cancer of lung, 233
    in cystic fibrosis, 262–263
    in emphysema, 93
    forced (see Forced expiratory maneuver)
    in lung disease, obstructive, 38–47
    in pneumoconiosis, 207
Expiratory reserve volume (ERV) decrease
    in asthma, 114
    in bronchiectasis, 103
    in bronchitis, chronic, 82
    in cystic fibrosis, 263
    in emphysema, 93
    in lung disease, obstructive, 47
Expiratory volume, forced (see Forced expiratory volume)
Exudate, 326

F

Fascia, 326
Fatigue: in idiopathic respiratory distress syndrome, 247
Febrile, 326

FEF (*see* Forced expiratory flow)
Fetus (*see* Circulation, fetal)
FEV (*see* Forced expiratory volume)
Fibrillation: atrial, 319
Fibrin, 326
Fibrinolytic, 326
Fibroelastic, 326
Fibrosis, 326
    cystic (*see* Cystic fibrosis)
Fissure, 326
Fistula, 326
Flail chest, 166–173
    alveolar hyperventilation with hypoxemia in, 169
    alveoli in, 166
    anatomic alterations of lungs in, 167
    blood gases in, 169
    blood pressure in
        increase, 169
        systemic, decrease in, 169
    central venous pressure increase in, 169
    chemoreceptor stimulation in, peripheral, 167–168
    chest wall paradoxical movement in, 170
    clinical manifestations, cardiopulmonary, overview, 167–170
    cyanosis in, 170
    etiology, 167
    heart output increase in, 169
    heart rate increase in, 169
    lung capacities in, 168
    lung function in, 168
    lung volumes in, 168
    management, general, 170–171
    oxygen in, supplemental, 171
    references for, 309–311
    respiratory rate increase in, 167–170
    rib fracture in, 166
    venous admixture in, 169
    ventilatory failure with hypoxemia in, 169
    x-ray in, chest, 170
Flare, 326
Flora: normal, 333
Flourescent antibody microscopy, 326
Flow
    expiratory (*see* Expiratory flow)
    Poiseuille's law for, 42–43, 44, 352–353
    -volume loop, 36
        information obtained from test, 36

    normal, 37
    obstructive pattern, 38
    restrictive pattern, 39
Foramen ovale, 326
Forced expiratory capacity:
    increase in asthma, 114
Forced expiratory flow (FEF)
    in sleep apnea, 290
    25%–75%, 33–34
        decrease in asthma, 114
        decrease in bronchiectasis, 103
        decrease in bronchitis, chronic, 82
        decrease in cancer of lung, 233
        decrease in cystic fibrosis, 262
        decrease in emphysema, 93
        decrease in obstructive lung disease, 38
        decrease in pneumoconiosis, 207
    200–1200, 32–33, 34
        decrease in asthma, 114
        decrease in bronchiectasis, 103
        decrease in bronchitis, chronic, 82
        decrease in cancer of lung, 233
        decrease in cystic fibrosis, 262
        decrease in pneumoconiosis, 207
Forced expiratory maneuver
    effort-dependent portion, 40, 41
    effort-independent portion, 40, 41
Forced expiratory volume
    /forced vital capacity ratio
        decrease
            in asthma, 114
            in bronchiectasis, 103
            in bronchitis, chronic, 82
            in cancer of lung, 233
            in cystic fibrosis, 262
            in emphysema, 93
            in pneumoconiosis, 207
    in 1 second
        decrease in obstructive lung disease, 38
        forced vital capacity ratio, 35
    timed, 32, 33
        decrease in asthma, 114
        decrease in bronchiectasis, 103
        decrease in bronchitis, chronic, 82
        decrease in cancer of lung, 233

    decrease in cystic fibrosis, 262
    decrease in emphysema, 93
    decrease in obstructive lung disease, 38
    decrease in pneumoconiosis, 207
Forced inspiratory flow: in sleep apnea, 290
Forced vital capacity (FVC) 31, 32, 33
    decrease
        in asthma, 114
        in bronchiectasis, 103
        in bronchitis, chronic, 82
        in cancer of lung, 233
        in cystic fibrosis, 262
        in emphysema, 93
        in lung disease, obstructive, 38
        in pneumoconiosis, 207
    /FEV ratio (*see* Forced expiratory volume/forced vital capacity ratio)
Fossa, 326
Fracture: of rib in flail chest, 166
FRC (*see* Functional residual capacity)
Fremitus
    tactile, 6
        path of, 7
    vocal, 6
        path of, 7
Friedländer's bacillus, 124
Functional residual capacity (FRC), 32
    decrease
        in bronchiectasis, restrictive, 103
        in cancer of lung, 233
        in flail chest, 168
        in fungal diseases, 224
        in Gullain-Barré syndrome, 273
        in kyphoscoliosis, 198
        in lung disease, restrictive, 37–38
        in myasthenia gravis, 281
        in pleural effusion, 190
        in pneumoconiosis, 206
        in pneumonia, 128
        in pneumothorax, 179
        in pulmonary edema, 138
        in respiratory distress syndrome, adult, 161
        in respiratory distress syndrome, idiopathic, 243
        in sleep apnea, 290
        in tuberculosis, 216

increase
  in bronchiectasis, 103
  in bronchitis, chronic, 82
  in cystic fibrosis, 263
  in emphysema, 93
  in lung disease,
    obstructive, 47
Fungal diseases, 221–228
  alveolar hyperventilation
    with hypoxemia in, 224
  anatomic alterations of lungs
    in, 221
  antifungal agents in,
    225–226
  decrease in emphysema,
    93
  decrease in obstructive
    lung disease, 38
  blood gases in, 224
  blood pressure increase in,
    224
  chest assessment in, 224
  chest expansion decrease in,
    224
  clinical manifestations,
    cardiopulmonary,
    overview, 223–225
  cough in, 224
  cyanosis in, 224
  etiology, 221–223
  heart output increase in,
    224
  heart rate increase in, 224
  hemoptysis in, 224
  lung capacities in, 224
  lung function in, 224
  lung volumes in, 224
  management, general,
    225–226
  medications in, 225–226
  oxygen in, supplemental,
    226
  pain in, chest, 224
  pleural effusion in, 188, 224
  references for, 313
  respiratory rate increase in,
    223–224
  sputum production in, 224
  ventilatory failure with
    hypoxemia in, 224
  x-ray in, chest, 225
Fungus: dimorphic, 324
FVC (see Forced vital
  capacity)

G

Galactosemia, 326
Gas(es)
  blood (see Blood gases)
  equation, alveolar, ideal,
    349
  symbols for, 343
  tension, 339

Gastric juice, 327
Gastrointestinal tract disease:
    causing pleural effusion,
    189
Genioglossus muscle: in
    obstructive sleep apnea,
    284
Genus, 327
Globulin, 327
Glossary, 317–342
Glossopharyngeal nerve, 327
Glycolysis, 327
Glycoprotein, 327
Goblet cell, 60
Grunting: expiratory, in
    idiopathic respiratory
    distress syndrome,
    244–245
Guillain-Barré syndrome,
    270–277
  anatomic alterations in, 271
  autonomic nervous system
    dysfunction in, 274
  blood gases in, 273
  bronchial secretion
    mobilization in, 275
  chest assessment in, 273
  clinical manifestations
    cardiopulmonary,
    overview, 273–274
    noncardiopulmonary,
    common, 272–273
  complement-activating
    antibodies in, 272
  cyanosis in, 273
  etiology, 271–272
  hyperinflation techniques in,
    275
  lung capacities in, 273
  lung function in, 273
  lung volumes in, 273
  management, general,
    274–275
  oxygen in, supplemental,
    275
  plasmapheresis in, 274–275
  references for, 316
  ventilatory failure with
    hypoxemia in, 273
  x-ray in, chest, 273–274

H

HCO$_3^-$
  in carbon dioxide
    transportation, 51
  decrease
    in alveolar
      hyperventilation,
      50–52
    in asthma, early stages,
      115
    in bronchiectasis, early
      stages, 104

  in bronchitis, chronic,
    early stages, 83
  in cancer of lung, early
    stages, 234
  in cystic fibrosis, early
    stages, 263
  in emphysema, early
    stages, 94
  in epiglottitis, early
    stages, 255
  in flail chest, early stages,
    169
  in fungal diseases, early
    stages, 224
  in kyphoscoliosis, early
    stages, 198
  in laryngotracheobronchi-
    tis, early stages, 255
  in pleural effusion, early
    stages, 190
  in pneumoconiosis, early
    stages, 207
  in pneumonia, early
    stages, 129
  in pneumothorax, early
    stages, 179
  in pulmonary edema,
    early stages, 138
  in pulmonary embolism,
    early stages, 148
  in respiratory distress
    syndrome, adult, early
    stages, 161
  in tuberculosis, early
    stages, 216
  increase
    in asthma, advanced
      stages, 115
    in bronchiectasis,
      advanced stages, 104
    in bronchitis, chronic,
      advanced stages, 83
    in cancer of lung,
      advanced stages, 234
    in cystic fibrosis,
      advanced stages, 263
    in emphysema, advanced
      stages, 94
    in epiglottitis, advanced
      stages, 255
    in flail chest, advanced
      stages, 169
    in fungal diseases,
      advanced stages, 224
    in Guillain-Barré
      syndrome, 273
    in kyphoscoliosis,
      advanced stages, 198
    in laryngotracheobronchi-
      tis, advanced stages,
      255
    in myasthenia gravis, 281
    in pleural effusion,
      advanced stages, 190

HCO₃⁻ *(cont.)*
  in pneumoconiosis,
    advanced stages, 207
  in pneumonia, advanced
    stages, 129
  in pneumothorax,
    advanced stages, 180
  in pulmonary edema,
    advanced stages, 138
  in pulmonary embolism,
    advanced stages, 148
  in respiratory distress
    syndrome, adult,
    advanced stages, 161
  in respiratory distress
    syndrome, idiopathic,
    245, 247
  in sleep apnea, 290
  in tuberculosis, advanced
    stages, 216
  in ventilatory failure,
    acute, 53
  in ventilatory failure,
    chronic, 55
  relationships of, 50–52, 53
Heart
  arrhythmia in sleep apnea,
    291
  failure
    congestive, causing
      pleural effusion,
      187–188
    with pulmonary edema,
      140
  output
    increase in asthma, 114
    increase in bronchiectasis,
      104
    increase in bronchitis,
      chronic, 82
    increase in cancer of lung,
      234
    increase in cystic fibrosis,
      263
    increase in emphysema,
      94
    increase in epiglottitis,
      255
    increase in flail chest, 169
    increase in fungal
      diseases, 224
    increase in kyphoscoliosis,
      198
    increase in
      laryngotracheobronchitis,
      255
    increase in pleural
      effusion, 190
    increase in
      pneumoconiosis, 207
    increase in pneumonia,
      129
    increase in pneumothorax,
      179

  increase in respiratory
    distress syndrome,
    adult, 161
  increase in respiratory
    distress syndrome,
    idiopathic, 243
  increase in tuberculosis,
    216
  in lung disease, 57
  patterns in sleep, 285–286
  rate
    increase in asthma, 114
    increase in bronchiectasis,
      104
    increase in bronchitis,
      chronic, 82
    increase in cancer of lung,
      234
    increase in cystic fibrosis,
      263
    increase in emphysema,
      94
    increase in epiglottitis,
      255
    increase in flail chest, 169
    increase in fungal
      diseases, 224
    increase in kyphoscoliosis,
      198
    increase in
      laryngotracheobronchitis,
      255
    increase in pleural
      effusion, 190
    increase in
      pneumoconiosis, 207
    increase in pneumonia,
      129
    increase in pneumothorax,
      179
    increase in pulmonary
      embolism, 149–150
    increase in respiratory
      distress syndrome,
      adult, 161
    increase in respiratory
      distress syndrome,
      idiopathic, 243
    increase in tuberculosis,
      216
  in lung disease, 57
  sounds *(see* Sounds, heart)
Hematocrit, 327
Hematopoiesis, 327
Hemoglobin: in cyanosis, 17
Hemophilus influenzae
  B in acute epiglottitis, 254
  in bronchiectasis, 105
  in bronchitis, chronic, 83
  pneumonia due to, 125
Hemoptysis, 61, 327
  in bronchiectasis, 105
  in cancer of lung, 234
  in fungal diseases, 224

  in pneumonia, 129
  in pulmonary embolism, 151
  in tuberculosis, 216
Hemorrhage, 327
Hemothorax: pleural
    separation due to,
    parietal, 189
Heparin, 327
Hepatic hydrothorax: causing
    pleural effusion, 188
Hepatosplenomegaly, 327
Heterozygote, 327
Hilus, 327
Histamine, 327
Histoplasma capsulatum,
    221–222
  spore in alveolus, 220
Histoplasmosis, 221–222
  disseminated, 222
  latent asymptomatic, 222
  self-limiting primary, 222
  x-ray in, chest, 225–226
Homozygote, 328
Hormone, 328
  adrenocorticotropic, 317
    in myasthenia gravis, 282
Household measurement
    equivalents, 351
Humoral, 328
  agents causing
    vasoconstriction in
    pulmonary embolism,
    149
Hyaline membrane: in IRDS,
    240
Hydrogen ions: stimulating
    central chemoreceptors,
    28
Hydropneumothorax
  after thoracentesis in pleural
    effusion, 191
  x-ray in, chest, 191
Hydrostatic, 328
Hydrostatic pressure
  decreasing, methods for,
    141
  increase in pulmonary
    edema, 136
Hydrothorax: hepatic, causing
    pleural effusion, 188
Hydrous, 328
Hypercapnea, 328
Hypercarbia, 328
Hypercoagulation, 328
Hyperinflation, 328
  alveolar *(see* Alveoli,
    hyperinflation)
  techniques, 348–349
    in cancer of lung, 237
    in Guillain-Barré
      syndrome, 275
    in kyphoscoliosis, 200
    in myasthenia gravis, 283
    in pleural effusion, 193

in pneumonia, 130
in pulmonary edema, 139
in respiratory distress
    syndrome, adult, 162
Hyperplasia, 328
Hyperpnea, 328
Hyperresonant percussion
    note, 8
    in alveolar hyperinflation,
        10
    in pneumothorax, 182
Hypertension, 328
    in pulmonary embolism,
        148–149
Hypertrophy, 328
Hyperventilation, 328
    alveolar (see Alveoli,
        hyperventilation)
Hypogammaglobulinemia: and
    bronchiectasis, 102
Hypoperfusion, 328
Hyperproteinemia, 328
Hypotension: systemic, in
    pulmonary embolism,
        149
Hypoventilation, 328
    alveolar, 54
Hypoxemia, 328
    with alveolar
        hyperventilation (see
        Alveoli,
        hyperventilation with
        hypoxemia)
    with ventilatory failure (see
        Ventilation, failure with
        hypoxemia)
Hypoxia, 328
    alveolar, causing
        vasoconstriction in
        pulmonary embolism,
        149
    with vasoconstriction, 69

I

Iatrogenic, 328
Iatrogenic pneumothorax, 175,
    177
IC: definition, 31
Idiopathic, 329
Idiopathic respiratory distress
    syndrome (see
    Respiratory distress
    syndrome, idiopathic)
Ileocecal valve, 329
Ileus, meconium, 331
    in cystic fibrosis, 265
Imaging: lung, perfusion,
    abnormalities in
    pulmonary embolism,
    152
Immunoglobulin, 329
Immunologic mechanism, 329
    in asthma, 112–113

Immunotherapy, 329
    in cancer of lung, 236
Incubation period, 329
Infant, respiratory distress
    syndrome (see
    Respiratory distress
    syndrome, idiopathic)
Infarction, 319
    myocardial, 332
Infection
    in bronchiectasis, 102
    in bronchitis, chronic, 82, 86
    in emphysema, 93, 96
Influenza virus
    in pneumonia, 126
INH: in tuberculosis, 218
Inhaled irritants
    in bronchitis, chronic, 86
    in emphysema, 93, 96
Inotropic agents, positive, 329,
    348
    in bronchiectasis, 107
    in bronchitis, chronic, 86
    in emphysema, 97
    in pulmonary edema, 141
Inspection, 4–6
Inspiration: muscles during,
    accessory, 61–64
Inspiratory capacity:
    definition, 31
Inspiratory flow: forced, in
    sleep apnea, 290
Inspiratory reserve volume
    (IRV)
    decrease
        in asthma, 114
        in bronchiectasis, 103
        in bronchitis, chronic, 82
        in cystic fibrosis, 263
        in emphysema, 93
        in lung disease,
            obstructive, 47
    definition, 31
Inspiratory stridor (see Stridor,
    inspiratory)
Intercostal retraction, 72–73,
    329
    (See also Sternal intercostal
        retractions)
Interferon: in cancer of lung,
    236
Interstitial, 329
Intrapleural pressure, 329
    decrease in pulmonary
        edema, 137
    negative, increase in
        idiopathic respiratory
        distress syndrome,
        243–244
Intrapleural space
    breath sounds in, 183
    in pneumothorax, 180
Intubation (see Endotracheal
    intubation)

Iodine, 329
Ion, 329
Irritants (see Inhaled irritants)
IRV (see Inspiratory reserve
    volume)
Ischemia, 329
Isoniazid: in tuberculosis, 218
Isotope, 330
IVC, 329

J

J receptors, 30
Juxtapulmonary-capillary
    receptors, 30

K

Kartagener's syndrome, 102
Kerley lines, 330
    B, 140
Kinetic, 330
Klebsiella pneumoniae,
    124–125
Kulchitsky cell, 330
Kyphoscoliosis, 197–201
    alveolar hyperventilation
        with hypoxemia in, 198
    anatomic alterations of lungs
        in, 197
    blood gases in, 198
    blood pressure increase in,
        198
    bracing in, 199
    bronchial secretion
        mobilization in, 200
    chest assessment in,
        198–199
    clinical manifestations,
        cardiopulmonary,
        overview, 197–199
    cor pulmonale in, 198
    cough in, 198
    cyanosis in, 198
    electrical stimulation in,
        200
    etiology, 197
    heart output increase in,
        198
    heart rate increase in, 198
    hyperinflation techniques in,
        200
    lung capacities in, 198
    lung function in, 198
    lung volumes in, 198
    management, general,
        199–200
    oxygen in, supplemental,
        200
    polycythemia in, 198
    references for, 312
    respiratory rate increase in,
        197–198
    sputum production in, 198
    surgery of, 200

Kyphoscoliosis *(cont.)*
  ventilatory failure with
      hypoxemia in, 198
  x-ray in, chest, 199
Kyphosis: definition, 197

L

Lactic acid, 330
Lactic acidosis, 57
Lamina propria, 60
Landmarks: external, 5
Laryngotracheobronchitis,
    253–259
  accessory muscles in, 256
  aerosol mist in, cool, 257
  alveolar hyperventilation
      with hypoxemia in, 255
  anatomic alterations of
      upper airway in, 253
  antibiotics in, 257
  blood gases in, 255
  blood pressure increase in,
      255
  chest assessment in, 256
  clinical manifestations,
      overview, 255–256
  cyanosis in, 256
  endotracheal intubation in,
      257
  etiology, 254
  heart output increase in,
      255
  heart rate increase in, 255
  history, 255
  management, general,
      256–257
  oxygen in, supplemental,
      256
  physical findings, 255
  respiratory rate increase in,
      255
  sternal intercostal
      retractions in, 256
  stridor in, inspiratory, 256
  ventilatory failure with
      hypoxemia in, 255
  x-ray in, neck, 256
Law *(see* Poiseuille's law)
Legionella pneumonia, 126
Length
  conversions, 352
  English system, 352
  metric, 351, 352
Lethargy, 330
Leukocytes, 330
  polymorphonuclear, 335
Leukopenia, 330
Ligamentum nuchae, 330
Light-headedness: in
      pulmonary embolism,
      149
Linea alba, 330
Lipid, 330

Lipoid pneumonitis: and
    pneumonia, 128
Lipid
  measure, 350
  metric, 350
Lubb-dub sounds: of heart,
    origin of, 15
Lumen, 330
Lung
  (See also Pulmonary)
  abscess with pleural
      effusion, 192
  adenocarcinoma, 230, 232
  anatomic alterations
    in asthma, 111
    in bronchiectasis, 101
    in bronchitis, chronic, 81
    in cancer of lung,
        231–232
    in cystic fibrosis, 261
    in emphysema, 91
    in flail chest, 167
    in fungal diseases, 221
    in kyphoscoliosis, 197
    in pleural effusion, 187
    in pneumoconiosis,
        203–204
    in pneumonia, 123
    in pneumothorax, 175
    in pulmonary edema, 135
    in pulmonary embolism,
        145
    in respiratory distress
        syndrome, adult,
        159–160
    in respiratory distress
        syndrome, idiopathic,
        241–242
    in tuberculosis, 213
  black, 205
  cancer *(see* Cancer of lung)
  capacity *(see under*
      Capacity)
  carcinoma *(see* Carcinoma of
      lung)
  coal miner's, 205
  compliance
    decrease, relationship to
        work of breathing,
        24–27
    decrease, in ventilatory
        frequency and tidal
        volume, 26
    decrease, in
        volume-pressure curve,
        26
    increase, in
        volume-pressure curve,
        26
    in ventilatory patterns,
        24–27
  compression with atelectasis
      in chest anomalies,
      196

  consolidation
    bronchial breath sounds
        in, auscultation of, 12
    whispered voice sounds
        in, auscultation of, 15
  disease, 2
  disease, obstructive
    air trapping in, 13
    airway resistance equation
        in, 46
    alveolar hyperinflation in,
        13
    Bernoulli's principle and,
        42
    compression mechanism
        and, dynamic, 40–46
    lung capacities in, 47–48
    lung function in, 31–37
    lung volumes in, 47–48
    Poiseuille's law and, 42–46
  disease, references for,
      299–300
  disease, restrictive
    lung capacities in, 37–38,
        39
    lung function in, 31–37
    lung volumes in, 37–38,
        39
  function
    in asthma, 114
    in bronchiectasis, 103
    in bronchitis, chronic, 82
    in cancer of lung,
        233–234
    in cystic fibrosis, 262–263
    in emphysema, 93
    in flail chest, 168
    in fungal diseases, 224
    in Guillain-Barré
        syndrome, 273
    in kyphoscoliosis, 198
    in lung disease,
        obstructive, 31–37
    in lung disease,
        obstructive, expiratory
        maneuver, 38–47
    in lung disease,
        obstructive, lung
        volumes and capacities,
        47–48
    in lung disease,
        restrictive, 31–37
    in lung disease,
        restrictive, volumes and
        capacities, 37–38
    in myasthenia gravis, 281
    in pleural effusion, 190
    in pneumoconiosis,
        206–207
    in pneumonia, 128
    in pneumothorax, 179
    in pulmonary edema, 138
    in respiratory distress
        syndrome, adult, 161

in respiratory distress
    syndrome, idiopathic, 243
in sleep apnea, 290
in tuberculosis, 215–216
fungal diseases (see Fungal
    diseases)
imaging, perfusion,
    abnormalities in
    pulmonary embolism,
    152
landmarks, external, 5
normal, 60
patterns in sleep, 285–286
volumes (see under
    Volumes)
Lymph, 330
Lymph node, 331
Lymphangitis carcinomatosa,
    330
Lymphatic insufficiency: in
    pulmonary edema, 136
Lymphatic vessels, 331
Lymphocyte: in Guillain-Barré
    syndrome, 270

M

Macrophage, 331
    in Guillain-Barré syndrome,
        270
    in respiratory distress
        syndrome, idiopathic,
        240
Malnutrition: in cystic fibrosis,
    265
Mandibular advancement: in
    sleep apnea, 293
Manubrium, 5
Mast cell, 331
Mathematics, 352–353
Measles: causing pneumonia,
    128
Measurements: units of,
    350–352
Mechanoreceptor, 331
Meconium ileus, 331
    in cystic fibrosis, 265
Medications
    in asthma, 117
    in bronchiectasis, 106–107
    in bronchitis, chronic, 86
    cardiotonic, 321
    in cystic fibrosis, 265–266
    in emphysema, 96–97
    in fungal diseases, 225–226
    in myasthenia gravis, 282
    in pneumonia, 131
    in pulmonary edema, 141
    in respiratory distress
        syndrome, adult, 163
    in sleep apnea, 292
    in tuberculosis, 217–218
Mendelian pattern: standard,
    in cystic fibrosis, 262

Meningitis, 331
Mesothelioma, 331
    malignant, causing pleural
        effusion, 188
Metaplasia, 331
Methylphenidate: in sleep
    apnea, 292
Methylxanthine, 331
Metric length, 351, 352
Metric liquid, 350
Metric volume, 351
Metric weight, 350, 351
Metronidazole, 347
Micronefrin: in
    laryngotracheobronchitis
    and epiglottitis, 257
Microscopy: fluorescent
    antibody, 326
Microvilli, 331
Miner's phthisis, 205
Mitosis, 331
Mitral valve, 331
Monitoring: in asthma, 117
Mononucleosis, 331
Morphine sulfate: in
    pulmonary edema, 141
Mucociliary clearing action,
    332
Mucolytic agents
    in bronchiectasis, 106
    in bronchitis, chronic, 86
    in cystic fibrosis, 265
Mucus, 332
    accumulation in cystic
        fibrosis, 260
    -controlling agents, 346
    plugging in cystic fibrosis,
        260
    production in asthma, 13
Muscle(s)
    accessory
        in asthma, 114
        in bronchiectasis, 104
        in bronchitis, chronic, 83
        in cystic fibrosis, 263
        in emphysema, 94
        in epiglottitis, 256
        during expiration, 64–67,
            68
        during inspiration, 61–64
        in laryngotracheobronchi-
            tis, 256
    fiber
        in Guillain-Barré
            syndrome, 270
        in myasthenia gravis, 278
    genioglossus, in obstructive
        sleep apnea, 284
    oblique
        external, 64–65
        internal, 65–66
    pectoralis major, 62–63, 64
    rectus abdominis, 64
    scalene, 62

smooth, 338
sternocleidomastoid, 62, 63
transversus abdominis,
    66–67
trapezius, 63–64, 65
Myambutol: in tuberculosis,
    218
Myasthenia gravis, 278–283
    ACTH in, 282
    anatomic alterations in, 279
    blood gases in, 281
    bronchial secretion
        mobilization in, 283
    chest assessment in, 281
    clinical manifestations
        cardiopulmonary,
            overview, 281–282
        noncardiopulmonary,
            common, 280–281
    corticosteroids in, 282
    cyanosis in, 281
    etiology, 279–280
    hyperinflation techniques in,
        283
    lung capacities in, 281
    lung function in, 281
    lung volumes in, 281
    management, general,
        282–283
    medications in, 282
    oxygen in, supplemental,
        283
    references for, 315
    thymectomy in, 282–283
    ventilatory failure with
        hypoxemia in, 281
    x-ray in, chest, 281–282
Mycobacterium: in
    tuberculosis, 214, 215
Mycoplasma
    in Guillain-Barré syndrome,
        272
    pleural effusion due to, 188
    pneumonia due to, 127
Myelin, 332
    in Guillain-Barré syndrome,
        270
Myelinated nerve fiber (see
    Nerve, myelinated
    fiber)
Myeloma, 332
Myocardial infarction, 332
Myocarditis, 332
Myocardium, 332
Myopathy, 332

N

Neck
    collar in sleep apnea, 294
    x-ray in
        laryngotracheobronchitis
        and epiglottitis, 256
Necrosis, 332

transformed data into the statistical package's own "system file." In SPSS for DOS, you can deal with the *command or program file* by using its editor: Press the function key F9 to save the program you have compiled or edited, and later press F3 to call it back. In SPSS for Windows, you only need to click your mouse. On the other hand, you use certain language in the program rather than the function keys or mouse to deal with the *raw data* as well as the *system file*: Use GET, TRANSLATE FROM, or DATA LIST FILE to get data input, and SAVE OUTFILE to produce the data management output. When switching between different computer systems (e.g., the PC and the mainframe), you will need to use the command EXPORT to produce a portable file and later IMPORT to read it into any other computer system. When you run the program, you will need another file to save your results. In SPSS/PC+, the results of a whole session are cumulatively and automatically saved in a file called SPSS.LIS. But if you do not rename that file, next time you run SPSS over again it will automatically be overwritten by the new results. Therefore, you had better save your results in a file with a different name. The command is "SET LISTINGS FILE= file name", which should be put at the beginning of the program. Later on you can use a word processor to read the file (by specifying the type as ASCII text file) and edit it. You can print out the analysis results automatically by putting the command "SET PRINT ON" on top of the SPSS program (make sure your printer is on). Or you can print the results from the word processor, but oftentimes you need to make the font smaller to avoid messing up the format on the screen.

It should be noted that you need to read the computer package manuals or take courses in computer applications to appropriately operate the various kinds of computer programs. Computer language is very rigid and you should take great care in using it. SPSS/PC+, for example, requires you to use a period to end each command. If you forget one, you will only get an error message. There are now good texts available combining statistics with the use of the computer, such as: George and Mallery, 1995; Dometrius, 1992; Aron and Norman, 1997; Rowland, Arkkelin, and Crisler, 1991; and Grimm and Wozniak, 1990. It will greatly help if you have prepared yourself in both computer applications and statistics before you further study or review the topic of data analysis. The SPSS manuals are also good, and are said to have greatly helped sell the software product.

Neoplasm (*see* Tumor)
Nephritis, 332
Nephrotic syndrome: causing
    pleural effusion, 188
Nerve
    afferent, 317
    efferent, 324
    glossopharyngeal, 327
    myelinated fibers
      in Guillain-Barrè
        syndrome, 270
      in myasthenia gravis,
        278
    parasympathetic, 60
    phrenic, pacemaker, in
      sleep apnea, 293
    somatic, 338
Nervous system
    autonomic, dysfunction in
      Guillain-Barré
      syndrome, 274
    central, stimulants in sleep
      apnea, 292
Neuroendocrine, 332
Neuromuscular junction, 332
Newborn
    lung disease of, references
      for, 300–301
    respiratory distress
      syndrome (*see*
      Respiratory distress
      syndrome, idiopathic)
Nitrogen
    oxide, 332
    single-breath nitrogen test
      for closing volume and
      capacity, 36
Nocturnal, 332
Nomogram, 333
Norepinephrine, 333
Nostrils: flaring, in idiopathic
    respiratory distress
    syndrome, 244
Nutrition: in emphysema, 96

O

Olfactory, 333
Oncotic pressure, 333
    decrease in pulmonary
      edema, 137
Orbicularis oculi, 333
Ornithosis: causing
    pneumonia, 127
Oropharynx: tongue in, in
    obstructive sleep apnea,
    284
Orthopnea, 333
Osmotic pressure, 333
Osteoporosis, 333
Oxygen
    chemosensitive cells, 29
      on carotid artery, 29
    content, 333

saturation, arterial, in sleep
    apnea, 289
supplemental
    in asthma, 117
    in bronchiectasis, 107
    in bronchitis, chronic, 86
    in cancer of lung, 237
    in cystic fibrosis, 266
    in emphysema, 97
    in epiglottitis, 256
    in flail chest, 171
    in fungal diseases, 226
    in Guillain-Barré
      syndrome, 275
    in kyphoscoliosis, 200
    in laryngotracheobronchi-
      tis, 256
    in myasthenia gravis, 283
    in pleural effusion, 193
    in pneumoconiosis, 210
    in pneumonia, 131
    in pneumothorax, 183
    in pulmonary edema,
      139–141
    in respiratory distress
      syndrome, adult, 163
    in tuberculosis, 218
    tension (*see* Pa_{O_2})
    therapy in sleep apnea, 292
Ozone, 333

P

Pacemaker: phrenic nerve, in
    sleep apnea, 293
Pa_{CO_2}
    decrease
      in alveolar
        hyperventilation,
        49–50
      in asthma, early stages,
        115
      in bronchiectasis, early
        stages, 104
      in bronchitis, chronic,
        early stages, 83
      in cancer of lung, early
        stages, 234
      in cystic fibrosis, early
        stages, 263
      in emphysema, early
        stages, 94
      in epiglottitis, early
        stages, 255
      in flail chest, early stages,
        169
      in fungal diseases, early
        stages, 224
      in kyphoscoliosis, early
        stages, 198
      in laryngotracheobronchi-
        tis, early stages, 255
      in pleural effusion, early
        stages, 190

      in pneumoconiosis, early
        stages, 207
      in pneumonia, early
        stages, 129
      in pneumothorax, early
        stages, 179
      in pulmonary edema,
        early stages, 138
      in pulmonary embolism,
        early stages, 148
      in respiratory distress
        syndrome, adult, early
        stages, 161
      in tuberculosis, early
        stages, 216
    increase
      in asthma, advanced
        stages
      in bronchiectasis,
        advanced stages, 104
      in bronchitis, chronic,
        advanced stages, 83
      in cancer of lung,
        advanced stages, 234
      in cystic fibrosis,
        advanced stages, 263
      in emphysema, advanced
        stages, 94
      in epiglottitis, advanced
        stages, 255
      in flail chest, advanced
        stages, 169
      in fungal diseases,
        advanced stages, 224
      in Guillain-Barré
        syndrome, 273
      in kyphoscoliosis,
        advanced stages, 198
      in laryngotracheobronchi-
        tis, advanced stages,
        255
      in myasthenia gravis,
        281
      in pleural effusion,
        advanced stages, 190
      in pneumoconiosis,
        advanced stages, 207
      in pneumonia, advanced
        stages, 129
      in pneumothorax,
        advanced stages, 180
      in pulmonary edema,
        advanced stages, 138
      in pulmonary embolism,
        advanced stages, 148
      in respiratory distress
        syndrome, adult,
        advanced stages, 161
      in respiratory distress
        syndrome, idiopathic,
        245, 247
      in sleep apnea, 290
      in tuberculosis, advanced
        stages, 216

in ventilatory failure,
    acute, 53
in ventilatory failure,
    chronic, 54–55, 56
relationships of, 50–52, 53
Pain, 30
    chest, 70–72
        in cancer of lung, 234
        in fungal diseases, 224
        nonpleuritic, 72
        in pleural effusion, 190
        pleuritic, 71–72
        in pneumoconiosis, 207
        in pneumonia, 130
        in pulmonary embolism,
            152
        in tuberculosis, 216
Palatine arch, 333
Palatopharyngoplasty: in sleep
    apnea, 293
Palpation, 6
Pancreas, 333
    juice, 333–334
Pancrease: in cystic fibrosis,
    266
Pancreatic enzymes: in cystic
    fibrosis, 266
Pa$_{O_2}$
    decrease
        in alveolar
            hyperventilation,
            49–50
        in asthma, advanced
            stages, 115
        in asthma, early stages,
            115
        in bronchiectasis,
            advanced stages, 104
        in bronchiectasis, early
            stages, 104
        in bronchitis, chronic,
            advanced stages, 83
        in bronchitis, chronic,
            early stages, 83
        in cancer of lung,
            advanced stages, 234
        in cancer of lung, early
            stages, 234
        in cystic fibrosis,
            advanced stages, 263
        in cystic fibrosis, early
            stages, 263
        in emphysema, advanced
            stages, 94
        in epiglottitis, advanced
            stages, 255
        in epiglottitis, early
            stages, 255
        in flail chest, advanced
            stages, 169
        in flail chest, early stages,
            169
        in fungal diseases,
            advanced stages, 224

in fungal diseases, early
    stages, 224
in Guillain-Barré
    syndrome, 273
in kyphoscoliosis,
    advanced stages, 198
in kyphoscoliosis, early
    stages, 198
in laryngotracheobronchi-
    tis, advanced stages,
    255
in laryngotracheobronchi-
    tis, early stages, 255
in myasthenia gravis, 281
in pleural effusion,
    advanced stages, 190
in pleural effusion, early
    stages, 190
in pneumoconiosis,
    advanced stages, 207
in pneumoconiosis, early
    stages, 207
in pneumonia, advanced
    stages, 129
in pneumonia, early
    stages, 129
in pneumothorax,
    advanced stages, 180
in pneumothorax, early
    stages, 179
in pulmonary edema,
    advanced stages, 138
in pulmonary edema,
    early stages, 138
in pulmonary embolism,
    advanced stages, 148
in pulmonary embolism,
    early stages, 148
in respiratory distress
    syndrome, adult,
    advanced stages, 161
in respiratory distress
    syndrome, adult, early
    stages, 161
in respiratory distress
    syndrome, idiopathic,
    245, 246–247
in sleep apnea, 290
in tuberculosis, advanced
    stages, 216
in tuberculosis, early
    stages, 216
in ventilatory failure,
    acute, 53
in ventilatory failure,
    chronic, 54–55
Paracentesis, 334
Paradoxical, 334
Parainfluenza virus
    in laryngotracheobronchitis,
        254
    pneumonia due to, 127
Paralysis: flaccid, 326
Paramyxovirus, 334

Parasympathetic nerve, 60
Parasympatholytic agents, 345
    in asthma, 117
    in bronchiectasis, 106
    in bronchitis, chronic, 86
    in cystic fibrosis, 265
    in emphysema, 96
Parenchyma, 334
Paroxysmal, 334
Patent ductus, 334
PCWP, 336
Peak expiratory flow rate,
    (PEFR), 34, 35
    decrease
        in asthma, 114
        in bronchiectasis, 103
        in bronchitis, chronic, 82
        in cancer of lung, 233
        in cystic fibrosis, 263
        in emphysema, 93
        in obstructive lung
            disease, 38
        in pneumoconiosis, 207
Pectoralis major muscles,
    62–63, 64
Pectoriloquy (see Whispered
    pectoriloquy)
PEFR (see Peak expiratory
    flow rate)
Pendelluft, 168, 334
    in pneumothorax, 179
    with sucking chest wound,
        176
Penicillin, 347
Pentamidine, 347
    aerosolized, in pneumonia,
        131
Percussion, 7–8
    abnormal notes, 8
    dull notes, 8
        in alveolar consolidation,
            9
    hyperresonant (see
        Hyperresonant
        percussion note)
    normal lung, 9
    path of, 8
    technique, 7
Perfusion-ventilation (see
    Ventilation-perfusion)
Peribronchial, 334
Peritoneal dialysis, 334
    pleural effusion due to, 188
pH, 334
    decrease
        in asthma, 115
        in cancer of lung,
            advanced stages, 234
        in epiglottitis, advanced
            stages, 255
        in flail chest, advanced
            stages, 169
        in Guillain-Barré
            syndrome, 273

pH (cont.)
  in laryngotracheobronchitis, advanced stages, 255
  in myasthenia gravis, 281
  in pleural effusion, advanced stages, 190
  in pneumonia, advanced stages, 129
  in pneumothorax, advanced stages, 180
  in pulmonary edema, advanced stages, 138
  in pulmonary embolism, advanced stages, 148
  in respiratory distress syndrome, adult, advanced stages, 161
  in respiratory distress syndrome, idiopathic, 245, 247
  in sleep apnea, 290
  in ventilatory failure, acute, 53
  increase
    in alveolar hyperventilation, 50–52
    in asthma, early stages, 115
    in bronchiectasis, early stages, 104
    in bronchitis, chronic, early stages, 83
    in cancer of lung, early stages, 234
    in cystic fibrosis, early stages, 263
    in emphysema, early stages, 94
    in epiglottitis, early stages, 255
    in flail chest, early stages, 169
    in fungal diseases, early stages, 224
    in kyphoscoliosis, early stages, 198
    in laryngotracheobronchitis, early stages, 255
    in pleural effusion, early stages, 190
    in pneumoconiosis, early stages, 207
    in pneumonia, early stages, 129
    in pneumothorax, early stages, 179
    in pulmonary edema, early stages, 138
    in pulmonary embolism, early stages, 148
    in respiratory distress syndrome, adult, early stages, 161

  in tuberculosis, early stages, 216
  normal
    in bronchiectasis, advanced stages, 104
    in bronchitis, chronic, advanced stages, 83
    in cystic fibrosis, advanced stages, 263
    in emphysema, advanced stages, 94
    in fungal diseases, advanced stages, 224
    in kyphoscoliosis, advanced stages, 198
    in pneumoconiosis, advanced stages, 207
    in tuberculosis, advanced stages, 216
    in ventilatory failure, chronic, 55
  relationships of, 50–52, 53
Phagocytosis, 334
Phalanges, 334
Pharmacologic agents (see Medications)
Phenotype, 335
Phenylketonuria, 335
Phlegmasia alba dolens, 335
Phosgene, 335
Phosphodiesterase, 335
Phrenic nerve pacemaker: in sleep apnea, 293
Phthisis
  black, 205
  miner's, 205
Physiologic dead space: calculation, 349
Physiology
  references for, 297–298
  respiratory, symbols and abbreviations in, 343–345
Plaques: pleural, 209
Plasmapheresis: in Guillain-Barré syndrome, 274–275
Pleomorphic, 335
Pleura
  diseases, 187–195
    etiology, 187–189
    references for, 311–312
  effusion (see Pleural effusion below)
  friction rub, 13–14
  intrapleural (see Intrapleural)
  parietal
    during pain, 71
    pathologic fluids separating, 189
  parietal, separation of
    chylothorax causing, 189
    empyema causing, 189

  hemothorax causing, 189
  plaques, 209
  rupture causing valvular pneumothorax, 177
  visceral, 342
Pleural effusion, 186–195
  alveolar hyperventilation in, 190
  anatomic alterations of lungs in, 187
  blood gases in, 190
  blood pressure in
    increase, 190
    systemic, decrease in, 190
  central venous pressure increase in, 190
  chest assessment in, 190
  clinical manifestations, cardiopulmonary, overview, 189–192
  collagen vascular disease causing, 189
  cough in, 190
  cyanosis in, 190
  dialysis causing, peritoneal, 188
  etiology, 187–189
  exudative
    causes, 188–189
    mesothelioma causing, malignant, 188
    pneumonia causing, 188
  fungal disease causing, 188, 224
  gastrointestinal tract disease causing, 189
  heart failure causing, congestive, 187–188
  heart output increase in, 190
  heart rate increase in, 190
  hydrothorax causing, hepatic, 188
  hyperinflation techniques in, 193
  with lung abscess, 192
  lung capacities in, 190
  lung function in, 190
  lung volumes in, 190
  malignant, 188
  management, general, 193
  nephrotic syndrome causing, 188
  oxygen in, supplemental, 193
  pain in, chest, 190
  in pneumonia, 129
  in pulmonary edema, 138
  pulmonary embolism causing, 148, 188
  references for, 311–312
  respiratory rate increase due to, 189–190
  subpulmonic, 192

thoracentesis in, 193
  hydropneumothorax after, 191
  transudate in, 187
  tuberculosis causing, 216, 188
  ventilatory failure in, 190
  x-ray in, chest, 191–192
Pleurisy, 335
Pleuritic chest pain, 71–72
Pleuritis, 335
Pneumoconiosis, 203–211
  alveolar hyperventilation with hypoxemia in, 207
  anatomic alterations of lungs in, 203–204
  blood gases in, 207
  blood pressure increase in, 207
  chest assessment in, 207–208
  chest expansion decrease in, 207
  clinical manifestations, cardiopulmonary, overview, 206–208
  coal worker's discussion of, 205
    emphysema in, focal, 205
  cor pulmonale in, 207
  cough in, 207
  cyanosis in, 207
  digital clubbing in, 207
  etiology, 204–206
  expiratory maneuver in, 207
  heart output increase in, 207
  heart rate increase in, 207
  lung capacities in, 206
  lung function in, 206–207
  lung volumes in, 206
  management, general, 208–210
  oxygen in, supplemental, 210
  pain in, chest, 207
  polycythemia in, 207
  references for, 312
  respiratory rate increase in, 206
  sputum production in, 207
  ventilatory failure with hypoxemia in, 207
  x-ray in, chest, 208
Pneumocystis carinii pneumonia, 128
Pneumonia, 122–133
  adenovirus, 127
  alveolar consolidation in, 122
  alveolar hyperventilation with hypoxemia in, 129
  analgesics in, 131
  anatomic alterations of lungs in, 123

antibiotics in, 131
bacteria causing, 123–126
  gram-negative organisms, 124–126
  gram-positive organisms, 123–124
blood gases in, 129
blood pressure increase in, 129
chest assessment in, 129
chest expansion decrease in, 130
clinical manifestations, cardiopulmonary, overview, 128–130
cough in, 129
cyanosis in, 129
etiology, 123–128
  tabular data on, 124
heart output increase in, 129
heart rate increase in, 129
Hemophilus influenzae, 125
hemoptysis in, 129
hyperinflation techniques in, 130
influenza virus causing, 126
Klebsiella causing, 124–125
Legionella, 126
lung capacities in, 128
lung function in, 128
lung volumes in, 128
management, general, 130–131
medications in, 131
Mycoplasma, 127
ornithosis causing, 127
oxygen in, supplemental, 131
pain in, chest, 130
parainfluenza virus, 127
pentamidine in, aerosolized, 131
pleural effusion in, 129
  exudative, 188
Pneumocystis carinii, 128
pneumonitis and aspiration, 128
  lipoid, 128
Pseudomonas aeruginosa, 125
references for, 305–306
respiratory rate increase in, 128
respiratory syncytial virus, 126–127
Rickettsiae, 127
rubella causing, 128
sputum production in, 129
Staphylococcus, 124
Streptococcus, 123
thoracentesis in, 131
varicella causing, 128

ventilatory failure with hypoxemia in, 129
viral causes, 126–127
x-ray in, chest, 130
Pneumonitis
  aspiration, and pneumonia, 128
  lipoid, and pneumonia, 128
Pneumotaxic center, 27
Pneumothorax, 174–185
  alveolar collapse in, 174
  alveolar hyperventilation with hypoxemia in, 179
  anatomic alterations of lungs in, 175
  blood gases in, 179–180
  blood pressure in
    increase, 179
    systemic, decrease in, 179
  central venous pressure increase in, 179
  chemoreceptor stimulation in, peripheral, 178–179
  chest assessment in, 182
  chest diameter increase in, 180
  clinical manifestations, cardiopulmonary, overview, 178–182
  cyanosis in, 180
  etiology, 175–177
  heart output increase in, 179
  heart rate increase in, 179
  hydropneumothorax (see Hydropneumothorax)
  hyperresonant percussion notes in, 182
  iatrogenic, 175, 177
  intrapleural space in, 180
  lung capacities in, 179
  lung function in, 179
  lung volumes in, 179
  management, general, 182–183
  oxygen in, supplemental, 183
  pendelluft in, 179
  references for, 311
  respiratory rate increase in, 178–179
  spontaneous, 175, 177
  tension, 181
  traumatic, 175, 176–177
  valvular
    chest wall wound causing, 176
    pleural rupture causing, 177
  venous admixture in, 178
  ventilatory failure with hypoxemia in, 180
  x-ray in, chest, 180–182

Poiseuille's law
  for flow, 42–43, 44,
    352–353
  lung disease and,
    obstructive, 42–46
  for pressure, 43–45, 46, 353
  rearranged to simple
    proportionalities, 45–46
  significance of, 42
Polyarteritis nodosa, 335
Polycythemia, 67–69, 335
  in bronchiectasis, 104
  in bronchitis, chronic, 83
  in cystic fibrosis, 263
  definition, 67
  in emphysema, 94
  in kyphoscoliosis, 198
  in pneumoconiosis, 207
  viscosity in, increase in,
    67–69
Polymyxin, 347
Polyneuritis, 335
Polyneuropathy, 335
Polyradiculitis, 335
Polyradiculoneuropathy, 335
Postpartum, 335
Postural drainage, 335
Pressure, 335
  atmospheric, 319
  central venous (see Central
    venous pressure)
  continuous positive airway,
    in sleep apnea, 293
  driving, 324
  equal-pressure point, 40
  hydrostatic (see Hydrostatic
    pressure)
  intrapleural (see Intrapleural
    pressure)
  negative-pressure ventilation
    in sleep apnea, 293
  oncotic, 333
    decrease in pulmonary
      edema, 137
  osmotic, 333
  Poiseuille's law for, 43–45,
    46, 353
  pulmonary wedge, increase
    in pulmonary edema,
    139
  systolic, 339
  transpulmonary, 340
  -volume (see
    Volume-pressure)
Prophylactic, 336
Propranolol, 336
Prostaglandin F, 336
Proteolytic, 336
Protriptyline: in sleep apnea,
  292
Pseudomonas
  aeruginosa: causing
    pneumonia, 125
  in cystic fibrosis, 261

Psittacosis: causing
  pneumonia, 127
Pulmonary, 336
  (See also Lung)
  angiography, in pulmonary
    embolism, 152, 154
  artery, chemosensitive cells
    and baroreceptors on,
    29
  capillary wedge pressure,
    336
  circulation, 336
  edema (see Edema,
    pulmonary)
  embolectomy, 154
  embolism (see Embolism,
    pulmonary)
  function (see Lung function)
  hypertension, in pulmonary
    embolism, 148–149
  reflex, 57
  shunt (see Shunt,
    pulmonary)
  tuberculosis (see under
    Tuberculosis)
  vessels, 336
    in hypoxic
      vasoconstriction, 69
    in pulmonary embolism,
      149
  resistance, 336
  wedge pressure increase in
    pulmonary edema, 139
Pulse paradoxus, 336
  in asthma, 115–116
Pursed-lip breathing, 67
  in asthma, 114
  in bronchiectasis, 104
  in bronchitis, chronic, 83
  in cystic fibrosis, 263
  in emphysema, 94
Purulent, 336
PVR, 336
Pyrazinamide: in tuberculosis,
  218

Q
Quinolone, 347

R
Racemic epinephrine: in
  laryngotracheobronchitis
  and epiglottitis, 257
Radiography (see X-ray)
Radiotherapy: in cancer of
  lung, 236
Rectus abdominis muscle, 64
Reflex(es)
  aortic baroreceptor, 30
    in pulmonary embolism,
    148
  carotid sinus baroreceptor,
    30

in pulmonary embolism,
    148
  deflation, 30
  irritant, 30
  pulmonary, 57
Reid index, 85
  increase in chronic
    bronchitis, 84–85
REM inhibitors: in sleep
  apnea, 292
REM sleep, 286
Residual capacity: decrease in
  fungal diseases, 224
Residual volume (RV)
  decrease
    in bronchiectasis,
      restrictive, 103
    in flail chest, 168
    in Guillain-Barré
      syndrome, 273
    in kyphoscoliosis, 198
    in lung disease,
      restrictive, 37
    in myasthenia gravis, 281
    in pleural effusion, 190
    in pneumoconiosis, 206
    in pneumonia, 128
    in pneumothorax, 179
    in pulmonary edema, 138
    in respiratory distress
      syndrome, adult, 161
    in respiratory distress
      syndrome, idiopathic,
      243
    in sleep apnea, 290
    in tuberculosis, 215
  definition, 31
  increase
    in asthma, 114
    in bronchiectasis, 103
    in bronchitis, chronic,
      82
    in cystic fibrosis, 263
    in emphysema, 93
    in obstructive lung
      disease, 47
  /total lung capacity ratio
    increase
      in asthma, 114
      in bronchiectasis, 103
      in bronchitis, chronic,
        82
      in cystic fibrosis, 263
      in emphysema, 93
Respiratory care
  in cancer of lung, 237
  in myasthenia gravis, 283
  references for, 299
Respiratory components: of
  lower brain stem, 27
Respiratory disease
  chest assessment, 3–78
  classification, 4
  clinical manifestations, 3–78

Respiratory distress syndrome
  adult, 158–165
    alveolar hyperventilation
      with hypoxemia in, 161
    anatomic alterations of
      lungs in, 159–160
    antibiotics in, 163
    blood gases in, 161
    blood pressure increase
      in, 161
    chest assessment in, 162
    clinical manifestations,
      cardiopulmonary,
      overview, 161–162
    corticosteroids in, 163
    cyanosis in, 162
    diuretics in, 163
    etiology, 160–161
    heart output increase in,
      161
    heart rate increase in, 161
    hyperinflation techniques
      in, 162
    lung capacities in, 161
    lung function in, 161
    lung volumes in, 161
    management, general,
      162–163
    medications in, 163
    oxygen in, supplemental,
      163
    references for, 308–309
    respiratory rate increase
      in, 161
    substernal intercostal
      retractions in, 162
    ventilatory failure with
      hypoxemia in, 161
    x-ray in, chest, 162
  idiopathic, 240–251
    anatomic alterations of
      lungs in, 241–242
    blood gases in, 245–247
    blood pressure increase
      in, 243
    chest assessment in, 248
    clinical manifestations,
      cardiopulmonary,
      overview, 243–248
    cyanosis in, 248
    etiology, 242–243
    expiratory grunting in,
      244–245
    fatigue in, 247
    fetal circulation in, 246
    HCO_3 increase in, 245,
      247
    heart output increase in,
      243
    heart rate increase in, 243
    intrapleural pressures in,
      negative, increase in,
      243–244
    lung capacities in, 243

    lung function in, 243
    lung volumes in, 243
    management, general, 248
    nostrils in, flaring, 244
    Pa_{CO_2} increase in, 245, 247
    Pa_{O_2} decrease in, 245,
      246–247
    pH decrease in, 245, 247
    references for, 313–314
    respiratory rate increase
      in, 243
    type I cell, 240
    type II cell, 240
    ventilatory failure with
      hypoxemia in, 245–247
    x-ray in, chest, 245
  infant (see idiopathic above)
Respiratory function
  airway resistance equation
    and, 46
  compression mechanism
    and, dynamic, 40–46
  Poiseuille's law and, 42–46
Respiratory group
  dorsal, 27
  ventral, 27
Respiratory physiology:
    symbols and
    abbreviations in,
    343–344
Respiratory rate
  increase, 23–30
    in asthma, 114
    in bronchiectasis, 103
    in bronchitis, chronic, 82
    in cancer of lung, 233
    in cystic fibrosis, 262
    in emphysema, 93
    in epiglottitis, 255
    in flail chest, 167–170
    in fungal diseases,
      223–224
    in kyphoscoliosis,
      197–198
    in laryngotracheobronchi-
      tis, 255
    in pleural effusion,
      189–190
    in pneumoconiosis, 206
    in pneumonia, 128
    in pneumothorax,
      178–179
    in pulmonary edema, 137
    in pulmonary embolism,
      146–148
    in respiratory distress
      syndrome, adult, 161
    in respiratory distress
      syndrome, idiopathic,
      243
    in tuberculosis, 215
Respiratory syncytial virus
  in laryngotracheobronchitis,
    254

    pneumonia due to, 126–127
Reticular formation, 337
Rheumatism: "desert," 223
Rhinovirus: in
    laryngotracheobronchitis,
    254
Rhonchi, 12–13
  in asthma, 13
Rib fracture: in flail chest, 166
Ribonucleic acid, 337
Rickettsiae: causing
    pneumonia, 127
Rifadin: in tuberculosis, 218
Rifampin: in tuberculosis, 218
RNA, 337
Roentgenography, 337
Rubella: causing pneumonia,
    128
Rupture: pleural, causing
    valvular pneumothorax,
    177
RV (see Residual volume)

S

S_2: split in pulmonary
    embolism, 16, 150
Salmonella typhi: in
    Guillain-Barré
    syndrome, 272
Salt: in cystic fibrosis, 266
Scalene muscle, 62
Scanning: lung, in pulmonary
    embolism, 152
Scapula, 5
  inferior angle, 5
Scintillation camera, 337
Scoliosis
  definition, 197
  kyphoscoliosis (see
    Kyphoscoliosis)
Semilunar valve, 337
Septicemia, 337
Septum, 337
Serotonin, 337
Shunt
  anatomic, 18
  capillary, 18
  equation, 21
    classic, 21
  pulmonary, 18–19, 20
    clinical significance of, 24
    type in respiratory
      disease, 21
Shuntlike effect, 18–19
Sibilant, 337
Silicate, 337
Silicosis: discussion of, 205
Single-breath nitrogen test: of
    closing volume and
    capacity, 36
Sinus
  aortic, baroreceptors, 29
  carotid (see Carotid sinus)
  tachycardia, 337

Sleep
  apnea, 285–296
    arrhythmia in, 291
    blood gases in, 290
    central, 288
    central nervous system
      stimulants in, 292
    continuous positive airway
      pressure in, 293
    cyanosis in, 290
    clinical manifestations,
      cardiopulmonary,
      overview, 290–291
    diagnosis, 288–289
    hemodynamic changes in,
      acute, 290–291
    lung function in, 290
    management, general,
      291–294
    mandibular advancement
      in, 293
    medications in, 292
    methylphenidate in, 292
    mixed, 288
    neck collar in, 294
    obstructive, 284, 287
    oxygen saturation in,
      arterial, 289
    oxygen therapy in, 292
    palatopharyngoplasty in,
      293
    phrenic nerve pacemaker
      in, 293
    protriptyline in, 292
    references for, 316
    REM inhibitors in, 292
    sawtooth pattern in, 290
    sleep posture in, 292
    surgery in, 293
    tongue-retaining device
      in, 294
    tracheostomy in, 293
    types, 286–288
    ventilation in, mechanical,
      293
    ventilation in, mechanical,
      continuous, 293
    ventilation in,
      negative-pressure, 293
    weight reduction and, 292
    x-ray in, chest, 291
  cardiopulmonary patterns in,
    characteristic, 285–286
  non-REM, 285
  REM, 286
  stages, 285–286
Smoking (see Cigarette
    smoking)
Sodium: elevation in sweat in
    cystic fibrosis, 265
Sounds
  breath (see Breath sounds)
  heart
    abnormalities in pulmonary
      embolism, 150–151

lubb-dub, origin of, 15
  normal, review of, 14–15
  second, in pulmonary
    embolism, 150
  third, in pulmonary
    embolism, 151
  voice, whispered,
    auscultation of, 14
    in lung consolidation, 15
Spasm, 338
Sphygmomanometer, 338
Spine: curvature, posterior
    and lateral, 196
Spirometry: abbreviations in,
    344
Sputum, 338
  frothy in pulmonary edema,
    138
  positive, in tuberculosis, 215
  production, 58–61
    in asthma, 115
    in bronchiectasis, 105
    in bronchitis, chronic, 83
    in cancer of lung, 234
    in cystic fibrosis, 263
    in fungal diseases, 224
    in kyphoscoliosis, 198
    in pneumoconiosis, 207
    in pneumonia, 129
    in pulmonary edema, 138
    in tuberculosis, 216
    types of, 60–61
Staphylococcus
  aureus in acute epiglottitis,
    254
  in cystic fibrosis, 261
  organism, diagram of, 125
  pneumonia due to, 124
Stasis, 338
  venous, 341
Status asthmaticus, 338
Sternal intercostal retractions
  in epiglottitis, 256
  in laryngotracheobronchitis,
    256
Sternal notch, 5
Sternocleidomastoid muscles,
    62, 63
Sternum: body of, 5
Streptococcus
  in bronchiectasis, 105
  in bronchitis, chronic, 83
  in epiglottitis, acute, 254
  organism, diagram of, 124
  pneumonia due to, 123
Streptomycin: in tuberculosis,
    218
Stridor, inspiratory, 253
  in epiglottitis, 256
  in laryngotracheobronchitis,
    256
Stroke volume, 338
Subarachnoid space, 338
Substernal retraction, 72–73
  intercostal, in ARDS, 162

Sulfur dioxide, 338
Surfactant, 338
Swan-Ganz catheter, 339
Sweat: sodium and chloride
    elevation in, in cystic
    fibrosis, 265
Symbols, 343–344
  for blood, 343
  for gas, 343
Sympathomimetic, 339
Sympathomimetics, 344–345
  in asthma, 117
  in bronchiectasis, 106
  in bronchitis, chronic, 86
  in cystic fibrosis, 265
  in emphysema, 96
  in pulmonary edema, 141
Synaptic cleft: in myasthenia
    gravis, 278
Syncope, 339
  in pulmonary embolism, 149
Syncytial, 339
Systole, 339

T

Tachycardia, 339
  sinus, 337
Tachypnea, 339
Tactile fremitus, 6
  path of, 7
Technetium-99m, 339
Tension
  carbon dioxide (see Pa_{CO_2})
  of gases, 339
  oxygen (see Pa_{O_2})
  pneumothorax, 181
  surface, 338
Tetracycline, 347
Thoracentesis, 339
  in pleural effusion, 193
    hydropneumothorax after,
      191
  in pneumonia, 131
Thoracic (see Chest)
Thrombocytopenia, 340
Thromboembolic, 340
Thrombolytics: in pulmonary
    embolism, 154
Thrombophlebitis, 340
Thrombus, 340
"Thumb sign:" in edematous
    epiglottitis, 257
Thymectomy, 340
  in myasthenia gravis,
    282–283
Thymus, 340
Tidal volume (V_T)
  decrease
    in bronchiectasis,
      restrictive, 104
    in cancer of lung, 234
    in flail chest, 168
    in fungal diseases, 224
    in kyphoscoliosis, 198

in lung disease,
  restrictive, 37
in pleural effusion, 190
in pneumoconiosis, 206
in pneumothorax, 179
in pulmonary edema, 138
in respiratory distress
  syndrome, adult, 161
in respiratory distress
  syndrome, idiopathic,
  243
in tuberculosis, 216
definition, 31
increase
  in asthma, 114
  in bronchiectasis, 103
  in bronchitis, chronic, 82
  in cystic fibrosis, 263
  in lung disease,
    obstructive, 47
TLC (see Total lung capacity)
Tongue
  in oropharynx in obstructive
    sleep apnea, 284
  -retaining device in sleep
    apnea, 294
Total lung capacity (TLC), 32
  decrease
    in bronchiectasis, 104
    in cancer of lung, 234
    in flail chest, 168
    in fungal diseases, 224
    in Guillain-Barré
      syndrome, 273
    in kyphoscoliosis, 198
    in lung disease,
      obstructive, 47
    in lung disease,
      restrictive, 37–38
    in myasthenia gravis, 281
    in pleural effusion, 190
    in pneumoconiosis, 206
    in pneumothorax, 179
    in pulmonary edema, 138
    in respiratory distress
      syndrome, adult, 161
    in respiratory distress
      syndrome, idiopathic,
      243
    in sleep apnea, 290
    in tuberculosis, 216
  /residual volume ratio (see
    Residual volume/total
    lung capacity ratio)
Toxemia, 340
Toxin, 340
Trachea, 340
  in croup, 252
Tracheobronchial
  clearance, 340
  tree, 59
    cartilaginous structures, 60
    epithelial lining, 58, 61
    histology of, 58–61
    size changes, normal, 43

Tracheobronchitis (see
    Laryngotracheobronchitis)
Tracheostomy, 340
  in sleep apnea, 293
Tracheotomy, 340
Transfusion, 340
Transpulmonary pressure,
    340
Transversus abdominis muscle,
    66–67
Trapezius muscles, 63–64, 65
Trauma, 341
Traumatic pneumothorax, 175,
    176–177
Tricuspid valve, 341
Trypsin, 341
Tuberculosis, 212–219, 341
  alveolar hyperventilation
    with hypoxemia in, 216
  anatomic alterations of lungs
    in, 213
  blood gases in, 216
  blood pressure increase in,
    216
  bronchiectasis and, 102
  cavitation in, 212
  chest assessment in, 216
  chest expansion decrease in,
    216
  clinical manifestations,
    cardiopulmonary,
    overview, 215–217
  cough in, 216
  cyanosis in, 216
  diagnosis, 215
  ethambutol in, 218
  etiology, 214
  heart output increase in,
    216
  heart rate increase in, 216
  hemoptysis in, 216
  isoniazid in, 218
  lung capacities in, 215–216
  lung function in, 215–216
  lung volumes in, 215–216
  management, general,
    217–218
  medications in, 217–218
  miliary, 214
  oxygen in, supplemental,
    218
  pain in, chest, 216
  pleural effusion in, 216
  positive culture in, 215
  postprimary stage, 213
  primary, 213
  primary infection stage, 213
  primary infections in, 212
  pyrazinamide in, 218
  references for, 312–313
  reinfection, 213
  respiratory rate increase in,
    215
  rifampin in, 218
  secondary stage, 213

sputum in
  positive, 215
  production, 216
streptomycin in, 218
ventilatory failure with
  hypoxemia in, 216
x-ray in, chest, 216–217
Tumor
  benign, 231
  definition, 231
  malignant, 231
  (See also Cancer)
T wave, 341

U

Ulcerate, 341
Units: of measurement,
  350–352
Uremia, 341
Urokinase, 341

V

Vaccinia, 341
Vagus, 341
Valve
  aortic, 319
  ileocecal, 329
  mitral, 331
  semilunar, 337
  tricuspid, 341
Valvular pneumothorax (see
    Pneumothorax, valvular)
Vancomycin, 347
Vaponefrin: in
    laryngotracheobronchitis
    and epiglottitis, 257
Varicella: causing pneumonia,
    128
Varicose bronchiectasis, 100,
    101
Variola, 341
Vasoconstriction, 341
  alveolar hypoxia causing, in
    pulmonary embolism,
    149
  humoral agents causing, in
    pulmonary embolism,
    149
  with hypoxia, 69
VC (see Vital capacity)
V_D (see Dead space
    ventilation)
Vein
  admixture (see Venous
    admixture)
  bronchial, 60
  central (see Central venous
    pressure)
  stasis, 341
Vena cava
  inferior, 329
  superior, 338
Venous admixture, 19–23
  in alveolar consolidation, 49

Venous admixture (cont.)
  automobile accident victim
    and, 22–23
  in flail chest, 169
  in pneumothorax, 178
  in pulmonary embolism, 147
Ventilation, 341
  dead space, 19
  failure, definition, 52–53, 54
  failure with hypoxemia, 52–56
    in asthma, 115
    in bronchiectasis, 104
    in bronchitis, chronic,
      advanced stages, 83
    in cancer of lung, 234
    in cystic fibrosis, 263
    in emphysema, 94
    in epiglottitis, 255
    in flail chest, 169
    in fungal diseases, 224
    in Guillain-Barré
      syndrome, 273
    in kyphoscoliosis, 198
    in laryngotracheobronchi-
      tis, 255
    in myasthenia gravis, 281
    in pneumoconiosis, 207
    in pneumonia, 129
    in pneumothorax, 180
    in pulmonary edema, 138
    in pulmonary embolism,
      148
    in respiratory distress
      syndrome, adult, 161
    in respiratory distress
      syndrome, idiopathic,
      245–247
    in sleep apnea, 290
    in tuberculosis, 216
  failure in pleural effusion,
    190
  failure, respiratory diseases
    and, 55
  frequency
    airway resistance increase
      in, 26
    lung compliance decrease
      in, 26
  maximum voluntary, 35
  maximum voluntary (MVV),
    decrease of
    in asthma, 114
    in bronchiectasis, 103
    in bronchitis, chronic, 82
    in cancer of lung, 233
    in cystic fibrosis, 262
    in emphysema, 93
    in obstructive lung
      disease, 38
    in pneumoconiosis, 207
  mechanical
    in asthma, 117
    continuous, in sleep
      apnea, 293
    in sleep apnea, 293

    negative-pressure, in sleep
      apnea, 293
  patterns
    airway resistance in,
      24–27
    lung compliance in,
      24–27
  -perfusion, 16–18
  -perfusion ratio, 16
    decrease in, 18
    decrease in pulmonary
      embolism, 146
    increase in, 18
    normal, 17
Ventricle, 342
  gallop in pulmonary
    embolism, 151
  right, in pulmonary
    embolism, 151
Vernix, 342
Vessels
  collagen vascular disease
    causing pleural effusion,
    189
  lymphatic, 331
  pulmonary (see Pulmonary
    vessels)
Viruses
  adenovirus (see Adenovirus)
  influenza (see Influenza
    virus)
  parainfluenza (see
    Parainfluenza virus)
  paramyxovirus, 334
  pneumonia due to, 126–127
  respiratory syncytial (see
    Respiratory syncytial
    virus)
  rhinovirus in
    laryngotracheobronchitis,
    254
Viscus, 342
Vital capacity (VC)
  decrease
    in asthma, 114
    in bronchiectasis, 103
    in bronchitis, chronic, 82
    in cancer of lung, 233
    in cystic fibrosis, 263
    in emphysema, 93
    in flail chest, 168
    in fungal diseases, 224
    in Guillain-Barré
      syndrome, 273
    in kyphoscoliosis, 198
    in lung disease,
      obstructive, 47
    in lung disease,
      restrictive, 37
    in myasthenia gravis, 281
    in pleural effusion, 190
    in pneumoconiosis, 206
    in pneumonia, 128
    in pneumothorax, 179
    in pulmonary edema, 138

    in respiratory distress
      syndrome, adult, 161
    in respiratory distress
      syndrome, idiopathic,
      243
    in sleep apnea, 290
    in tuberculosis, 215
  definition, 31
  forced (see Forced vital
    capacity)
  forced (see Forced
    expiratory
    volume/forced vital
    capacity ratio)
  slow, 31
$V_{max\ 50}$
  decrease
    in asthma, 114
    in bronchiectasis, 103
    in bronchitis, chronic, 82
    in cancer of lung, 233
    in cystic fibrosis, 263
    in emphysema, 93
    in pneumoconiosis, 207
Vocal cords: in croup, 252
Vocal fremitus, 6
  path of, 7
Voice sounds, whispered,
    auscultation of, 14
  in lung consolidation, 15
Volume
  apothecary, 351
  closing (see Closing volume)
  conversions, 351
  expiratory reserve (see
    Expiratory reserve
    volume)
  -flow (see Flow-volume loop)
  inspiratory reserve (see
    Inspiratory reserve
    volume)
  lung
    abbreviations for, 343
    in asthma, 114
    in bronchiectasis, 103
    in bronchitis, chronic, 82
    in cancer of lung,
      233–234
    in cystic fibrosis, 263
    definitions, 31
    in emphysema, 93
    in flail chest, 168
    in fungal diseases, 224
    in Guillain-Barré
      syndrome, 273
    in kyphoscoliosis, 198
    in lung disease,
      obstructive, 47–48
    in lung disease,
      restrictive, 37–38, 39
    in myasthenia gravis, 281
    normal, overview of,
      31–32
    in pleural effusion, 190
    in pneumoconiosis, 206

in pneumonia, 128
in pneumothorax, 179
in pulmonary edema, 138
in respiratory distress
    syndrome, adult, 161
in respiratory distress
    syndrome, idiopathic,
    243
in tuberculosis, 215–216
metric, 351
percent, 342
-pressure curve
    compliance in, increase
        and decrease, 26
    normal, 25
residual (*see* Residual volume)
stroke, 338
tidal (*see* Tidal volume)
V̇/Q (*see* Ventilation-perfusion
    ratio)
V$_T$ (*see* Tidal volume)

W

Weight
    apothecary, 351
    avoirdupois, 351
    conversions, 351

measurement units, 350
metric, 350, 351
reduction and sleep apnea,
    292
Wheal, 342
Wheezing, 13
    in asthma, 13
Whispered pectoriloquy, 14
    definition, 14
Whispered voice sounds,
    auscultation of, 14
    in lung consolidation, 15
Work of breathing: relationship
    to lung compliance
    increase, 24–27

X

Xanthine (*see* Bronchodilators,
    xanthine)
Xenon-133, 342
Xiphoid process, 5
X-ray, chest
    in asbestosis, 209
    in asthma, 116
    in bronchiectasis, 105
    in bronchitis, chronic, 84
    in cancer of lung, 234–236

in cystic fibrosis, 264
decubitus, 323
in emphysema, 94–95
in flail chest, 170
in fungal diseases, 225
in Guillain-Barré syndrome,
    273–274
in histoplasmosis, 225–226
in hydropneumothorax, 191
in kyphoscoliosis, 199
in myasthenia gravis,
    281–282
in pleural effusion, 191–192
in pneumoconiosis, 208
in pneumonia, 130
in pneumothorax, 180–182
in pulmonary edema, 139
in pulmonary embolism, 152
in respiratory distress
    syndrome
    adult, 162
    idiopathic, 245
in sleep apnea, 291
in tuberculosis, 216–217
X-ray, neck
    in epiglottitis, 256
    in laryngotracheobronchitis,
        256

CHAPTER ELEVEN

Analyzing Your Data

The computer has become an indispensable tool in social and behavioral science research. In using a software package to conduct data analysis, you need to know how to specify your analysis procedures via menu selection (when the package offers this option) and/or typewriting. You also need to know how to run a program. In the convention of SPSS for DOS, for example, you call in your program or command file by pressing F3 and supplying the file name, place the cursor at where you want to run from, and then press F10 to start executing the program. In SPSS for Windows, you click the mouse to get the command file, highlight the part of the program that you want to apply to your data, and click the execution button to run it over. This chapter, however, will not focus on the computer techniques and operations. Rather, it will emphasize the ideas that lie behind the methods and procedures. In other words, we will talk about the purposes, principles, utilities, and limits of statistics with some major issues in building your analytical models.

Statistics is about the reduction of data as well as the generalization from sample information to the condition of a research population. Accordingly, the study is divided into two parts. The first is called descriptive statistics, and the second, inferential statistics.

We will be talking about a number of statistical techniques and procedures that are useful in data analysis. Yet students often feel at a loss when faced with a specific analytical task. Here a major organizing framework is the hierarchy of different *measurement levels*. Generally speaking, data obtained at higher measurement levels will have better mathematical properties. Therefore, any statistical procedure suitable for analyzing data obtained at a lower measurement